Making of America Project

The Actress in High Life

An Episode in Winter Quarters

Making of America Project

The Actress in High Life
An Episode in Winter Quarters

ISBN/EAN: 9783744664387

Printed in Europe, USA, Canada, Australia, Japan

Cover: Foto ©Thomas Meinert / pixelio.de

More available books at **www.hansebooks.com**

THE ACTRESS

IN

HIGH LIFE:

AN EPISODE IN WINTER QUARTERS.

"Grim-Visag'd War hath smooth'd his wrinkled front;
And now, instead of mounting barbed steeds,
To fright the souls of fearful adversaries,
He capers nimbly in a lady's chamber,
To the lascivious pleasing of a lute."

NEW YORK:
DERBY & JACKSON.
1860.

C. A. ALVORD, PRINTER, NEW YORK.

THE ACTRESS IN HIGH LIFE;

AN EPISODE IN WINTER QUARTERS.

CHAPTER I.

I was a traveler, then, upon the moor,
  I saw the hare that raced about with joy,
I heard the woods and distant waters roar,
  Or heard them nót, as happy as a boy;
  The pleasant season did my heart employ.
My old remembrances went from me wholly,
And all the ways of men so vain and melancholy

WORDSWORTH.

GENTLE READER: Wherever you may be, in bodily presence, when you cast your eyes on this page, let it for a few hours transport your complying spirit to a remote region and a bygone day. We may alter names without injury to our story; but every real character, or event, has its own time, place, and accidents; to tear it from them is like transplanting a tree from its native spot; it must be trimmed and pruned, and robbed of its due proportions and its natural grace.

Here, then, on this lovely day, near the end of the year 1812, you are in Alemtejo—the largest, poorest, and, in every sense, worst peopled province of Portugal. As its name implies, you are, as to Lisbon, beyond the Tagus. Hasten eastward over this sandy, arid plain, covered with a forest of stunted sea-pines, through whose tops the west wind glides with monotonous and melancholy moans, fit music for the wilderness around you. Nor need you loiter on this desolate moor, scantily carpeted with heaths of different kinds and varying hues. The drowsy tinkling of the cow-bell amidst yonder brushwood, the goats sportively clambering over that ledge of rocks, and those distant dusky spots upon the downs, which may be sheep, tell you that all life has not left the land. You may, perchance, on your journey, see a goatherd or a shepherd here or there; by rarer chance may meet some wayfarer like yourself, but as likely a robber as an honest man; and may find shelter, at least, in one of the few and comfortless *vendas*, the wretched inns the route affords.

You need not pause to gaze on many a wild scene, some beautiful, and even here and there a fertile spot; nor loiter in this provincial town—rich, perhaps, in Moorish ruins, but in nothing else—but hasten onward till you reach that elevated point, where the road, one hundred miles from Lisbon, winds over the ridge of yonder hill. The chilly night winds of the peninsula have gone to sleep. Here, even in midwinter, the sun at this hour shoots down scorching rays upon your head.

Seat yourself by the road-side, on this ledge of slate-rock, at the foot of the cork-oak, which so invitingly spreads out its sheltering arms. Here while you take breath, cast your eyes around you.

You are no longer in the midst of broken, desolate wastes. To the south-west rises the Serra d'Ossa—its sides clothed with evergreen oaks, and a dense growth of underbrush sheltering the wolf and the wild boar, while the northern slope of its rocky ridge is thatched with snow. Before you is spread out the valley of the Guadiana. Sloping downward toward the mighty stream, lie pasture, grove and field, gaily mingled together. There, to the east, sits Elvas, on a lofty hill, whose sides are covered with vineyards, oliveyards and orchards, and just north of it, on a yet loftier peak, with a deep narrow valley lying between them, stands the crowning castle of La Lippe, the strongest fortress in Portugal. Far beyond, but plainly seen through the clear atmosphere of the peninsula, now doubly transparent since it has been purified by the heavy rains which here usher in the winter, rises the blue mountain of Albuquerque, far away in Spanish Estremadura. Whichever way you look, Sierras, nearer or more distant, tower above the horizon, or fringe its utmost verge.

Among these scenes of nature's handiwork, a production of human art demands your attention. See, on your right, the beginning of the ancient aqueduct, reared by Moorish hands, which leads the pure mountain stream for three miles across the valley to the city seated on the hill. Here, the masonry is but a foot or two above the ground; below, the road will lead you under its three tiers of arches, with the water gliding an hundred feet above your head.

But here comes a native of this region to enliven, if not adorn, the landscape. This lean, swarthy young fellow, under his *sombrero* with ample brim, exhibits a fair specimen of the peasants of Alemtejo. His sheep-skin jacket hangs loosely from his shoulders, and between his nether garment and his clumsy shoes, he displays the greater part of a pair of sinewy legs, which would be brown, were they not so well powdered with the slate dust of the rocky road he travels. With a long goad he urges on the panting beasts, yoked to the rudest of all vehicles—the bullock cart of Portugal. Its low wheels, made of solid wooden blocks, are fastened to the axle-tree, which turns with them, and at every step squeaks out complaining notes under the burden of a cask of the muddy and little prized wine of the province, which is seeking a market at Elvas.

The carter is now overtaken by a peasant girl, who, with basket on her arm, has been gathering chesnuts and *bolotas* in the wood. They are no strangers to each other, and she exchanges her brisk, elastic step, for a pace better suited to that of the toiling oxen. The beauty of this dusky belle consists of a smiling mouth, bright black eyes, and youth and health. Though fond of gaudy colors, she is not over dressed. A light handkerchief rather binds her raven hair than covers her head. Her bright blue petticoat, scanty in length, and her orange-colored spencer, open in front, both well worn, and showing here and there a rent, but half conceal the graces of her form, and a pair of nimble feet, scorning the trammels of leather, pick their way skillfully along the stony path. That she does not contemn ornament, is shown by her one small golden ear-ring, long since divorced from its mate, and the devout faith which glows in her bosom is symbolized by the little silver image of our lady, slung from her neck by a silken cord, spun by her own silk worms, and twisted by her own hands. In short, she is neither beautiful, nor noble, nor rich; yet her company seems instantly to smooth the road and lighten the toils of travel to her swain. He helps himself, unasked, out of her basket, and urges her to partake of the stores of his leathern wallet—hard goat's cheese—and the crumbling loaf of *broa*, or maize bread. Soon in deep and sweet conference, in their crabbed, but expressive tongue, he forgets to make occasional use of his goad, and thus keeping pace with the loitering bullocks, they go leisurely along. Let them pass on, and wait for better game.

Turn and look at this cavalcade toiling up toward you. A sudden bend in the road has brought it into view, and its aspect, half native, half foreign—its mixed civil and military character—attract attention. Two mounted orderlies, in a British uniform, lead the way, and are followed by a clumsy Lisbon coach, every part of it well laden with luggage. It is drawn by four noble mules, such as are seldom seen out of the peninsula, deserving more stylish postillions than those who, in ragged jackets, greasy leathern breeches and huge jack boots, are urging them on. Two men sit at ease on the coach box. One, a tall young fellow, looks at a distance like a field-officer in a flashy uniform, but is only an English footman in a gaudy livery, who needs the training of a London winter or two, in a fashionable household, to make him a flunky of the first water. The other, an old man, with a severe countenance, is plainly dressed, but, with a less brilliant exterior, has a more respectable air than his companion. He, too, is the man in authority as, from time to time, he directs the party and urges them on in somewhat impatient tones.

If you are familiar with the country and the times, you may imagine that some British general officer has been so long in the peninsula, that he has adopted the style and equipage of Cuesta, and some other Spanish leaders, and fallen into their habits of slow and dignified motion. You will think it high time for him to be sent home, that some one less luxurious and stately, but more alert and energetic, may fill his place. One look into the coach will undeceive you. Its chief occupant is a lady, whose years do not exceed nineteen; and she is evidently no native of Alemtejo, nor of Portugal; and might have been sent out hither as a specimen of what a more northern country can occasionally produce. While she looks out with deep, yet lively interest on the scenery before and around her, you naturally gaze with deeper interest only upon her. Her companion is her maid, some years older than herself, who might be worth looking at, were her mistress out of the way.

One of the orderlies, turning in his saddle, now points out the city to the old man, who, in turn, leans over to the coach window, and calls out, "My lady, there is Elvas!"

"And my father is in Elvas!" She leans eagerly out of the window; but the front of the clumsy vehicle obstructs the view, and she calls out, "Stop the coach, Moodie, and let me out. I will not go one step further until I have taken a good look at Elvas."

The old man testily orders a halt. The footman opens the door, and the lady springs lightly out, followed by her maid. Neglecting all other objects in sight, she gazes long and eagerly at the city seated on the hill. The interest she shows is no longer merely that of observant curiosity, but is prompted by the gushing affections of the heart. In Elvas, besides much new and strange, there is something known and loved.

She now begins to question the orderlies as to the exact spot where her father has quartered himself; but the old man interrupts her:

"You have traveled a long way, my lady, to get to Elvas, but you will never reach it while you stand looking at it and spiering about it."

"Very true, old Wisdom. How comes it that you are always in the right? Let us push on now, and in an hour," she exclaims, stepping into the coach, "I will see my father, for the first time since I was fourteen."

The coach moves on, but too slowly for her. Leaning out of the window, and surveying the road, she calls out gaily, "Our way lies down hill, Moodie, and they tell me that mules are so sure-footed that they never stumble. Pray buy or borrow that long goad from the young gentleman in the sheep-skin jacket. By skillful use of it you might mend our pace, and bring us sooner to Elvas."

We will leave this impatient lady to hasten on to Elvas, whether expedited or not by the use of the goad, to inquire the occasion of her journey thither.

For five years the peninsula has been one battle-field, and the present has been one of unceasing activity to the British troops. Beginning the year by suddenly crossing the frontier and investing Ciudad Rodrigo, they had taken it by storm in January, while the French were preparing to relieve it. Equally unexpectedly crossing the Tagus and the Guadiana, they had sat down before the strong fortress of Badajoz, and to save a few precious days, in which Soult and Marmont might have united their hosts to its rescue, they, in April, took it in a bloody assault, buying immediate possession at the price of more than a thousand precious lives. No sooner had the disappointed Marshals withdrawn their armies to less exhausted regions, than the forts of Almarez were surprised in May, and the direct route of communication between them cut off. The British army then invaded Spain on the side of the kingdom of Leon: the forts of Salamanca fell before them in June, and in July the battle of Salamanca crushed the French force in that quarter, and opened the road to Madrid to the British, who, driving thence the intrusive king, acquired the control of all central Spain. But, at length, in October, the castle of Burgos defied their utmost efforts, unaided by a siege-train. The French hosts from north, south and east, abandoning rich provinces and strong fortresses they had held for years, gathered around them in overwhelming numbers; and slowly, reluctantly, and with many a stubborn halt, the English general retraced his steps toward Portugal. The prostrated strength of both armies put an end to the campaign. The French gave up the pursuit, being too hungry to march further, or to fight any more; and the discipline and appetites of the British soldiers were indicated, on their march through the forests bordering the Huebra, by the fusilade opened on the herds of swine, which were fattening on the acorns there. For a moment their commander thought himself surprised, and that the country, for miles around, was the scene of one wide-spread skirmish with the foe. Even hanging a few of his men did not put a stop to the disorder. Late in November the troops were permitted to pause for rest, in the neighborhood of Ciudad Rodrigo, with their energies prostrated and their discipline relaxed through the sieges and battles, the continual marches, the exposure and the want of a campaign so long and arduous as this. Strange it seemed to them, after going so far, and doing and suffering so much, that they should end the campaign where they had begun it. Yet they had done much: wrenching the larger and richer half of Spain out of the grasp of the French, and changing their possession of the country to a mere invasion of it.

Such toils need long rest. Privations and sufferings like theirs should be repaid by no scanty measure of plenty and enjoyment. The troops went into winter quarters chiefly between the Douro and the Tagus; but, as an army in this country is always in danger of starvation, a brigade was sent over into Alemtejo, at once, to make themselves comfortable, and to facilitate getting up supplies from a province which now had something in it: as, for four years, the French had been kept out of it.

Accordingly, it was absolutely refreshing to see the liberal provision made for the almost insatiable wants of this brigade—for among them our story lies. They proved themselves good soldiers, to a man, in their zeal to refresh and strengthen themselves against the next campaign, by enjoying, to the full, every good thing within their reach. The officers, especially, ransacked the country for every commodity that could promote enjoyment; and what Alemtejo could not furnish, Lisbon and London must provide. Nothing was too costly for their purses, no place too distant for their search. Doubtless, the veterans of the greatest of all great captains were permitted for a time to run a free and joyons career in Capua; and this brigade, besides having a little corner of Portugal to themselves, somewhat out of sight of the commander-in-chief and of Sir Rowland Hill, enjoyed the further advantage of being led by a good soldier in the field; and a free-liver in garrison and camp, who looked upon his men in winter quarters, after a hard campaign, somewhat in the light of school-boys in the holidays, and was willing to see the lads enjoy themselves freely.

Lord Strathern, a veteran somewhat the worse for wear, had entered the army a cadet of a Scotch family, more noble than rich. At length, the obliging death of a cousin brought him a Scotch peerage, and an estate little adequate to support that dignity. High rank, and a narrow estate, form an inconvenient union; so he stuck to the profession which he loved, and, being a widower, entrusted his only child, a daughter, to a sister in Scotland.

Though he had seen little of domestic life, he was an affectionate man. The briskness of the last campaign, and the number of his friends who dropped off in the course of it, strongly warned him that if he would once again see his daughter, now attaining womanhood, it would be well to lose no time about it. So, one morning, during the retreat from Burgos, after issuing the brigade orders for the day, he penned an order to his sister in Scotland, to send out the young lady, with proper attendants, under the care of the wife of any officer of rank who might be sailing for

Lisbon. There she would be within reach, and he might find leisure to visit her.

His sister would have protested against this had she had an opportunity; but the order of the father, and the affectionate and adventurous spirit of the daughter, at once decided the matter. On her arrival, however, in Lisbon, her father was too busy establishing his brigade in comfortable quarters, to meet her there; and the military horizon giving promise of a quiet winter, he summoned her to join him at Elvas.

The brigade had been for some weeks living in clover in their modern Capua, when Lady Mabel Stewart joined her father. A Portuguese provincial town, with its filthy streets and squalid populace, could be no agreeable place of residence to a British lady. Lord Strathern felt this, and, looking about him, found a large building in the midst of an orchard without the walls of Elvas, and more than half-way down the hill. It had been erected by one of the monastic societies of the city, as a place of occasional retirement for pleasure, or devotion, or both. The French had summarily turned them out of it five years before, and so thoroughly plundered them, at the same time, that they had not since found heart or means to repair and refurnish it. Accordingly, it was a good deal dilapidated. But the refectory and the kitchen took his lordship's eye. The former could dine half the officers of the brigade at a time, and the latter allowed abundant elbow-room to cooks and scullions, while preparing the feast. So, here he established the headquarters of his brigade, and here Lady Mabel Stewart made her appearance in the new dignity of womanhood, to preside over his household.

CHAPTER II.

"Oh sovereign beauty, you whose charms
All other charms surpass;
Whose lustre nought can imitate,
Except your looking-glass.

Southey, *from the Spanish.*

The arrival of Lady Mabel Stewart was a god-send to the young officers of the brigade. Already the sources of interest afforded by the country around, began to fail them. Few men can long make a business of mere eating and drinking; red-legged partridges were getting scarce in that neighborhood, and boar hunting in the mountain forests was distant, laborious, and too often, fruitless of game. The scenery of the country, the costume and habits of the people, now familiar to their eyes, palled upon their tastes. They wanted something new to interest them, and were particularly delighted when this novelty came from home. But, above all, the black-haired, dark-eyed daughters of this sunny region grew many shades browner in their eyes. We look not at the daffodils when the lily rears its head. A new and higher order of beauty, rare even at home, now demanded homage, and it was freely paid.

Lord Strathern, a social and jovial man, had always been a favorite with his subalterns, but now his popularity attained its acme. His open house became headquarters, even more in a social than a military sense. It was a little court, and Lady Mabel played the queen regnant there.

Justly proud of her, her father encouraged this, taking all the attention she attracted as compliments to himself; and the gentlemen displayed great ingenuity in devising various excuses for being in frequent attendance at headquarters, in the service of her ladyship. Lieutenant Goring, the best horseman in the —— light dragoons, a squadron of which had been sent hither with the brigade, to fatten their emaciated steeds on the barley and maize of Alemtejo, established himself, uninvited, in the post of equerry, and sedulously devoted himself to training the beautiful Andalusian provided for Lady Mabel's own saddle. Of course, he had to be in attendance when she took the air on horseback. Major Warren, from a free, heedless sportsman, who followed his game for his own pleasure, became gamekeeper, or rather, grand huntsman, bound to lay the feathered, furred, and scaly tribes under contribution to supply her table and tempt her delicate appetite. A proud and happy man was he when skill or fortune enabled him to lay the antlered stag or tusked boar at her feet, and expatiate on the incidents of his sylvan campaign. He, of course, must be often invited to partake of the social meal. Captain Cranfield, of the engineers, had just returned from Badajoz, where he had been repairing shattered bastions, and patching up curtains sadly torn by shot and shell. He found Lady Mabel busy renovating, modernising and adorning the rude and comfortless apartments of her monastic quarters. Immediately his pencil, his professional ingenuity and skill are devoted to her service. He appoints himself architect, upholsterer and improver-general to the household. He designed elegant curtains, with graceful festoons for the misshapen windows, tasteful hangings to conceal bare walls of rough-hewn stone, picturesque screens to hide unsightly corners; and arranged and put them up with as much skill as if, with a native genius for it, he had been bred to the business. The commonest materials became rich chintz and costly arras in his hands, mahogany, or rose-wood, at his bidding. One morning so spent put him on an easier footing with Lady Mabel than a dozen casual meetings; and he quite got the weather gage of both equerry and huntsman, securing frequent and easy intercourse, while advising and assisting her in his inter-menial capacity, whereas these gentlemen's spheres of official duty lay properly out of doors. But he soon found a dangerous rival to take the wind out of his sails, in the person of Major Lumley, who, possessing great taste and skill in music, accidentally heard Lady Mabel singing in one room, while he was conversing with her father in the next. "She has," thought and said the major, "the sweetest voice in the world; and it only needs a little more cultivation to make it heavenly!" Lord Strathern thought so too. The major's instructive talents were put into requisition, and, from private practice, her father led her on, somewhat reluctant, to more public display, and soon the major and herself discoursed exquisite music to the ears of a score of officers, at a musical soirée. If, with the powers, she did not acquire the confidence of a *prima donna*, it was not his lordship's fault. Had propriety permitted, he would have brought up the brigade in close column of divisions, to hear Lady Mabel sing; and he could not help saying to the gentlemen beside him: "I have heard you young fellows talk about the nightingale, and have even known some of you spend hours in the moon-lit grove, listening to their music, but my bird from foggy Scotland can out-warble a wood full of them." And no one felt disposed to contradict him.

How many others, irresistibly attracted, sought, each in his own way, to make himself agreeable, we will not undertake to say. Perhaps Ensign Wade, who, not yet eighteen, had just been rubbing off the school-boy in the last campaign, was the most madly in love with her; unless he was surpassed by little Captain Hatton, who, being but five feet three, had, to the great injury of his marching powers, magnanimously added an extra inch to his boot heels, that Lady Mabel might not look too much down upon him, when so happy as to stand beside her.

Hers was a curious position for a lady, and, yet, more for one so young. She instinctively looked round for the countenance and support which only female companions could give. But, of the very few ladies with the brigade, Mrs. Colonel Colville was at Portalegre, where her husband's regiment was quartered, the wife of Major Grey was shut up with him in his sick room; Mrs. Captain Howe had come out from home less to visit her husband than to cure her rheumatism in the balmy climate of Elvas; and the wife of Captain Ford had just, very injudiciously, presented him with two little Portuguese, who might have made very good Englishmen, had they first seen the light in the right place. If the brigade had suffered heavy loss in the last campaign, the ladies of the brigade were absolutely *hors de combat*, and could not furnish Lady Mabel even a sentinel in the shape of a chaperon. She felt that this was awkward; but, said she to herself, "If there were any impropriety in my situation here, Papa would not open his house so freely to the officers of the brigade." For she loved and admired him far too much to doubt his judgment on such a point. Now, Lord Strathern had dined the better part of his life at a regimental mess table; and when promotion at length removed him from that genial sphere, he felt selfish and solitary, if he took his dinner and wine without, at least, a corporal's guard of his brother officers around him. So far from deeming his daughter's arrival a reason for excluding them, she was a strong ally, and a delightful addition to his means of entertaining his friends. So she found herself suddenly the centre of a circle, composed of gentlemen only, most of them unmarried, young and gay, and admiring her. In short, Lady Mabel was finishing off her education in a very bad school, worse, perhaps, than a Frenchified academy, devoted to the education of the extremities, in the shape of music, dancing and gabbling French, with a dash of mental and moral training in the development of the sickly imagination of the head and the empty vanities of the heart.

For a time the dilapidated condition of kitchen and refectory restricted the scale of hospitality at head-quarters. But Lady Mabel soon completed her reforms of house and household, in which she found old Moodie an able assistant. Captain Cranfield had to bring his labors of love to an end, and Lord Strathern celebrated the event by feasting a large party of his friends.

While the company was assembled, Lady Mabel led a party of the first comers through the apartments, to admire the results of the labor and taste bestowed upon them. Some of the more prying peeped into the kitchen to see what was going on there.

"I am glad to see," said Captain Hatton, "that though this is a monastic house, and this a fast day, we shall not have to dine orthodoxly, on *bacalhao* and *sardinhas*."

"Nor be bored with the long Latin grace," said Major Warren, "which the very walls of the refectory are tired of hearing and not understanding."

"Would rendering it into English reconcile you to its length?" asked Lady Mabel.

"Not in the least. I think nothing so heterodox as a long grace, while soup and fish grow cold."

"I am told," said Lady Mabel, ascending to the apartment above, "that this was the abbot's own room."

"That is very likely," said Captain Hatton, "from its neighborhood to the kitchen."

"It is not exactly the apartment," she continued, "which I would design for a lady's withdrawing room. But, if it satisfied the holy father before it was thus improved, it is too good for a heretic like me. I sometimes feel myself a profane intruder here, and, when I call to mind whom this building belongs to, and see so many red-coated gentry stalking at ease through dormitory, refectory and cloisters, I think of rooks who have fled the rookery, before a flock of flamingoes who usurp their place."

"The pious crows," said Captain Hatton, "would forgive our intrusion, did they see the bird of paradise that attracts us hither."

"Put a weight on your fancy, Captain Hatton," said Lady Mabel. "Such another flight and it may soar away altogether. Pray observe the admirable effect of those hangings, with which Captain Cranfield has concealed the dark and narrow passage that leads to the oratory."

Major Warren was provoked at the general admiration of Cranfield's taste and skill, and stung by the repeated thanks with which Lady Mabel repaid his labors, so he endeavored to turn them into ridicule.

"It is a thousand pities, Cranfield, that these happy designs should perish with their temporary use. Let me beg you to send a sketch of them to Colonel Sturgeon, the head of your department. They should be preserved among the draughts and plans of the engineer corps."

Cranfield was about to make angry answer, but Lady Mabel anticipated him by saying: "doubtless, whenever Colonel Sturgeon has occasion to turn monkish cloisters into ladies' bowers, it will save him a world of trouble to avail himself of these designs.

At this moment dinner was announced. Colonel Bradshawe, resolving that his juniors should not have Lady Mabel all to themselves, availed himself of his right of precedence, to hand her into the room, and seated himself at her right hand.

Full thirty guests occupied the space between her father's portly, but martial figure, and her seat at the head of the table; and though, Minerva-like in air and form, she presided there with exquisite grace, she shrunk from this long array, and sought a kind of privacy in devoting her attention, somewhat exclusively, to the senior colonel of the brigade. Knowing how important a matter dining was in his estimation, she soon made a conquest of him, by her judicious care in supplying his wants, tickling his palate, and coinciding in his tastes. She even, for his benefit, called into requisition the unwilling service of old Moodie, who had habitually taken his post behind her, like a sentinel, not troubling himself about the wants of the guests. The colonel might have choked with thirst before he spontaneously handed him a decanter.

Colonel Bradshawe having made himself comfortable, next sought to make himself agreeable. "What a delightful contrast between my situation to-day, and this day year, Lady Mabel."

"Where were you then?"

"About this hour we were fording the Aguada, in a snow storm, to invest Ciudad Rodrigo."

"That was somewhat different from our present occupation."

"We soon finished that little job, however, before we had suffered many privations there. But it proved to be but the opening of a campaign, which I began, after a time, to think would never come to an end."

"And, unhappily," said Lady Mabel, "it did not end quite so well as it promised to do."

"Fortune is a fickle mistress, and fond of showing her character in war," said the colonel. "Sometimes she favors one party with a run of luck, then shifts suddenly over to the other side. So with individuals, only there she is most apt to work at cross purposes. One pretty fellow deserves to live forever, and gets knocked on the head in the first skirmish; another deserves to rise, and all his good service is overlooked or forgotten; another gets praise and promotion for what he never did, or ought never to have done. Some men have such luck! There is L'Isle now, who, after being pushed on as fast as money and family interest could shove him; what next happens to him? Why just for blundering into a Spanish village, and being nearly taken with his whole command, he is made a lieutenant-colonel on the spot."

"That is a curious result of such a blunder."

"Curious, but true. This is capital port," interjected the colonel, emptying his glass. "We drank no such stuff as this during the last campaign. I would not disgust you with a detail of our privations; but you must know, Lady Mabel, that during the whole march from Madrid to Burgos, and thence, in retreat, to Ciudad Rodrigo, I never tasted a bottle of wine that deserved the name, except one of *Peralta*, of which I feel bound to make honorable mention. I met with it by great good luck at the posada at Buitrago; but when I called for another, it was so excellent that the landlord had drank all himself. The stuff we had to drink was made by pouring water on the skins of grapes already pressed. After they had been well macerated in it, it was allowed to ferment and grow sour, then sold to us at the price of good liquor."

"That accounts," said Lady Mabel, "for the provident care you lately showed, in laying in a stock of better liquor for your winter's use. Is it true that you sent a special agent to Xeres de la Frontera, to select the best sherry for the regimental mess?"

"Not exactly a special agent," said the colonel, disclaiming it with a gentle wave of the hand; "but, finding a trusty person, and a capital judge, going thither, we did charge him with a little commission that way."

"I was sorry to hear of your disappointment," added she, in a commiserating tone. "I am told that he found that the firm of Soult, Victor & Co., had already taken up all the oldest and best wine on credit, that is, without paying for it; and you had to put up with new and inferior brands, or go without any."

"It is but too true," said the colonel, with a sigh. "Those rascally Frenchmen had drained the country of everything worth drinking; our agent, very wisely, under the circumstances, made no purchase there, and I am glad of it; for I have since learned, that the Amontillado, which had been recommended to us as the dryest of sherry wines, is made from a variety of grapes plucked before they are ripe."

"How lucky," said Lady Mabel, in a congratulatory tone, "that you have since found out that this wine is made of sour grapes."

A faint suspicion that she was laughing at him induced him to change the topic. "You were never abroad before, I believe. This part of the country has some drawbacks; but I think you will find it, during the winter, a very pleasant part of the world."

"We will all endeavor to make it so to you, Lady Mabel," said Major Warren, who, impatient of his superior's monopoly, here tried to edge in a word. But the colonel cut him short with "That's a mere truism, Warren, a self-evident proposition. Let us have nothing more of that sort. One of the peculiarities of this climate, Lady Mabel, is that it has a double spring: one in February and another in April. Then we will see you take your appropriate place in the picture, representing the heyday of youth in the midst of spring, and beauty, surrounded by flowers."

She bowed low, in suppressing a laugh at this elaborate compliment, and said, "Will spring be so soon upon us?"

"In a fortnight you may gather the same flowers which at home you must wait for till May."

"Not the same flowers," said she, quickly. "Portugal has a Flora peculiar to itself, embracing very few of our native British plants. I am on my strong ground on this topic, being a pupil of Dr. Graham, who relieves his graver studies by striving to rival King Solomon in the knowledge of plants, 'from the cedar of Lebanon to the hyssop that grows on the wall.' I am pledged to carry home a vast *hortus siccus* for him."

"Oh! a scientific young lady—perhaps a little of a blue-stocking, too," said the colonel to himself. "I must hash up a dish to suit her peculiar taste. Though no botanist," continued he aloud, "there is one plant that has strongly attracted my attention, and I recommend it to yours; though your *hortus siccus* will hardly contain a fair specimen of it."

"What is that?" said she, on the *qui vive* to hear of some rare plant.

"It is the cork-oak," said the colonel, solemnly. "Its rough exterior has led tourists and artists, and even naturalists, to treat it with neglect, while it is daily contributing to the comfort, delight, and civilization of the world."

"It may, perhaps," said Lady Mabel, hesitating, "be said to do all that you attribute to it."

"Does it not strike you as passing strange, Lady Mabel, (*apropos* to our subject, pray take a glass of wine with me,) that the Romans, who were, doubtless, a great and a wise people, should have been masters of Spain and Gaul, and of their forests of cork trees for centuries—that these Romans," continued he, growing eloquent on the subject, "who had the tree in their own country, though not, perhaps, in the full perfection of its cortical development, and did apply its bark to a number of useful purposes, including, occasionally, that of stoppers for vessels, should yet never have attained to the systematic use of it in corking their bottles!"

"Strange, indeed," said Lady Mabel. "It was shutting their eyes against the light of nature; for, we may say, that the obvious final end of the cork tree is to provide corks for bottles."

"A great truth well expressed," said the colonel. "Such an oversight has hardly a parallel; unless it be in their invention of printing and never using it. For we see, in the baker's name, stamped on the loaves found in Pompeii, and words impressed on their pottery and other articles, what amounts to stereotype printing; yet they never went on to separate the individual letters, and so become compositors and printers in the usual sense of the art. But they could certainly get on better without printing than without corks."

"Undoubtedly. For the world may—indeed, has—become too full of books; while there is little fear of its becoming too full of bottles; they get emptied and broken so fast."

"I wonder whether Horace," continued Colonel Bradshawe, with a thoughtful air, "when he opened a jar of Falernian, was obliged to finish it at a sitting, to prevent its growing sour? Wine out of a jar! Think of that. With a wooden or earthen stopper, made tight with pitch. Think of having your wine vinho-flavored with pitch! like the *vinho verde* of these Portuguese peasants, out of a pitchy goat-skin sack."

Lady Mabel looked nauseated at the idea, and the colonel swallowed a glass of Madeira, to wash away the pitchy flavor. "Yes," said he, shaking his head gravely, "they must have often felt sadly the want of a cork. How would it be possible to confine champagne (I am sorry this cursed war prevents our getting any,) until it is set free with all its life and perfection of flavor, just at the moment of enjoyment! They had glass, too, and used glass, these Romans, yet persevered in keeping their wine in those abominable jars. It proves how little progress they had made in the beautiful art of glass-blowing; and, of course, (here the colonel took up a decanter of old Madeira and replenished his glass, after eyeing approvingly the amber-colored liquor,) they were ignorant that wines that attain perfection by keeping, ripen most speedy in light-colored bottles."

"Indeed!" said Lady Mabel, "I did not know that. But I learn something new from you every moment."

"And that," said he, nodding approvingly at her, "is something worth knowing. I doubt, after all, whether these Romans, with the world at their beck, really knew much of the elegant and refined pleasures of life. Setting aside their gladiatorial shows, and the custom of chaining the porter by the leg to the door-post, that he might not be out of the way when friend or client called on his master, and similar rude habits, there is enough to convict them as a gross people. They put honey in their wine, too! What a proof of childish, or rather, savage taste! Lucullus' monstrous suppers, and Apicius' elaborate feasts, are better to read about than to partake of. Give me, rather, a quiet little dinner of a few well-chosen dishes and wines, and three or four knowing friends, not given to long stories, but spicy in talk, and I will enjoy myself better than 'the noblest Roman of them all.'"

"But, Colonel Bradshawe, how did you become so familiar with Roman manners? Many of us know something of their public life, their wars, conquests, seditions and laws; but you seem to have put aside the curtain, and peered into the house, first floor, garret and cellar."

"You overrate my learning, Lady Mabel; my tastes naturally lead me to inform myself on some points that may seem to lie out of the common road. Some people take the liberty of calling me an epicure. I admit it so far as this: I hold it to be our duty to enjoy ourselves wisely and well. Much as I esteem a knowing *bon vivant*, I despise an ignorant glutton, or undiscriminating sot. To know how to make the most of the good things given us, is, at once, a duty and a pleasure. This conviction has led me to heighten what are called our epicurean enjoyments, by investigating the history of cookery, the literature of the vineyard, and other cognate branches of learning."

"You have devised a happy union of intellectual and sensual pleasure, well calculated to heighten both."

"Why were these good things given us," said the colonel, gracefully waving his hand over the table, "but that we should ascertain their uses, and apply them accordingly?"

"I begin to understand your philosophy, in letting none of the good things of life run to waste, but rather receiving them all in the spirit of thankfulness."

"In those few words you express the essence of my philosophy."

"There may be," continued Lady Mabel, "as much piety, and certainly more wisdom, in frankly enjoying the good things given us, than in despising the world which God made, and rejecting the blessings it teems with, like these self-tormenting ascetics, the monks and friars around us."

"Heaven help your simplicity, Lady Mabel! They

only pretend to do so, the hypocrites! Rest assured, every one of these fellows is on the sly."

"What! No exceptions? Is it true of every one—

'His eyes are set on heaven, his heart on earth?'"

"It fits them to a man!" said the colonel. "Their vocation is securing to themselves the good things of this world, by promising to others the blessings of the next: and as for the friars, true to their motto, *Nihil habentes et omnia possidentes*, they profess to hold no special property, merely that the whole country might be bound to maintain them. They know the value of the good things of this life, and how to enjoy them in a corner."

"These odd-looking monks and friars attract me much," said Lady Mabel: "perhaps they will not bear a close inspection; but, with all my prejudice against them, I must own, that many seem truly devout, and the friars, at least, very zealous in their labors among the people."

"Yet the people, except the women," said Bradshawe, "are losing faith in their greasy reverences."

"Women are everywhere more devout than men," she answered; "and I do indeed observe their greasy reverences, as you call them, conversing oftener with our sex than yours."

"Observe more closely, Lady Mabel, and you will see that they are most zealous for the conversion of the young women, the tender lambs of the flock. They care little for a tough, smoke-dried, old woman's soul." This was said with a knowing wink, and caused some merriment among his juniors within ear-shot.

A gradual but perceptible change was coming over the colonel's manner, which Lady Mabel did not like. In fact, Lord Strathern had pushed the bottle briskly, though sometimes slighting it himself, as did many of his guests; but Bradshawe made it a point of conscience to take toll every time it passed him. He had, moreover, violated one of his own maxims, in talking incessantly while imbibing his liquor; so she took advantage of the next pause in his conversation to leave the table.

CHAPTER III.

You are a gentleman of excellent breeding, admirable discourse, of great admittance; authentic in your place and person, and generally allowed for your many warlike, courtlike, and learned preparations.—*Merry Wives of Windsor.*

So time ran merrily on in Elvas, and most merrily at headquarters; thanks to Lord Strathern's hospitality, and to the elegance, variety and life Lady Mabel gave to the brilliant circle she attracted thither.

Entering her father's sitting-room one morning, she found him in conference with a gentleman whom she had nevér seen before. They were so much engrossed in conversation, that she had time to remark, unobserved, that he was young, handsome, and an officer of rank, but thin and pallid, as if just released from long confinement in a sick room. She was about to withdraw, when the stranger, turning to take a paper from the table, saw her. After an abstracted look of admiring curiosity, as if gazing on a fine picture, unexpectedly placed before him, he recollected himself, and rose from his chair.

"This must be Lady Mabel Stewart. Pray, my lord, psesent me to your daughter."

"What, *Ma Belle*, are you here? L'Isle, let me

make you known to my daughter. Like yourself, she occupies a distinguished post in the brigade, though not quite so well defined as yours."

Lady Mabel acknowledged this addition to her acquaintance; then said, "but I see you are busy, papa."

"Not at all," said he, thrusting some papers into his portfolio, "sit with us here;" and he drew a chair for her. "L'Isle has been so long in his sick room, that a little of our pleasant company will do him good. You must have suffered much from solitude, L'Isle, as well as from your wounds."

"Surgeons and servants were my sole companions. Their rude hands, too, convinced me that our sex were never meant for nurses. A sister of mercy would have been an angel of light; and if young and good-looking, she might have made a convert of me to her church."

Lady Mabel could perceive that her father treated his companion with unusual consideration, and L'Isle was induced to prolong his visit for an hour and more. He was certainly well-bred and well-informed, and seemed disposed to make himself agreeable; yet there was something in his manner that puzzled and annoyed her. It was not the little reserve which he exhibited toward her father, yet more than to herself. It was not that he was out of spirits; for he was quite animated at times. It seemed to be a feeling of— Lady Mabel's self-satisfaction did not permit her immediately to perceive what this feeling was.

"So," said she to herself, when L'Isle had taken his

leave, her father accompanying him out of the room, "So this is the veritable Lieutenant-Colonel L'Isle! After hearing of him daily for three weeks, I have now seen him in real life, or rather, half alive; for the cadaverous gentleman seems to have had at least half his life let out of him in that last affair. This is the glass in which the young lieutenants and ensigns of the brigade dress themselves. As Colonel Bradshawe says, there is no need to distribute copies of the articles of war among them. They may all be condensed into one injunction: 'Be just like Lieutenant-Colonel L'Isle, and you will rise like him; and deserve to rise—if you have as strong family interest to back you.' But he seems to have suffered much from his wounds, poor fellow, and in spite of family interest, to have been very near leaving his regiment vacant for another aspirant."

"By-the-bye," said Lady Mabel, as a new light flashed upon her, "he seemed to pity me all the time he was talking to me. That was it! A condescending commiseration in every look, and in every word he uttered. I am very much indebted to him for his sympathy." Here she assumed a haughty air. "But we certainly do not know ourselves; for I cannot, for the life of me, discover what he sees so pitiable about me. He is, doubtless, a very over-weening fellow—I do not like him at all!" And, with a haughty wave of the hand, she dismissed an imaginary personage from her presence, and moved off with dignity to her own room. Now, be it remembered, that Lady Mabel, walking in "maiden meditation, fancy free," among the officers of the brigade, had never, until this moment, thought it worth while to ask herself, as to any of them, whether she liked him or not.

While she was thus meditating and soliloquizing, L'Isle had mounted his horse, and was riding slowly back to his quarters, meditating and soliloquizing, too.

"What on earth was Lord Strathern dreaming of, when he brought his daughter out here—and such a daughter—to preside over his house and his table? She might as well take her seat at the head of a regimental mess-table. We know his habits of life. He cannot dine comfortably without half a dozen fast fellows about him. To make it worse, has a new set every day. And with his notions of hospitality, all are made free of the house. Of course, they become her companions, and to such a degree of freedom, that she can only get out of their way by shutting herself up in her chamber. She can scarcely have a female companion an hour in the week; for the few of our ladies here have no leisure to be trotting out of Elvas, down to headquarters, to play chaperon to a young girl who ought to be in England."

"Here is a man," continued L'Isle to himself, in an indignant tone, and so loud that his servant spurred up from behind him to see if he was wanted. "Here is a man who has been near forty years in the service, and has not yet found out what kind of women are made out of these garrison girls. Bold, flippant creatures, light infantry in petticoats, destitute of the delicacy and modesty, without which a woman may be honest by good luck, but can never be a lady deserving the name.

"She seems to retain yet the air and manner, and, I trust, the modesty and purity of mind that should grace such beauty. But how will it be six months hence? Her situation is absolutely improper. Lord Strathern has shown himself no more fit to bring up such a daughter, or even to take charge of her, after some fitter person has brought her up, than he is to say mass." For here L'Isle's eye fell on a fat priest, toiling up the hill beside him. "Though he may be as fit for that as some of these gentry. No more fit," continued he, struggling after another simile, "than for a professor of Greek literature." For during his late solitude his thoughts had often wandered back to his old haunts, before he had broken off a promising career at Oxford, to join the first British expedition that had come out to Portugal nearly five years ago.

"I am sorry for her, upon my soul I am. She would make so fine a woman in proper hands! I wonder if some remedy cannot be found against the effects of her father's folly—his forgetfulness of what is due to maiden delicacy and the privacies of domestic life!"

L'Isle was still meditating on this interesting subject when he dismounted at his own quarters, one of the best houses on the *praça*, or public square of Elvas.

Lady Mabel was right in supposing that family interest had something to do with putting L'Isle at the head of a regiment when just twenty-four. Such instances have been common enough in the British service—and not rare in others, in all ages of the world. Family interest, or something very like it, put Alexander, at the age of twenty, at the head of an army with which he went on conquering to the end of his short life. The same influence put Hannibal, at twenty-seven, at the head of an army with which he continued for seventeen years to shake the foundations of Rome. Family interest thrust forward such men as Edward the Black Prince, the fifth Harry of England, and the fourth Henri of France. This, too, thrust forward the great Condè to offer to France the first fruits of his heroism, when victor at Rocroi, at twenty-two. So, too, with Gustavus Adolphus, Turenne, Eugene of Savoy, and Frederick the Great. Family interest, not of the most creditable kind, turned the courtier Churchill into the conquering Marlborough; and his nephew, the gallant young Berwick, found that being, somewhat irregularly, the son of an English king, helped him much in obtaining the command of the armies of France. Just at this time the son of an earl, and the brother of a governor-general of India, pushed on by family interest, was proving himself not unfit to direct the efforts of the British arms. It is curious to see in these, and many an instance more in military history, how aptly family interest has come into play. It is likely that these men were not the mere creatures of accident, but had each merits of his own, and in spite of whispered insinuations, so had Lieutenant-Colonel L'Isle, though nephew and heir to an earl. Having chosen his profession, he followed it laboriously and gallantly, as if he had not been heir to an acre—but bore his fortunes on the point of his sword.

He had just reached Elvas, after spending six tedious weeks at Ciudad Rodrigo, under the surgeon's hands. He now found his own hands full of regimental business—accumulated against his arrival—and being a prompt man, set himself to work, though yet little fit for it.

Though he had seen Lady Mabel but once, he was not suffered to forget her. Every young officer he met, and many of the older, had something to say of her, some comment to make on the attractions at headquarters, some details to give of the witty things said, and the graceful things done by Lady Mabel; for she said many happy things, and did many things well, and was, at all events, sure of admiration. All this only the more convinced L'Isle that her position was very inappropriate to one so beautiful and young.

After some days he began to think himself guilty of gross neglect in not having called on the lady at headquarters. Disliking, however, to make one of an admiring crowd, he showed his strategy in choosing well his time, and called on Lady Mabel on the day and at the hour when an inspection of the troops having been ordered, every officer was at his post except himself—yet too weak to be expected to put himself at the head of his regiment.

On calling, he was immediately admitted. Lady Mabel apparently had been reading in the room in which she received him. He now saw her for the first time alone, and she was by no means aware what a critical examination she was undergoing. Her manner was different from what he had expected. With quiet politeness she received his visit as one of mere etiquette to the lady at headquarters. That repose of manner might indicate a cold disposition, or might cover strength of character and depth of feeling, not given to perpetual demonstrations, but showing vigor and animation, with telling effect, at the right time. There was no indication of that craving for company, of the *ennui* at being thrown upon her own resources for a whole morning, so common with young women brought up in a crowd, and habitually surrounded by admirers. "As yet," thought L'Isle, "she has escaped that." He even thought he could perceive that he had interrupted her in some occupation, which would be resumed the moment he left her; that his visit was a parenthesis awkwardly thrust in between, and breaking the connection of her morning hours.

Lady Mabel expressed some surprise at his being at leisure just at this time, but added: "I suppose you are yet too weak to burden yourself with such mere formalities as parades and inspections."

L'Isle was a martinet, and this a military heresy. "Keeping the troops up to the mark, fit for instant service, is not a matter of form; and that is the end of parades and inspections. But," added he, smiling,

"I am not surprised at your mistake; for I find, on coming to Elvas, that many of my brother officers have embraced the same opinion. They have got tired of these formalities, and dispense with them as often as they can. But I must not find fault with them, while indulging myself as an invalid longer than is absolutely necessary. Confinement and idleness have made me a little lazy."

An air of languor, and the marks of recent suffering, fully excused what he called his laziness. They did something more for him by exciting Lady Mabel's sympathy, putting her at ease, and inducing her to exert herself to entertain him; and during their conversation L'Isle was quietly on the watch for each indication of character his fascinating companion might betray.

Presently she rested her elbow on a thick quarto on the table beside her. L'Isle then observed that it was a Portuguese and English dictionary, and saw a volume of Count Ericeira's works beside it.

"I see, Lady Mabel, that you do not mean to remain ignorant of the language of the people you have come among."

"I wish not to remain ignorant. But between my own dullness and the want of a master, I make wonderfully slow progress. It is very provoking, particularly to a woman, to be in the midst of a people whom she can neither talk to nor understand."

"It is certainly better," said L'Isle, "to learn to fight before we go into battle, and to speak a people's language before we throw ourselves among them."

"Very true. But I have been thrown very unexpectedly among these Portuguese. I came out merely to visit my father, you know. That is, he sent for me, not having seen me for years. That must account," said she, laughing, "for my joining the brigade. I am not even a volunteer among you; nor shall I subject myself to the articles of war."

"You are a traveler, then, and not a soldier," said L'Isle.

"I am a daughter," she answered, "and in that character I come. But, beside the pleasure of being with my father, an opportunity to see outlandish places and people was no small inducement. I have my full share of curiosity and love of adventure; I want, too, to know the people I am among; and that is impossible, without speaking their language."

"But I think you are misdirecting your efforts, and wasting your time," said L'Isle. "The Spanish will be of more permanent value, and almost equally useful here on the frontier. The one is a language widely spread and a noble one. The other, though exceedingly well adapted to conversation, has but a narrow range, and may one day be merged in the superior tongue. The literature of the Spanish, too, is the richer, though both are poor enough."

"I am glad to hear you say that; for I have already made some little progress in Spanish. I have read a few books, and moulded my tongue to the utterance of a long list of conversational phrases. I would now gladly exchange my French for Spanish or Portuguese. What a pity it is, that the languages of different countries are not, like their coins, exchangeable one for another."

"Unfortunately," said L'Isle, laughing, "that exchange is a slow process; and exact equivalents are seldom found."

"It is too provoking," continued Lady Mabel, "after having been at so much pains to learn French, not to be at liberty to go to France, to show the natives how well I can speak their tongue. True, I have access to their books, which are, perhaps, better than themselves."

"That is not saying much for their books," said L'Isle contemptuously. Their literature is much overvalued. Its chief merits are variety and bulk.'

"Do you think so? That is not the opinion I have heard expressed."

"Very true. The world is full of false opinions and bad taste. But a literature, whose great epic poem is the *Henriade*, may be abundant but cannot be rich. A language, in which you cannot make verse without the jingle of rhyme, may be clear and copious, but is wanting in melody and force. Take away from French literature Gil Blas and the *memoires*, and were all the rest lost, its place might be easily filled with something better. With these exceptions, there is little worth doing into English or any other tongue. And after all, Gil Blas is only a renegade Spaniard in a French uniform; and, undoubtedly, it is not genius, but merely their intense vanity and egotism, that enables them to excel in writing their own memoirs. Besides, unlike most other people, their books are as immoral as themselves."

"Well," said Lady Mabel, looking at him in some surprise, yet half convinced of the truth of what he had been saying. "It must certainly be a great comfort to you to entertain so thorough a contempt and dislike for the people you have to fight against."

"Perhaps it is," said L'Isle, laughing at her observation and his own warmth. "It may not be in the spirit of Christianity or of chivalry, but it is exceedingly true to our nature, to dislike our enemies, and heartily, too. But to return to our subject. You wish to learn Spanish, and I can provide you a capable and zealous teacher."

"I am much obliged to you; where is he to be found?"

"I will bring him here, any day and hour you may appoint."

"Then I will fix an early hour, and take a lesson every day."

"The truth is," said L'Isle, hesitating and somewhat confused, "it is very difficult to find a Spaniard who speaks English well enough to teach you his own tongue."

"But you said just now that would find me such a master."

"But not a Spaniard. I hear," said L'Isle, putting a bold face on the matter, "that several of my brother officers have been permitted to make themselves useful to you in various capacities. For instance, on looking round this room, I see more than one achievement of Captain Cranfield's, and hear that Major Lumley's skill in music has been called into play. Now I am behind no one in zeal for your service."

"So you, yourself, are the Spanish master, whom you, yourself, would recommend?"

"I assure you I do not know where to find another."

"Your offer is exceedingly tempting," said Lady Mabel, bowing ironically low. "But I am too much in debt already to the gentlemen in his majesty's service. To turn one of his colonels into my Spanish master would be seriously to misemploy his precious time. I would feel that I was robbing my country. Is it not positive treason to aid and abet the king's enemies? Then it is negative treason, to divert from his service any of the king's friends."

"But you forget that I am an invalid, not yet fit for duty."

"You are getting more fit for it every day. My invalid tutor would become a sound colonel long before I had made much progress under his tuition."

"But I would not object to relaxing from my military duties, and prolonging my invalid condition in your service."

"Let me beg that you do no such thing, but hasten

to get so well as to forget your wounds, and the awkward occasion on which you received them."

"Why," said L'Isle, in some surprise, "what have you heard of that occasion?"

"Perhaps you, like some other people, do not care to be reminded of your blunders," said Lady Mabel, mischievously.

"Blunders?" said L'Isle, "I do not see how a soldier can avoid exposing himself occasionally to the risk of being shot, sabred, or bayoneted. What blunder of mine have you heard of?"

"Merely that on the approach of a French column, you, instead of rejoining the main body, in great alarm hid yourself and your men in a little Spanish village too mean to have a name. The French found you out, and kept you shut up there in great trepidation for five or six hours, while they were cutting away your barricades, beating in the doors, and tearing off the roofs of the houses. Your case was as desperate as that of a rat in a trap; and when your friends came to your relief, they had to knock a great many of the French in the head before they could persuade them to let you slip out. But, by some lucky misunderstanding at headquarters, you were soon after made a lieut. colonel."

"Do you know," said L'Isle, laughing, "that this is, to me, quite a new version of that little affair? Did you hear whether we did the French any damage, while they beset us so closely?"

"Nothing was said on that score. So I suppose you did them little harm."

"It is lucky for me that your informant had not the reporting of this affair at headquarters."

"It is said that you had that more adroitly done by your own friends."

"They give me credit at least for good diplomacy," said L'Isle. "Or, at all events, it is a good thing to have a friend at court—that is, at the elbow of the commander-in-chief. And it seems that I have one there. But still you make a great mistake in declining my services as a teacher of the Spanish tongue. I may be a blundering soldier, but have made myself thoroughly master of the languages of the Peninsula, and have a decided aptitude for teaching. Let me begin by warning you against a blunder we English always commit, in trying to speak a tongue not our own, with the mouth half open, and the hands in the pockets. Now, when you address a foreigner in his own tongue, speak with much noise and vociferation, opening your mouth wide and using much action. The ideas you cannot convey in words, you must communicate by gesticulation, the more emphatic the better."

"What!" said Lady Mabel. "Would you have me go scolding and gesticulating at every foreign fellow I meet with, and become notorious throughout Elvas as the British virago?"

"There is no danger of that," said L'Isle. "They would only say that you have as much vivacity as a native, and soon begin to understand you."

"I have made the acquaintance of some ladies of Elvas. As yet our intercourse has been limited to a few formal visits, and a few set phrases mingled with pantomime. But some of them are disposed to be very sociable, and, through their teaching, I hope to be able soon to bear my part in the most sprightly and sentimental conversation. You shall see what an apt scholar I am under the tuition of my own sex."

"I trust you will be on your guard against cultivating too great an intimacy with these people," said L'Isle. "You do not know what Portuguese and Spanish ladies are."

"What are they?"

"A thorough knowledge of them would only satisfy you that they are gross in language, particularly the Spaniards, indelicate in their habits, careless of propriety, lax in morals, and, with all their grace, vivacity, and elegance, very unfit companions for you. In short, the purity of mind, true refinement of manners, and scrupulous propriety of conduct we look for in a lady, are almost unknown among them."

"What a shocking picture you paint of our friends here. You must know them exceedingly well," added Lady Mabel, in innocent surprise, "to justify your abusing them so roundly."

"By report—only by report," said L'Isle hastily. "But I have had many opportunities of judging of the grossness of their conversation and manners. The Portuguese ladies are not gross in language, like the Spaniards; but are quite on a par with them in essentials, or rather the want of essentials."

"They are not at all indebted to your report, which has used them very roughly. You, perhaps, have been unfortunate in the samples you have met with; and, at least, do not know my new friends here in Elvas."

"I confess that I do not."

"Yet I must own that you have damped my ardor to cultivate an intimacy with them. Yet such is the situation of the two or three of our own ladies here, that these allies of ours afford the only female society at my command."

"In that respect your situation here must seem very strange to you."

"Strange, indeed, at first—but now I am getting accustomed to it. I begin to feel as if I held an official position in the brigade. I make great progress in knowledge of military affairs—am quite familiar, as you may perceive, with the details of the last campaign, and begin to understand both the technical language and the slang of our comrades; who give me plenty of their company, and right merry companions they are. But, perhaps," said she, looking at him doubtingly, "you may be able to understand me, and excuse my weakness, when I confess that there is still so much of the woman left in me that I do often long to slam the door in the face of the brigade, and have a good long confidential chat with some of my own sex."

"The want of that must be a sad privation to you."

"My only resource now is to get old Moodie and Jennie Aiken, my maid, together, and have a good home talk with them, which, for the time, may blot out the map of Portugal, and carry us back to Scotland."

"After that avowal," said L'Isle, rising from his chair, "I had better not trespass on you longer, lest I should have the door slammed in my face the next time I visit you." And he bowed and put an end to his visit."

As he rode homeward, he again brought Lord Strathern to trial, and soon found a verdict against him, of utter incapacity to take charge of such a daughter as heaven had blessed him with. L'Isle felt strongly tempted to take the vacant guardianship upon himself—but did not see just then how it was to be brought about.

He was buried in these thoughts when the sound of horses' feet aroused him; and looking up he saw Lord Strathern riding down toward him from the city gate, followed by a party of young officers. His lordship drew up as he approached, and said: "L'Isle, I am glad to see you look so much like taking the field again. Why, your ride has actually brought a color into your cheeks." In truth, L'Isle had turned somewhat red on seeing suddenly before him the very man he had just been condemning in secret tribunal. "We cannot let you play invalid much longer," his lordship continued. "We begin to miss you sadly.

By the by, I have just been inspecting the troops. Their condition is not exactly what I would wish. But the less we say about the matter—only—I am glad the French are not just now in the neighborhood."

"But they have not told us how long they meant to stay away," suggested L'Isle.

"We won't see them soon, however," said his lordship carelessly. "Well, L'Isle, I will begin to put you on duty by having you to dine with me to-morrow. These noisy fellows I have with me to-day would be too much for your nerves. We will have a quieter party, and I will not insist on your doing your full turn of duty at the bottle."

"I will obey you, my lord, with the greatest pleasure, particularly as you are so considerate as to the bottle. I have just been paying my respects, for the first time, to Lady Mabel."

"Well, if you did not bore her by the length of your visit—a thing she sometimes complains of—she will be glad to see you again to-morrow." And Lord Strathern rode off—with a merry party at his heels.

CHAPTER IV.

Celia.—Here comes Monsieur Le Beau.
Rosalind.—With his mouth full of news.
Celia.—Which he will put on us as pigeons feed their young.
Rosalind.—Then shall we be news-crammed.

As You Like It.

The next morning Colonel L'Isle was seated in his room, wrapped in his cloak, with a *brasero* filled with wood embers at his feet; for it was one of those windy, chilly days, not uncommon in this fluctuating climate, and he was still invalid enough to be keenly sensitive to these sudden changes of temperature. He was, too, so completely wrapped up in his meditations, that his servant had twice to announce that the adjutant was in the next room.

"Here, already!" said L'Isle; "I did not expect him until ten o'clock." He looked at his watch. "But it is ten already. Here have I been thinking for two hours, and have never once thought of the regiment. I am acquiring a sad habit of day-dreaming, or, rather, my mind has not yet recovered its tone. Ask Lieutenant Meynell to walk in here."

The regimental business was soon dispatched, and the adjutant, who was a capital newsmonger, began to detail the local news of the day. L'Isle liked to keep himself informed of what was going on around him, on the easy terms of listening to the adjutant. But this morning he seemed to tire soon at the details of small intelligence, much of which was of a sporting character, such as this: "Warren has succeeded in buying the famous dog at Estremoz; they say he will collar a wolf without ceremony, and throttle him single-handed; and he has the knack of so seizing a wild boar, that he can never bring his tusks to bear upon him."

"I hope," said L'Isle, "that Warren will show us many trophies of his prowess, or his dog's rather, in the hunt."

"He had to pay well for him, though. Fifty moidores was the least his owner would take for him."

"I sincerely trust that Warren will get fifty moidores' worth of sport out of him."

"He went out yesterday to try him," continued Meynell, "but Hatton, who was with him, got such a fall (he is a villainous rider, without knowing it), that they had great trouble in getting him back here, and it broke up the day's sport."

"Is he much hurt?" asked L'Isle.

"No permanent injury. But he fell on his head, and, at first, they thought the time come for firing blank-cartridges over him."

"I trust, if Hatton is bent on dying in the field, he will choose some occasion when they do not fire blank-cartridges."

As his colonel seemed little interested in his sporting intelligence, the adjutant turned to a topic that looked a little more like business. "I see that Commissary Shortridge has got back."

"Ah!" said L'Isle, suppressing a yawn, "where has he been?"

"He has been to Lisbon."

"What carried him there?" mechanically asked the colonel, evidently not caring to know.

"Business of the commissariat, he says."

"So I suppose," said L'Isle, carelessly.

"But I suppose no such thing," said Meynell. "The first thing these fellows think of is not the supply of the troops, but their own comfort. He only went to Lisbon to bring his wife here."

"What!" said L'Isle, with sudden interest, "is Mrs. Shortridge in Elvas?"

"Yes. She came with him last night."

"And is she to remain here any time?"

"As long as we stay," answered Meynell, surprised at the interest his superior now showed at his intelligence. "That is, if Shortridge can establish her here comfortably. You know, since the king's money has been passing through his hands, and some of it has stuck to his palms, he has begun to give himself airs. He speaks with the most gentlemanly disgust of the narrow and inconvenient lodgings they are obliged to put up with. He told me they were in the dirtiest part of the town, in the midst of the filthiest of these Portuguese, and sooner than let Mrs. Shortridge stay there, he will take her to Portalegre, or back to Lisbon."

"There will not be the least need of that," said L'Isle, quickly; "this house is large and convenient enough"—and he looked round the apartment into the room beyond—"and is one of the best situated in Elvas."

"But you are occupying it yourself, sir. What good will that do, Shortridge?"

"Oh, I will give it up to Shortridge. It is quite thrown away on a bachelor like me. Now I am on duty again, I prefer being near the regiment, and shall take rooms at the barracks."

"Shortridge will be exceedingly obliged to you. But," added Meynell, fishing for information, "I did not think you cared a farthing whether the commissary got into good quarters or no."

"The commissary!" said L'Isle, looking round on his companion with an air of surprise; then he added, in a tone of contempt, "he may lie in a ditch. Many a better man has done it. It is Mrs. Commissary for whom I would find good quarters."

"Oh, indeed!" said Meynell, elevating his eyebrows a good deal, "I overlooked that. But I was not aware that you had ever seen her."

"Oh, many times: in Lisbon, last year. Indeed, on one occasion I did her a well-timed service."

"What was that?—if I may be allowed to ask."

"Why, Mrs. Shortridge, though an excellent woman, is a little afflicted with the disease of sight-seeing, and had thrust herself, with a party of other heretics, into the Patriarchal Church, to witness the rending of the veil. Do you know what that means, Meynell? I believe you are not well drilled in theology."

"Not popish theology."

"Nor any other, I fear. However, a large detachment of the live and dead saints were there, and, certainly, half the rabble of Lisbon. In the rush of this devout crowd, Mrs. Shortridge got separated from her party, and, between alarm and exhaustion, fell, fainting, on the pavement. She would soon have been trampled to death, had I not picked her up and carried her out bodily. I had to swear awfully at the rabble to make them give way."

"That was no small service," said Meynell; then, glancing at the colonel's thin form, "I am afraid you could not repeat it just now. Mrs. Shortridge is a plump little body."

"I suppose not. Yet there is no knowing what exertions a man might make to save a pretty woman. However, she has been very grateful ever since, and whenever we meet we are excellent friends. I am glad Shortridge has brought her here. She is a different sort of person from himself. She has some very pleasant traits of character—in fact, she is a very good woman," and he sank into a reverie, apparently thinking over Mrs. Commissary's good qualities.

Meynell had nothing more to tell, and, hopeless of extracting any thing more, now took leave. But when he had gone out of the room, his colonel called him back to inquire where Shortridge was now lodged. Having given as precise an answer as he could to this question, the adjutant departed, trying as he went, to frame such a definition of a good woman as would fit his view of this case.

This little conversation seemed to have revived L'Isle a good deal. He looked out of the window and pronounced the wind to have fallen, and that, after all, it was a very pleasant day. Calling his servant to bring his boots and brush his clothes, he was soon after on the *praca* of Elvas.

This exhibited a busy scene; for the troops quartered in Elvas created a market, and drew a concourse of people from the surrounding country. Asses laden with, or just unladen of, country produce, were grouped about the square, each with his nose tied up in a net, that he might not eat his saddle or panniers. Bullock carts were seen here and there, among them, many of the oxen lying down with their legs doubled under them, taking advantage of the halt to enjoy their *siesta*. A crowd of peasants hovered about, and the sonorous Spanish mingling with the abrupt and nasal Portuguese, the short black jackets and *montero* caps, among the hats and vests, generally brown, showed that many of these men had come across the Spanish border. Here was the pig merchant, with his unquiet and ear-piercing merchandise, and the wine merchant, with his pitchy goat-skin sacks, full of, and flavoring the *vinho verde* Colonel Bradshawe so much abhorred. Here were peasant women, with poultry, and sausages, and goats'-milk cheese; and young girls, persuasively offering for sale the contents of their baskets, oranges, chesnuts, bolotas, and other fruits and nuts. Here, in the crowd, was a monk; there, a secular priest, and of friars a plenty. And here, in the midst of them, were the broad-faced English soldiers, touching their caps as L'Isle passed among them—their faces growing broader as they remarked to each other, that there was still something left of the colonel. Here, too, were the lounging citizens of Elvas, who might have personified *otium cum dignitate*, or plain English laziness, but for the presence of some of the gentlemen of the brigade, who were sauntering about with their hands in their pockets, as if caring for nothing, and having nothing to do, or at once too proud and lazy to do it—not much caring which way their steps led them, but expecting, of course, every one to get out of their way. Yet a spark of interest would, at times, shine out from them at the sight of a neat figure, or a pretty face, among the rustic belles, whose love of bright and strongly contrasted colors in dress, attracted the eye, and gave variety to the scene.

Some of these gentlemen stopped L'Isle to talk with him. But, avoiding any prolonged conversation, he hastened across the *praca*, into one of the narrow and uncleanly streets, along which he picked his way, wishing that he had authority, for a few days, to turn the good people of Elvas, clergy and all, into scavengers, and enter on a thorough purification of the place, beginning with the persons of the people themselves. A moral purification might possibly follow, but could not possibly precede this physical cleansing. Walking along, divided between these thoughts and the necessity of looking for the place he was searching for, he heard himself called by some one behind him. He turned; it was Commissary Shortridge himself, who being rather pursy, was a little out of breath through his exertions to overtake him.

Now, there were a good many things that L'Isle despised. But, if there was any thing that he did despise beyond all others, it was a commissary—a fellow who makes his gains where all other men make their losses; who devotes himself to his country's service for the express purpose of cheating it; who seizes the hour of its greatest want and weakness, to bleed it most freely; who, as often as he can, *sells* to his country straw for hay, chaff for corn, and bones for beef; the master-stroke of whose art is to get passed, by fraudulent vouchers, accounts full of imaginary articles, charged at fabulous prices; in short, a man who loves war more than Mars or Achilles; reaping, amidst its blood and havoc, a rich harvest in safety. Our commissary was not quite equal in professional skill to some of his brethren. Perhaps he had some small remnant of conscience left, or of patriotism, or of loyalty, or of caution, which withheld him from plundering king and country with both hands. Nevertheless, from being an unprosperous London tradesman, he had, in a few years, contrived to line his pockets exceedingly well, and had now grown ambitious of social position.

How came it then, when the commissary had expressed very copiously his delight at seeing Colonel L'Isle again, and yet more at seeing him so much better in health and strength than he had dared to hope, L'Isle condescendingly gave him to understand that the pleasure of this meeting was not all on the commissary's side? When Shortridge congratulated him on his promotion, and yet more on the high deserts that had drawn it upon him, L'Isle's manner implied that the commissary's good opinion gave him greater confidence in himself. How could L'Isle do this? Simply because the proudest and best of us can tolerate, and even flatter, those we despise, when we have urgent occasion to use them.

The commissary then said, "I have brought Mrs. Shortridge with me to Elvas."

"I am very glad to hear it," answered L'Isle, without betraying that he knew it before. "Even one English lady is a precious addition to our society in this dull place."

"Mrs. Shortridge has never forgotten your rescuing her from under the feet of the idolatrous rabble of Lisbon. She is still a strong friend of yours, and will be delighted to see you, as soon as she is mistress of a decent apartment."

"Where is she now?"

"Not far from here—but in such an abominable hole, that a lady is naturally ashamed to be caught there by any genteel acquaintance."

"I am truly sorry to hear that she is so badly lodged."

"Our officers," said Shortridge, "have taken up all the best houses; and the troops being quartered here has attracted such an additional population from the country around, that I was afraid I would have to carry Mrs. Shortridge to rooms in the barracks."

"That will never do," said L'Isle. "But, pray, if I am in her neighborhood, let me call on Mrs. Shortridge, and welcome her to Elvas."

Thus urged, the commissary led the way, and soon reached his lodgings. They found the lady in a room of some size, but dark, dirty, and offensive enough to eye and nose to disgust her with Elvas and drive her back to Lisbon, without unpacking the numerous trunks, baskets, band-boxes, and portable furniture which lumbered the room. These her man-servant was arranging, under her direction, while she was good-humoredly trying to pacify her maid, who, with tears in her eyes, was protesting that she could not sleep another night in that coal-hole, into which the people of the house had thrust her, and which they would persist in calling a chamber.

Mrs. Shortridge, a plump and pretty woman of eight-and-twenty, was a good deal fluttered at seeing such a visitor at such a time. She declared "that she did not know whether she was more delighted or ashamed to see Major—I beg your pardon—Colonel L'Isle, in such a place; we, who have been accustomed to a suite of genteel apartments wherever we went."

L'Isle cast his eye around the forlorn and dismal walls. "Let me beg you, Colonel L'Isle, to be conveniently near-sighted during your visit. I would not, for the world, have our present domicil, and our household arrangements, minutely inspected by your critical eye."

Without minding her protest, he completed a deliberate survey; then said, suddenly, "Why, Shortridge, how could you think of shutting up a lady in such a dungeon? If Mrs. Shortridge were not the best-tempered woman in the world, it would cause a domestic rebellion, and we would soon see her posting back to Lisbon, and London, perhaps, without leave or license. Do you forget how she yearns after the two little boys she left at home, that you venture to aggravate so her regrets at leaving England?"

"How can I help it?" said Shortridge, looking much out of countenance; "I have been into a dozen houses, and these rooms are the largest and least comfortless I can find."

"I would pitch my tent in the *praca*, and pass the winter in it," said L'Isle, "sooner than share with these people the pig-sties they call their houses."

"But a lady is not quite so hardy or fearless as a soldier," said Mrs. Shortridge, "and needs more substantial shelter and protection than a canvas wall."

"I have some thoughts of getting rooms in the barracks," said Shortridge; "but it is not pleasant for a lady to be in the midst of the rank and file."

"Of course not. By the by," said L'Isle, as if he

had just thought of it, "I intend, as soon as I get quite well, to take quarters at the barracks; I lodge too far from the regiment now. I may as well hasten my removal, and transfer my present abode to you. My house is large, well situated, and not more dilapidated than every thing else is in this country. It will suit Mrs. Shortridge as well as a Portuguese house can suit an English lady."

"But I cannot think of turning you out of it," said Mrs. Shortridge. "You are still an invalid, and need every comfort and convenience about you."

"I am nearly as well as I ever was in my life," answered L'Isle; "a little like the lean knight of La Mancha, it is true, but time and good feeding will soon cure that. And, let me tell you, good feeding is the order of the day here just now. I am only afraid we will eat up the country around, before the opening of the campaign. But my present house has a fault to me, which will be none to you. There is no stabling for my horses, unless I follow the Portuguese custom, and lodge them in the ground-floor of the house. I have to keep them at the barracks, and like to be so quartered that I can put my foot in the stirrup at a minute's warning."

The commissary and his wife made many scruples at accepting his offer, but L'Isle overruled them, and at length it was settled that he should march out at the end of three days, and Mrs. Shortridge and suite should garrison the vacant post.

"And now I will leave you," said L'Isle; "I will

finish my visit when you are more suitably lodged. I know how annoying it must be to a neat English woman to receive her friends in such a place as this." And he left Mr. and Mrs. Commissary full of gratitude for his attentions, and of a growing conviction that they were people of some importance and fashion.

The military gentlemen in Elvas had, most of them, abundant leisure on their hands, and, like the Athenians in St. Paul's day, spent their time in little else "than either to tell or to hear some new thing every day." Colonel Bradshawe, strolling about the *praca* with this praiseworthy object, had the luck to meet with Adjutant Meynell, and at once began to pump him for news. But the adjutant, being a man of the same kidney, needed no pumping at all. He at once commenced laying open to the colonel, under the strictest injunctions to secrecy, the thing weighing most on his mind, which was the curious little conversation he had just held with his own colonel, not forgetting to give a few extra touches to the expressions of satisfaction that the news of Mrs. Shortridge's arrival had called forth. After sifting and twisting the matter to their own satisfaction, they parted, and the colonel continued his stroll, chewing the end of the last news he had swallowed. An hour or so after, whom should he meet with, by the greatest good luck, but the commissary himself. Now, Shortridge was rather a favorite with the colonel, being a man who knew how to make himself useful. For instance, he was the very agent who had so judiciously declined purchasing the refuse sherry wines which Soult, Victor & Co. had contemptuously left on the market; while, with equal judgment and promptitude, he had laid in for the mess an abundant stock of the best port, malmsey and Madeira. Two such cronies, meeting for the first time for ten days, had much conference together; in the course of which the colonel learned all about the straits Mrs. Shortridge was put to for lodgings, and how she was to be relieved through the considerate kindness of L'Isle. This led to a minute account of the occasion on which their acquaintance began, and rather an exaggerated statement of the social relations existing between the aristocratic colonel and the Shortridge firm.

"I have been sometimes galled and ruffled by his haughty manner," said the commissary; "but now I know it is only his manner. He is very considerate of other people, and is getting more and more agreeable every day."

The commissary not having, like the colonel, nothing to do, now took his leave; a little surprised, however, seeing how glad Bradshawe had been to meet with him, at his not inviting him to dine that day with the mess, as he had often done before.

It was observed at the mess table of the —— regiment, that the colonel was in particularly fine spirits to-day. Always companionable, he this day enjoyed his dinner, his glass, and his jokes, and other men's jokes, with peculiar *gusto*. At length, however, the table grew thin. Duty, pleasure, satiety, and restlessness, took off man after man, particularly of the younger officers, and the colonel was left at last to the support of three or four of his special confidants, the stanchest sitters in the regiment.

Gathering them around him, he called for a fresh decanter, filled their glasses, and ordered the last servant out of the room. After slowly draining his glass, and dwelling awhile on the rich flavor of the wine, he remarked: "We certainly owe a debt of gratitude to Shortridge, for the good faith in which he executes these little commissions. They are, we should remember, quite beside his official duties. I never tasted better Madeira of its age in my life—it almost equals my lord's best, which is ten years older; and I do not think that Shortridge made more than two fair profits out of us. I met him, by the by, to-day, and would have had him to dine with us; but, for certain reasons, I think his best place, just now, is at home, watching over his domestic relations."

"What is there in them," exclaimed one of the party, "that needs such close watching?"

The colonel seemed for a moment to debate in his own mind the propriety of making a revelation, then said: "We are all friends here; and, while it is desirable in our profession, and in all others, to know thoroughly the men we live among, still there are many little things that are not to be published on parade, like a general order."

His discreet auditors assenting to this truth, he then gave a full detail of Adjutant Meynell's morning conversation with his colonel, painting broadly and brightly L'Isle's surprise and delight on hearing that Mrs. Shortridge was in Elvas. "What do you think of that, Fox?"

Captain Fox thought L'Isle very imprudent. "But he is young yet, and lacks secrecy and self-command."

"I had not well digested what Meynell had told me," continued Bradshawe, "when I met Shortridge, and lo! L'Isle had already found them out in their dirty lodgings," and the colonel went on to repeat and embellish Shortridge's narrative of L'Isle's kind attention, and the origin of their intimacy. Various were the comments of the company on the affair. But they all agreed to the justness of their colonel's criticism, when he remarked: "That scene in the Patriarchal Church must have been exceedingly well got up. I should like much to have been by. Have you ever remarked that a woman never faints out-and-out, when there is no man near enough, and ready enough, to catch her before she falls to the ground?"

This was a physiological fact, as to female fainting, that some of the company admitted was new to them.

"Now, you are all sharp fellows," said Bradshawe, with a patronizing wave of the hand; "and some of you profess to be men of intrigue; yet I doubt whether any one of you can tell me why the house is not handed over to Shortridge until at the end of three days."

One suggested one reason; another, another. But

wine had failed to sharpen their wits, and he scornfully rejected their solutions.

"Three days may be needed," said he, gravely, "to fit a double set of keys to every lock in the house. Shortridge will have one. L'Isle may keep the other, and with it the power of letting himself in and out at any minute of the twenty-four hours."

How stupid did his companions think themselves. The thing was now patent to the dullest apprehension.

"It is curious," continued the colonel, "that Shortridge, so keen a fellow in all business transactions (for both we and the government have found him too sharp for us before now), should be in these little delicate domestic relations such an egregious gull. You all know I do not view these little matters from the parson's point of view; but still, there is a propriety to be observed. To think," continued Bradshawe, with a countenance of comic horror, "of his proposing to make our friend Shortridge lie in a ditch, for his accommodation! Our punctilious comrade is getting to be a very bare-faced fellow. Just snatched from the brink of the grave, too," added he, in a sudden fit of pious indignation. "What a deliberate, cold-blooded fellow!"

Having thus, by fitting a few chance hints to each other, brought out a pretty piece of Spanish intrigue, that would have delighted Calderon or Lope de Vega, the colonel emptied the decanter by filling the glasses all round, and each man emptying his glass, the company dispersed.

CHAPTER V.

I praise God for you, sir: your reasons at dinner have been sharp and sententious, pleasant without scurrility, witty without affectation, audacious without impudence, learned without opinion, and strange without heresy.—*Love's Labor Lost.*

L'Isle, meanwhile, after spending an unwonted time at his toilet, drew himself up to the utmost of the five feet ten which nature had allotted to him, to shake off the stoop which he imagined himself to have contracted during his long hours of languor and suffering. He then inspected himself most critically in the glass, to see how far he had recovered his usual good looks. But that truthful counsellor presented to him cheeks still sunken and pallid, and sharpened features. The clear gray eye looked out from a cavern, and the rich nut-brown hair hung over a brow covered with parchment. His lean figure no longer filled the uniform which once fitted it so well. He stood before his glass in no peacock mood of self-admiration; but was compelled to own that he was not, just now at least, the man to fascinate a lady's eye; so he resolved to take Lady Mabel by the ear, which is, in fact, the surest way to catch a woman.

Lord Strathern kept his promise: to have no noisy

fellows at dinner to-day. Perhaps an occasional visitor, who hovered near, the gout, made him more readily dispense with his more jovial companions. The only guest, beside L'Isle, was Major Conway, of the light dragoons.

A party of four is an excellent number for conversation, especially if there be no rivalry among them. The major had served long in India, but had arrived in the Peninsula only toward the end of the last campaign. He wished to learn all he could of the country, the people and the war; and nearly five years of close observation, industrious inquiry, and active service had rendered L'Isle just the man to gratify his wishes. Lord Strathern, too, in a long and varied military career, had seen much, and the old soldier had not failed to lay in a stock of shrewd observation and amusing anecdote. So that, to a young listener like Lady Mabel, eager to learn and quick to appreciate, two or three hours glided away in striking and agreeable contrast with the more jovial and somewhat noisy festivities of yesterday and many a previous day. L'Isle made no attempt to engross her attention. Major Conway had left a wife in England, which shut out any feelings of rivalry with him. L'Isle was thus quite at his ease, and showed to much advantage; for it is surprising how agreeable some people can make themselves when they are bent upon it. He combined the qualities of a good talker and a good listener; was communicative to the major; yet more attentive to his lordship; and most careful, above all things, to turn the conversation to topics interesting to Lady Mabel, who, while listening, asking questions, and offering an occasional remark, was fast coming to the conclusion that L'Isle, young as he was, was by far the best informed and most considerate man in the brigade. She more particularly wondered how, while tied down to his military duties, he had found time to master the languages, history, topography, and even the antiquities of the peninsula. He knew personally many a Spaniard and Portuguese who had made himself conspicuous for good or ill, at this fearful crisis of his country's history. He thoroughly understood the people, with all their virtues and their vices, that perhaps outweigh those virtues; yet he seemed by no means to despise them. Amidst the too common baseness and corruption, he could paint vividly their nobler traits, and illustrate them by many a pointed anecdote and thrilling narrative. Lady Mabel could not help thinking what a delightful companion he would be on a tour through these countries, if she found so much pleasure in merely listening to his account of what he had seen and witnessed there.

"Traveling is my passion," said Lady Mabel. "From childhood I have longed to see foreign lands, and to find myself surrounded by outlandish people. I suppose it is owing to my having been kept close at home, yet encouraged to follow the footsteps of travelers over page after page of their rambles. My journey hither, through the wilderness of Alemtejo, has but whetted my appetite. And there is something peculiarly fascinating in the idea of traveling in Spain, the land of adventure and romance."

"Just now is no good time for such a journey," said L'Isle; "there are too many French and other robbers besetting the roads."

"There would be too little of romance and too much of adventure in meeting with them," said she. "It is most provoking to be thus tantalized; the cup at my lips, and I cannot taste of it; Spain in sight, and I cannot explore it. I am eager to visit the Alhambra and Escurial, and other show-places, and take a long ramble in the Sierra Morena. I would wish to engage the most skillful *arriero* in all Spain, and, mounted on his best mule, roam all over the country, through every mountain-pass, and across every desolate plain, and make a pilgrimage to every spot hallowed by poetic or historic fame. I would search out, as a shrine of chivalry, each field on which the Cid displayed the gleaming blade of *Tizona*, and on which the hoofs of his *Babieca* trampled on the Moor. I wonder if my guide could not show me, too, the foundation-stones of the manor-house of the good knight of La Mancha, the site at least of the bower of Dulcinea del Toboso, and Gil Blas' robbers' cave?"

"Just at this time," said L'Isle, "the cave of Captain Rolando and his comrades, being in the north of Leon, is particularly inaccessible, for there are some ninety thousand similar gentry wintering between us and it."

"Those fellows have been very quiet of late, and it will probably be some time before they are stirring again," said Lord Strathern.

"We will give them reason to bestir themselves as soon as the corn is grown enough to fodder our horses," answered L'Isle. "Meanwhile, Lady Mabel, there is much worth seeing in Portugal. All is not like the wilderness of Alemtejo. If you will believe the Portuguese, it was not to the imagination of the poet, but to the eye of the traveler in Lusitania, that we owe the poetic pictures of the Elysian fields. All the Portuguese agree that their country is crowded with the choice beauties and wonders of nature, and they certainly should know their own country best. I have seen enough of it to satisfy me, that though but a little corner of the smallest of the continents, it is a lovely and remarkable part of the earth. Its beautiful mountains, not sublime, perhaps, like the Alps and Pyrenees, but exquisitely rich and wonderful in coloring, with a variety of romantic and ever-shifting scenery, are perhaps unrivaled in Europe; its grand rivers, often unite on their banks the wildest rocks with the loveliest woodland scenes; its balmy climate fosters in many places an ever green foliage and a perpetual spring."

"From your description of the country," said Lady Mabel, "one might take you for a Portuguese."

"Yet they themselves have little perception of the real beauties of nature," said L'Isle. "They will lead you away from the loveliest scene in their land, to point out some curiosity, more to their taste; some miraculous image, some saintly relic brought by angels from the Holy Land, or, perhaps, some local natural phenomenon, which has a dash of the wonderful about it. For instance, when at Braga, three years ago, with my hands full of business, and anxious at the same time to learn all I could of the country around, my Portuguese companion compelled me to waste a precious hour in visiting a famous spring in the garden of a convent of St. Augustine. The water, you must know, is intensely cold, and if a bottle of wine be immersed in it, it is instantly turned into vinegar."

"Did you see that?" asked Lady Mabel.

"When I called for a bottle of wine, the good fathers told me they had given all they had to a detachment of Portuguese troops that marched by the day before—a charity more wondrous than the virtue of the spring."

"Yet it is a pity you could not test the virtues of this wonderful spring," said she.

"Not more wonderful," said L'Isle, "than the fountain in the village of Friexada. Its water, too, is excessively cold, and of so hungry a nature, that in less than an hour it consumes a joint of meat, leaving the bones quite bare."

"You of course tested that," said she.

"Unluckily," said L'Isle, "our party had only one leg of mutton in store, and were too hungry to risk their dinner in the fountain's maw."

"You are a bad traveler," said Lady Mabel, "and seem never to have with you the means of testing the truth of what you are told."

"I take with me a good stock of faith," said L'Isle, "and believe, or seem to believe, all that I am told. This pleases these people wonderfully well, and keeping them in good humor is the main point just now. There is, however, near Estremoz, which place you passed through coming hither, a curiosity of somewhat a similar kind. It is a spring which is dry in winter, but pours out a considerable stream in summer. Its waters are of so petrifying a quality, that the wheels of the mills it works are said to be soon turned into stone."

"I trust, for your credit as a traveler," said Lady Mabel, "that you will be able to say that you, for once, proved the truth or falsehood of what you heard."

"I did, and found them incrusted with stone. But that is not so curious as the prophetic spring of Xido, which foretells to the rustics around a fruitful season, by pouring forth but little water, or a year of scarcity by an abundant flow. These are little things; but were I to run over each class of objects of curiosity or interest this country affords, I would soon convince you that you were already in a land of wonders and rare sights."

"But even here I am trammeled. Papa did not come out here to examine the curiosities of the country, or to hunt out picturesque scenery, Moorish antiquities, or Roman ruins, and I cannot go scampering over the neighborhood with an escort of volunteers from the brigade or the Light Dragoons. It is true that Mrs. Captain Howe, who is a great *connoisseuse* in nature and art, has promised to be my guide in exploring the country as soon as she gets rid of her rheumatism. But from the number of her flannel wrappers, I infer that there is no hope of her soon extending her explorations beyond the walls of her room."

"You must indeed feel the want of a companion to free you from the awkwardness of your situation; here with no company but those rude comrades his majesty has sent out hither."

"My want is so urgent that were it not for my loyalty, I would now exchange a crack regiment for a companionable woman."

"I am glad, then, to be able to tell you that a lady has arrived in Elvas, who may be very useful in filling up this awkward gap in the circle of your acquaintance!"

"A lady? An English lady? Who is she?"

"An English lady. One old enough to be your chaperon, and young enough to be your companion. She has some other merits too, not the least of which, in my estimation is that she professes to be a great friend of mine."

"A crowning virtue, that," said lady Mabel."

"It does not blind me, however, to two or three faults, and a misfortune she labors under."

"What then are her faults?"

"The first is, that she is, it must be confessed, rather simple."

"Simplicity may be a virtue. We will overlook that."

"Then she sometimes clips the king's English!"

"There is no statute against it, like clipping his coin."

"She is afflicted, moreover, with an inveterate love of sight-seeing."

"That is a positive virtue. I have fellow-feeling with her. She would be no true woman if she ever lost her chance at a spectacle. But what is her misfortune?"

"She is the wife of a commissary," said L'Isle with a very grave face.

"Why L'Isle," said Lord Strathern, "has Shortridge brought his wife to Elvas?"

"Yes, my lord, they came last night. Yes, Lady Mabel; the woman who marries a commissary can hardly escape being the wife of a knave!"

"But I really believe," said his lordship, "that our rascal is the most honest fellow in the commissariat department."

"That is not saying much for his honesty."

"I hope for the honor of human nature," interposed Major Conway, "that there are honest men among commissaries?"

"It is no imputation on human nature to think otherwise," said L'Isle; "You might as soon hope there are honest men among pickpockets. For some good reason or other, honest men cannot follow either trade."

"That is one of your prejudices, L'Isle," said Lord Strathern, "and in them you are a true bigot. You are too hard upon poor Shortridge and his brethren. Shortridge is a very good fellow, though a little vulgar it is true. And he always cheats with a conscience, and so do many of his brethren."

"I shall have no scruples of conscience in making use of Mrs. Commissary, if I can," said Lady Mabel. "I hope she is of a sociable temper?"

"Quite so. And moreover, I forgot one trait that will make her particularly accessible to you. She is very fond of people of fashion, and a title secures her esteem.

"Then she belongs to me, for I shall not be wanting in attention to your newly arrived friend. How comes she to be your friend?"

L'Isle told Mrs. Shortridge's adventure in the Patriarchal church; mentioned the straits she was now in for lodgings, and his intention to yield his present quarters to her.

"Why Colonel L'Isle," exclaimed Lady Mabel, "you must be the very pink of chivalry. I do not know which most to admire, your gallant rescue of the dame, or your self-sacrificing spirit in finding her a home."

"You will make Shortridge jealous, L'Isle, by taking such good care of his wife," said Lord Strathern.

"Our sharp friend has too much sense," answered L'Isle, "to be guilty of such folly as that."

Major Conway setting the example, L'Isle now thought it time to take his leave, and he returned to his quarters with the air of a man who thought he had done a good day's work."

"I think," said Lord Strathern to his daughter, "that L'Isle is improving in manners."

"His manners are good, Papa. Were they ever otherwise?"

"I mean that he is becoming more conciliatory, and more considerate of other people. He has scarcely differed from me to-day, and certainly did not undertake to set me right, or contradict me even once, a habit he is *much* addicted to, and very unbecoming in so young a man! It is certainly, too, very kind of him to give up his comfortable quarters to the Shortridges, in their distress, particularly as I know he despises the man."

Now do not blunder on to the hasty conclusion, good reader, that L'Isle, having, at first sight, plunged over head and ears in love with Lady Mabel, had resolved to win and wear her with the least possible loss of time; that he was now investing the fortress, about to besiege it in form, and would hold himself in readiness to carry it by storm on the first opportunity. He acknowledged to himself no such intention; and he doubtless knew his own mind best. Without exactly holding the opinion of Sir John, as set forth by his follower, Bardolph, that a soldier is better accommodated than with a wife—he had often strenuously maintained, in opposition to some love-stricken comrade, that, in the midst of a bloody war, a soldier can give no worse proof of devotion to the lady of his choice, than urging her to become a promising candidate for early widowhood. He preached exceedingly well on this text, and it is but fair to believe that he would practice what he preached. No! in the interest he took in Lady Mabel's situation, he was actuated by no selfish or personal motives. He acquitted himself of that. Had he come across Lady Mabel's old Lisbon coach, beset by robbers, in her journey through the Alemtejo, he would have dashed in among them, sword in hand, like a true gentleman, and a good knight. Now, when he saw her surrounded by evils and embarrassments of a less tangible kind, the same spirit of chivalry brought him promptly to her aid.

Lady Mabel lost no time in adding Mrs. Shortridge to the list of her female acquaintances in Elvas, which, unlike that of her male friends was so short that this new comer was the only one available as a companion. This jewel of a companion, which elsewhere might have escaped her notice, was now seized upon as a diamond of the first water; and Mrs. Shortridge was happy and flattered to find herself the associate of a lady of rank, not to speak of her other merits.

It is not always similarity of character that makes people friends. It quite as often makes them rivals.

To have what your companion wants, and to need what he can afford you, is a better foundation for those social partnerships, often dignified with the name of friendship. The great talker wants a good listener; the sluggish or melancholic are glad of a companion who will undertake the active duty of providing conversation and amusement; he whose nature it is to lead, wants some one who will follow; and the doubting man welcomes as a strong ally, him who will decide for him. As Dogberry says, "when two men ride on a horse, one must ride behind," and the social, compliant and admiring temper of Mrs. Shortridge fitted in so well with the animated, impulsive, and vigorous spirit of Lady Mabel, that something very like friendship grew up between them.

Lady Mabel's habits now underwent a change, which proved that her late mode of life, and her morning and evening *levees* of epaulettes, had been quite as much the result of necessity as of choice. Her father's house was still much frequented by her gay and dashing comrades. But whenever there was a large company to dinner, or any other cause brought many of the gentlemen to head-quarters, she made a point of having Mrs. Shortridge at hand to countenance and sustain her; and in return she would often mount her horse early and canter into Elvas, followed only by a groom, to shut herself up with Mrs. Shortridge for a whole morning, doubtless in the enjoyment of those confidential feminine chats, for which she had longed so much. On these occasions the representatives of the ruder sex seldom gained admittance, except that L'Isle would now and then drop in for an hour, he being too great a favorite with Mrs. Shortridge to be excluded; and, for a time, he showed no disposition to abuse his special privilege.

It was on one of these occasions that L'Isle discovered that with all his assiduity in acquiring a thorough knowledge of the peculiar and interesting land in which he had now spent more than four years—an assiduity, on the result of which he much prided himself, and which had done him good service in his profession—there was still one important point that he had quite overlooked. He knew absolutely nothing of the botany of this region, nor, indeed, of any other. He made this discovery suddenly on hearing Lady Mabel express the interest she felt in this science, and her hope of finding many opportunities of pursuing it in a country whose Flora was so new to her. He at once began to supply this omission by borrowing from her half a dozen books on the subject. In two or three days he reappeared, armed with a huge bunch of wild flowers and plants, and professed to have mastered the technicalities sufficiently to enter at once on the practical study of the science in the field. Unless he deceived himself, he was an astonishing fast learner. Lady Mabel told him that she had heard that *poeta nascitur*, and now she believed it from analogy; for he was certainly born a botanist. He rebutted the sarcasm by showing that he had the terms stamen, pistil, calix, corolla, capsule, and a host of others at the tip of his tongue; though, possibly, had he been called upon to apply each in its proper place, he would have been like a certain student of geometry we once knew, who, by aid of a good memory alone, could demonstrate all Euclid's theorems, without understanding one of them, provided the diagrams were small enough to be hidden by his hand, so you could not detect him in pointing to the wrong angle and line.

January was gone, and the earlier of the two springs that mark this climate was opening beautifully. L'Isle displayed temptingly before Lady Mabel's eyes the wild flowers he had collected during a laborious morning spent on hill and plain, in wood and field, and urged her to lose no time in taking the field too, and making collections for the *hortus siccus* of which she talked so much, but toward which she had yet done nothing; while at the same time, she might, without trouble, indoctrinate him in the mysteries of this beautiful branch of natural history. Most of these flowers were new to her as living specimens. Her botanical enthusiasm was roused at the sight of them, and the offer of a pupil added to her zeal. When we know a little of any thing, it is very pleasant to be applied to for instruction by the ignorant, as it enables us to flatter ourselves that we know a great deal. And it is only the more gratifying when our voluntary pupil is otherwise well informed.

It was at once arranged that the party should take the field to-morrow. Mrs. Shortridge, it is true, had no particular taste for botany. If the flowers in her *bouquet* were beautiful, or fragrant, or both, she did not trouble herself about their history, names, class, order, or alliances; but pleasant company, fresh air, exercise, and new scenes, were inducements enough for her.

CHAPTER VI.

For thee my borders nurse the fragrant wreath,
My fountain murmurs and my zephyrs breathe;
Slow glides the painted snail, the gilded fly
Smooths his fine down to charm thy curious eye;
On twinkling fins my scaly nations play,
Or wind, with sinuous train, their trackless way.
My plumy pairs, in gay embroidery dressed,
Form with ingenious skill the pensile nest;
To Love's sweet notes attune the listening dell,
And Echo sounds her soft symphonious shell.

The Botanic Garden.

Betimes the next morning the botanical party were in the saddle. Mrs. Shortridge rode a mule, the especial favorite of the commissary, for her sure foot and easy gaits, and Lady Mabel was mounted on her Andalusian, on whose education Lieut. Goring had bestowed such pains: but on this occasion she ungratefully omitted to summon her equerry to attend her.

Descending the granite hill of Elvas, they rode westward across the fertile valley, their road shut in on either hand by luxuriant evergreen hedges; for here the dark clay soil was all under cultivation, and carefully laid out into garden, orchard, or field. They passed under the arches of the great aqueduct that stretched its tortuous length across the undulating vale; they paused to admire its peculiarity of style and structure, and the greatness of the work; to wonder at the crooked course it ran, and yet more at the little use the people of Elvas made of its waters for cleaning purposes. Then, hastening on, they found themselves, at the end of some five miles, in an open and elevated country. Dismounting here, they left the horses to the care of their servants. The riding skirts fell to the ground, the ladies stepped forth in walking costume, and the party commenced their ramble after flowers, plants, and scenery, directing their steps toward the high grounds to the northwest of Elvas.

For two or three hours they got on famously. There was much that was new, curious, and beautiful, to be gazed on and admired, wondered at, and collected. Lady Mabel, with the enthusiasm of a young botanist and a younger traveler, found treasures at every step. The gentle morning breeze came refreshingly down from the hills before them, laden with the perfumes of opening spring; the rich aroma of the gum-cistus, the fragrance of the wild rosemary, and many another sweet-scented plant, pervading the air, yet not oppressing the breath. Mrs. Shortridge expressed, rather strongly, perhaps, her delight at the contrast between the sweet-smelling country and the unsavory towns of the Portuguese. She quoted, with no little unction, the proverb: "God made the country, man made the town," as if she had never fully felt its force till now.

"We may say more broadly," observed L'Isle, "that God makes nature and man defiles it."

"I am truly glad," said Mrs. Shortridge, "that these filthy people have not been able to defile their whole land."

Gradually the sunbeams grew hotter, the mountain breeze became a sultry breath, the ground steeper and more rugged, and their accumulating floral treasures more and more cumbrous. Lady Mabel seemed to take delight in adding every moment to the load L'Isle carried. "You must know," she said, "that the pupil is always the packhorse on these occasions," and she insisted on Mrs. Shortridge bearing her share of the burden. This lady at first had talked incessantly, but had gradually less and less to say, and at length was reduced to silence from sheer want of breath. She had frequently to rest for a few minutes, and was coming fast to the conviction that rural excursions on a hot day, and flower-hunting over rough ground, were less pleasant than she thought at first. The hills, bare of trees, exposed them to the full power of the sun, yet were covered with a growth of tall heaths, mingled with patches of the *cistus ladaniferus*, which covers so much of the surface of the slaty hills of this region. The close growth and gummy exudations of this plant often made the thickets impenetrable, and forced the party to many a long circuit, in their efforts to reach the ridge of the high grounds. Mrs. Shortridge at length sat, or rather sunk, down upon a fragment of rock, and L'Isle came promptly to her aid.

"Colonel L'Isle," said she, panting, "I could not take another step up hill for all the flowers in Portugal."

"I am only astonished at your getting so far up. You are not used to climbing mountains."

"When Lady Mabel is at home in Scotland," said Mrs. Shortridge, "I suppose she walks up a mountain every morning, to get an appetite for breakfast. So it is in vain to attempt to follow her. But here she comes."

Lady Mabel now joined them; and L'Isle, pointing out a belt of low woods that wound along the hollow ground at no great distance below them, offered Mrs. Shortridge his arm, and induced her to make an effort to reach its shelter.

On drawing nearer to it, they found themselves in a rough path, made by the flocks of the neighborhood, which led them at first through thickets of evergreen shrubs, and then abruptly down the rocky and almost precipitous bank of that stream, which a mile or two below reached and supplied the aqueduct of Elvas.

Here the clear, cool waters glided over a rocky bed, and when they had quenched their thirst, the ladies found time to look around. On either hand they were shut in by masses of rock, which, with their stratified and fractured lines, resembled walls, the rude masonry of giants. A projecting crag shut out from sight the stream above them; but, attracted by the sound of falling waters, they pushed their way by a few careful steps round it, and full in view, and close at hand, the stream fell over a ledge of rock in a beautiful cascade, descending at once twenty feet into a rock-girdled pool, which in the course of ages it had hollowed out for itself. Here the water ran eddying round, as lingering on a spot it loved, and loath to resume its onward course.

The perpetually falling waters fanned and freshened the noonday air; while overhead, on every ledge that gave footing to their roots, the myrtle and laurustinus, mingled with the oleander, the rhododendron ponticum, and other evergreen shrubs, fed by the fostering moisture of the atmosphere, almost to the size of trees, spread out their luxurions branches to shut out each straggling sunbeam, and deepen the shade of the narrow dell almost to twilight. It was a cavern, with its vaulted roof removed, laying it gently open to the light of day, without its glare. The wood-pigeon amidst the boughs mingled his plaintive notes with the murmur of the falling water, and the speckled trout sported in the pool—now displaying his glistening scales at the surface, then suddenly and coyly hiding in some deep and dark recess.

Lady Mabel stood in silent, motionless delight, drinking in with eye, and ear, and breath, the thrilling sensations crowding on her in this enchanted spot. The exclamation in which Mrs. Shortridge's admiring surprise found vent, jarred on her young companions' nerves, and seemed to break a mystic spell.

The ladies were still wondering at the chance which had led them to this spot, so cool, shady and refreshing after their fatigues, and so charming in its happy grouping of wild, picturesque, and romantic features on a miniature scale, when one of L'Isle's servants stepped from behind the projecting crag, and spread a cloth over a large fragment of rock, the stratified surface of its upper side making no inconvenient table. Then, bringing forward a large basket, he lost no time in setting forth the materials of a light but elegant repast. It was now evident to the ladies that their arrival at this place of refuge and delight, neighboring so closely the bare mountain-side, was not so accidental as they had imagined, and they united in thanking L'Isle for his foresight, and lauding his taste.

Smaller fragments of rock were placed as seats for the ladies, and though they had not all the conveniences of a well-ordered dining-room, they only enjoyed themselves the more for the want of them, while L'Isle busied himself in doing the hospitalities of what Lady Mabel christened "Fairy Dell." The inducements were strong to remain here until the heat of the day was past. Mrs. Shortridge had had her fill of heat and fatigue, in scrambling over the rugged mountain. Lady Mabel had to place her botanical treasures with their stems in the water, to revive their already withering bloom and rear their drooping heads, before she could cull from their unwieldy bulk the specimens she wished to preserve. So, after their meal, the servant was sent to order the horses up to the nearest point that admitted of riding, while the party reposed themselves in the shade and rested from their labors, luxuriously enjoying the scene, sounds, and atmosphere around them.

"How did you happen to find this lovely spot?" asked Mrs. Shortridge.

"The truth is, I yesterday morning went over the same ground we have gone over to-day, and a good deal more," answered L'Isle. "Following this stream upward, I came to this spot. If you would hunt out the peculiar beauties of Portugal, you must follow the course of its rivers and rivulets. True as this is of many countries, it is most true of this. You may observe, Lady Mabel, that almost all the plants you have collected, and some flowers you have not met with to-day, were contained in the collection I brought you yesterday."

"I see that," said Lady Mabel. "But to-day's work is not therefore the less satisfactory. The true botanist—and I suppose you have found out that I make some pretensions to that character—is not content with merely having flowers, leaves, and parts of plants in his *hortus siccus*, or even abortive specimens in his garden and his hot-house: he wants to see the whole plant where nature placed it, and study its character and habits there. Who is satisfied with seeing a Turk in London? To know him as he is, we look for him in Constantinople, or, better still, in some province across the Bosphorus, seated on his own carpet, in his own shop, or in his coffee-house; or, better still, in his harem, with his customers, or neighbors, or his family of wives around him. How much does the Esquimaux in London resemble the Esquimaux seated on his sledge, shouting at his team of dogs, and posting over his frozen and trackless route, with a horizon of ice around him? That is traveling, and this is botany; and of all sciences botany best suits the traveler. Every variation of latitude, climate, or season, even the smallest changes of soil, elevation, or exposure, brings him to a new region, where he may make new acquaintances, or meet old friends. Through a love for botany the wilderness blooms to us like a garden, and the solitary places are made populous and glad."

Such an enthusiastic botanist must become an adept," said L'Isle. "I suppose you see in Portugal nothing but a land of rare and varied vegetation?"

"By no means. I am not wedded to one pursuit, or gifted with but one taste. I have eyes for other things beside flowers, and shall seize every opportunity of seeing and knowing something of the people of the country."

"The people, the real people," said L'Isle, "both of this country and of Spain, are the peasantry. They are chiefly agricultural countries, and the rural, or rather village population forms the bulk of both nations, and the best part of them."

"It is the peasantry, the dear, natural, picturesque peasantry that I most want to know."

"I am astonished to hear you say so, Lady Mabel. The ignorant, filthy, superstitious creatures!" exclaimed Mrs. Shortridge, with an air of infinite disgust. "Their *fidalgos*, as they call their gentry, are bad enough; but as for the common people, any familiarity with them, sufficient to enable you to know them, would be too disgusting. They may be picturesque; so let us confine them to their place in the picture. There alone it is that they do not bring their savor of garlic with them," and she here buried her pretty little turned-up nose in a bunch of Lady Mabel's most fragrant flowers.

"Give me those flowers, Mrs. Shortridge; you handle them so rudely, any one might see that you are no botanist. I had just laid them aside to be pressed. And as for the poor Portuguese, I mean to know them as well and despise them as little as I can, and even hope to learn something through them, if not from them. Colonel L'Isle, I have mastered already all the ordinary phrases of Portuguese salutation and compliment, which you know are much more various and cumbrous than in our direct, blunt English. I can already be as polite as the most courteous native, and that is, at least, the beginning of conversation. I can ask, too, for the necessaries of life, and inquire my road, should I chance to lose it. Let a woman alone for getting the tongues. I hold frequent conferences with Antonio Lobo, the peasant who keeps our orchard at head-quarters, and have daily talks with our Portuguese chamber-maid, and can find fault with her, not to say scold, in good set terms. The awkward creature gives me abundant provocation for scolding, and for not forgetting your advice about vociferation and gesticulation."

"You do well to remember it," said L'Isle; "it will help you on famously."

"I had some thoughts," she continued, "in order to lose no opportunity of familiarizing myself with these tongues, of saying my prayers in Spanish of a morning, and Portuguese at night. But a scruple of conscience deterred me from attempting, in prayer, to kill two birds with one stone."

"I think," said L'Isle, laughing, "that your scruple was not out of place."

"Yet you know that Charles V. held that God should never be addressed but in Spanish."

"A strange doctrine for a Papist, who was always praying to him in bad Latin," said L'Isle. "That opinion savors of heresy, and deserved the notice of the Inquisition."

"At all events," said Lady Mabel, "it is best not to pray to him in bad Spanish. But had I an opportunity of traveling through Spain and Portugal, and mixing freely with the people, I would show you how quickly both tongues could be mastered."

"I see little chance of your having that opportunity soon," said Mrs. Shortridge.

"I am afraid I must give up all hope of it. The *Santa Hermandad* no longer keep the roads safe; and all the knights of Alcantara and Calatrava to boot, of these degenerate days, would afford but little protection to a *demoiselle errante.*"

"I will offer you a more trusty escort than that of those false knights," said L'Isle. "I will place myself and regiment at your command."

"That is truly kind. I accept the offer; and when I set out on my travels, will send you on with it a march or two ahead, to clear the way, and make all safe for us, while Mrs. Shortridge and myself will follow at ease with our civic retinue, confident that you will have removed every danger from the path!"

"That arrangement would make the journey less pleasant to me than I hoped to find it."

"I thought your object was our safety, not your pleasure," said Lady Mabel.

"And for my part," said Mrs. Shortridge, "I do not care to travel any road which requires a regiment to make it safe. I am inquisitive enough, but my fears would be stronger than my curiosity."

"Well," Lady Mabel said, "I begin to despair of ever gratifying my longing after a rambling life. It is probably all for the best. I dare say I would have become a mere vagabond. But I had embraced a wide field in my contemplated travels: romantic Spain, la belle France, classic Italy, and that dreamy, misty Faderland. But I suppose that this war will last always, and for all practical purposes I may as well roll up the map of Europe."

"Do you seriously imagine that this war will last forever?" L'Isle asked.

"Why not forever, or, at least, for a long life time? It began before I was born, and may continue long after I am dead. I have no recollection of a state of peace, to make me think it the natural condition of nations."

"We are luckily not limited to our own experience in drawing our conclusions. Take my word for it, these wars are drawing to a close. I am only afraid that they will end before I am a Major-General."

"Why! Do you expect them to go on making a series of blunders at headquarters, like that in the affair of that unlucky Spanish village?"

"A series of blunders," L'Isle answered, "would be quite in accordance with the routine at the war-office, at least. So my expectations are not so unreasonable as you may imagine."

"Then let them blunder on as fast as possible, and make you a major-general, and a knight of the bath, too, if it please the king. Many of your family were knighted of old, and Sir Edward L'Isle will sound well enough until it be merged in the peerage. But mean while hasten to drive these French out of Spain, as the czar is driving them out of Russia; make Spain too hot, as Muscovy is too cold for them, that I may begin my travels at an early day."

L'Isle, out of countenance, made no answer to this sally. He did not like being laughed at, especially by Lady Mabel.

The rays of the declining sun now touched the tops only of the luxuriant shrubbery, that overhung this fairy dell. The heat of the day was passed, and clambering up the steep path to the more level ground, the party found their servants at hand with the horses, and rode slowly back toward Elvas.

Near the foot of the range of hills, L'Isle suddenly caught sight of three red coats, and saying, "I wonder what those fellows are doing so far from their quarters," he turned his horse out of the path, and rode toward them. They presently saw him approaching, and much to Lady Mabel's surprise and amusement, in which last feeling, Mrs. Shortridge joined, instead of waiting for him to come up, they immediately ran off different ways, seeking concealment from the thickets and hollows. Selecting one ot them for the chase, L'Isle pushed his horse boldly over the rough ground. But the soldier, finding the pursuit too hot, pulled off the coat which made him conspicuous, and folding it into small compass, pushed through an overgrown hedge and vanished. L'Isle was soon at fault, and had to give up the chase. He returned somewhat out of humor, with his horse somewhat blown.

"You are a bold rider," said Lady Mabel, "but those red foxes are too cunning for you. What made you chase them? What harm were they doing?"

"None that I know of—and had they let me speak to them I would have suspected none. But a soldier is always at mischief when he avoids being seen and identified by his officer. The men are allowed too much liberty in rambling over the country. No wonder we have so many complaints lodged against them."

"You had better speak to papa about it," said Lady Mabel, in simple confidence that so doing would set all to right.

"So I have, more than once. But he does not agree with me, and is opposed to what he calls needless restraint."

"Oh, if papa thinks so, you need not worry yourself about the matter. It is his business, and doubtless near forty year's experience has taught him what amount and kinds of restraint are needed, and what is merely burthensome and oppressive. I have heard him discuss these matters more than once."

She seemed so little disposed to think her father might be mistaken, that L'Isle did not venture to hint further the possibility of it. In that father, Lady Mabel had full faith, and also some of the faith of inexperience in the beautiful theory which teaches that the general knows best, that after him the second in command approaches nearest to infallibility, and so on through every gradation of rank, in all services, civil and military. Had she made an exception to the application of this rule, it would have been in her father's case; for she inclined to the belief, that notwithstanding the reputation and higher rank of the military men who stood between him and the commander-in-chief, her father was, after Wellington, the strongest bulwark against the torrent of invading French.

"I dare say that many of these poor fellows," observed Lady Mabel, "though they are but common soldiers, enjoy a stroll into the country as much as we do. In a rude way they admire picturesque beauty, and observe with interest, bird, beast and plant of a country so different from their own."

"I suspect," said Mrs. Shortridge, "they look chiefly for the picturesque spots frequented by the pigs and poultry of the peasants, and have a keen eye to detect where the fruits of the orchard are stored, and where the wine skins hang."

Lady Mabel was indignant at this suggestion. "It is a libel on the British army in general, and on our brigade in particular. They are soldiers, not robbers; and the king's troops are too well cared for to be driven to plunder for a living."

"But they may rob from love of mischief, of excitement, of excess, from mere idleness, or old habits," said L'Isle. "In recruiting we adopt a physical, and not a moral standard. A sound body, five feet some inches long, is all we look for, and we are glad to get it. A great many rogues fulfil these requisites, and get into the ranks; and though we charge ourselves with the moral as well as the physical training, we are not always successful. The sack of Badajoz, and of Ciudad Rodrigo bear witness to this."

They reached Elvas without further incident, and this proved but the first of many excursions made from time to time to points around that place. Thus, altogether with a view to her profit and pleasure,

L'Isle contrived to withdraw Lady Mabel frequently from the military throng at headquarters, and, with Mrs. Shortridge's aid, appropriate her to himself.

By this adroit manœuvre, L'Isle did not gain the good will of some of his brother officers, who found their share of her ladyship's society much curtailed. What cared L'Isle for that? No more than colonels usually care for the inclinations of subalterns. Many were the pleasant morning rambles on horseback and on foot that he took with the two ladies; and this mode of life agreed with him wonderfully well. Before long he recovered strength and activity to achieve some tall climbing after rare plants among the rocks and crags, which would have gained him great credit in an escalade. Occasionally too, while Mrs. Shortridge prudently, or indolently, kept the more level ground he would contrive to lead Lady Mabel to some elevated and perilous spot—and she boldly putting herself into difficulties, and not always seeing the way out of them, had to rely on his aid, and the supporting arm he delighted to afford her. And they gave to love for botany the credit of it all.

The zeal with which Colonel L'Isle followed up this new study, did not escape Colonel Bradshawe's watchful eye. So his satirical tongue had many a comment to make on the change in L'Isle's habits. To his own cronies Bradshawe dubbed him the bushman, not as being neighbor to the Hottentots, but from his often riding into Elvas, equipped like one of Malcolm's soldiers, marching from Birnam wood to Dunsinane.

"Our would be Achilles, laden with that huge bunch of materials for Lady Mabel's *hortus siccus*, thinks himself like Hercules with the distaff. To me he looks like a florist's apprentice, selling his flowers at a penny a bunch. It must be confessed though that the fellow has talents and tact. How completely has he contrived to shut out rivalry, by availing himself of my lady's weakness in imagining herself a great botanist, and providing her with a zealous and admiring pupil in his own person. And then to use so adroitly his accommodating temporary female friend in decoying his lawful love into the trap. She is certainly the finest girl of her day, and acres are good things, even though they be Scotch acres; for in the same proportion they are broader as well as more barren than English acres. The whole thing is admirable. It is a combination of means to a combination of ends, evincing genius of high order. Were I at the head of the war office, I would promote him on the spot."

"Poor Shortridge!" sighed Colonel Bradshawe, dropping at once from a tone of the highest admiration to one of deep commiseration, "can he possibly be blind to what is going on? And what is Lord Strathern dreaming of! What a pity one cannot interfere in these little matters, and put our friends on their guard! But Shortridge is so obtuse, and my Lord so self-willed and wrong-headed, that it would only make matters worse. Indeed, it is too late to help Shortridge, poor fellow! and we must console ourselves with the wise conclusion of the great bard:

> "He that is robbed, not wanting what is stolen,
> Let him not know it, and he's not robbed at all."

CHAPTER VII.

Whanne that April with his shoures sote
The droughte of March hath perced to the rote,
And bathed every veine in swiche licour,
Of which vertue engendred is the flour;
Whan Zephirus eke with his sote brethe,
Enspired hath in every holt and hethe
The tendre croppes, and the yonge sonne
Hath in the Ram his half cours yronne,
And smale foules maken melodie
That sleepen all night with open eye,
So pricketh hem nature in hir corages;
Than longen folk to gon on pilgrimages,
And palmeres for to seken strange strondes,
To serve halwes couthe in sondry londes.

Prologue to Canterbury Tales.

"Why, *Ma belle*, you are an indomitable excursionist!" exclaimed Lord Strathern one evening, when the botanical party, after a hard day's work in pleasure-hunting, returned to a late dinner at headquarters. "I wonder Mrs. Shortridge is not worn out in accompanying you."

"I take it easily, my Lord," said Mrs. Shortridge, "keeping the broadest and smoothest path I can find, like the wicked in Scripture, while Lady Mabel rambles about on either hand, having, I think, a liking for rough ground. Like the mountain goat, if she will forgive the comparison, she prefers the crag to the plain. If your Lordship saw the hardihood with which she puts herself into all sorts of perilous situations, until, at times, it needs all the aid Colonel L'Isle can give to extricate her, I fear you would put a stop to our jaunts."

"As yet my wardrobe has been the only sufferer," said Lady Mabel. "I have just taken off the third dress I have damaged past remedy."

"If you had been a boy, *Ma belle*, instead of a girl, you would have made a rare sportsman!"

"A sportsman, indeed! By this time I would have held a commission in his Majesty's service. Why, papa, I am a year older than ensign Wade, have almost as much beard to my chin, and, but for my sex, would make quite as good a soldier."

"I am content, however, to have you as you are, and would not exchange you for a regiment of the best boys in England."

"Better one daughter than a thousand sons," said Lady Mabel, "for they would make a cumbersome family."

"You are a cumbersome baggage yourself," said Lord Strathern. "Just see the endless litter of flowers, leaves, yea, branches of trees, with which you cumber the house. We will have to apply to the quartermaster for the use of a returning supply-train to convey your botanical treasures to Lisbon, and we will have to charter a vessel there to carry them home. Dr. Graham's study will not contain all you collect for him. You must have exhausted the neighborhood."

"In one sense I am afraid we have. Colonel L'Isle tells me that we have explored almost every part of the country immediately around Elvas."

"I am sorry we are tied down to this one spot," said her father. "As you have never been from home before, I would wish you to see as much as possible of this country. But I must stick close to the brigade, at hand for orders at any moment."

"I must be content," said Lady Mabel. "And, after all, it is better to see one place thoroughly, than to take a hasty glance at a dozen in the style of common-place travelers."

"I confess I am but a common-place traveler," said Mrs. Shortridge, "and would like to see a new place every day; though I have, I own, found more variety and amusement in exploring the neighborhood than I expected."

"You will shortly have an opportunity, Mrs. Shortridge," said L'Isle, "of visiting a very striking place by merely accompanying the commissary. He thinks of going to Evora to purchase cattle and grain for the troops, and Evora is well worth seeing, as well as the country you pass through in going thither."

"Ah! I would like the jaunt very much. But I did not know that the commissary was going thither."

"He is going, and you might accompany him," said L'Isle. "You could not indeed make the journey in your coach if you had one, for off this high road, from Lisbon to Madrid, there is scarcely a carriage-road in the country. But you are now quite at home, on the back of your sure-footed mule."

The truth was, L'Isle had himself suggested to the commissary that the country south of Evora was rich and productive, and that prices had not been raised there by the vicinity of the troops, and the demands of their market. At the same time he gave Shortridge to understand that he wished to get up a party to visit Evora, and Lady Mabel must be included in it.

"I will ask the commissary to-night when he is going," said Mrs. Shortridge; "and to take me with him, if he can."

Lady Mabel had listened with silent interest so far; but here she broke in upon their conference, just as L'Isle desired.

"Why, Mrs. Shortridge," she exclaimed, with a well-feigned air of one deeply wronged, "do you mean to desert me? After partaking of my pleasant excursions and botanical instructions (but I find you a very dull scholar), do you mean to go traveling about in search of adventures and rare sights, without even asking me to be of the party?—I, who am afflicted with a mania for traveling which can only be cured by being gratified? But such is woman's friendship."

"My dear Lady Mabel, how do you know that my lord would trust you so far under my care?

"So far!" said Lady Mabel, scornfully. "Did I not come from Scotland hither, braving the perils of the sea and of the wilderness, the stormy Bay of Biscay, and the desert of Alemtejo, teeming with robbers and wild beasts? With no guardian but old Moodie, whose chief merit is that of being a suspicious old Scot, with the fidelity and snappishness of a terrier."

"I am surprised now that I sent for you," said Lord Strathern, "considering the difficulties in the way of your coming. But you are here, and I thank God for it. But you would find it a long, rough ride to Evora, and the weather grows hotter every day."

"Rough roads are nothing to us who travel on horseback," Lady Mabel said, with the air of a cavalier; "and as for the distance, it is not much over a morning's ride. Colonel L'Isle, could not you ride there in a morning?"

"With relays of good horses, and good luck to my neck," said L'Isle, with a laugh. "It is about fifty miles; but one need not go the whole way in one day."

"Of course not," she answered. "We will not ride post, but take our ease, and see the country at our leisure."

"I see you intend going, *ma belle*," said Lord Strathern; "so I may as well give my consent with a good grace. But is the commissary able and willing to take charge of more than one lady, Mrs. Shortridge, who has a will of her own? I trust, too, L'Isle, that after giving these ladies a taste for rambling, you do not mean to desert them now. They may need your escort. Small parties are never safe traveling about this country. Our friends just hereabouts, especially, (I am sorry to-say it of them), are apt to fall in love with other men's goods, and have a strong throat-cutting propensity."

"Oh, there is nothing to fear, papa," said Lady Mabel. "Our troops occupy the country, and, if necessary, we will take Colonel L'Isle with us for further protection. Pray, Colonel L'Isle, how many robbers could you defend us from?"

"I would try to defend you against a hundred."

"But pray," said Mrs. Shortridge, "carry at least two servants, well armed."

"Certainly," said Lady Mabel; "we will do the thing effectually. They shall carry no baggage, but stuff their valises full of loaded pistols, as antidotes to Mrs. Shortridge's fears."

"I will join the party with pleasure, my lord. I suppose I can be spared from this post for a few days?" said L'Isle, well pleased to be urged to join in an excursion, secretly and ingeniously contrived by himself.

The ladies, delighted at the prospect of a pleasant journey and new scenes, were at once full of plans and preparations for their outfit on the road. Nor did they reckon without their host; for the commissary assented to their joining him the moment it was proposed. Colonel Bradshawe might amuse himself and his cronies by expressing astonishment at his blindness or complaisance, but Shortridge had good reasons for what he did. Since he had made money, both his wife and himself felt a strong craving for social promotion; and Colonel L'Isle and Lady Mabel were just the persons to lend them a helping hand in their efforts to ascend the social ladder. But with Shortridge this was just now but a secondary matter. The commander-in-chief had been lately giving a rough overhauling to the officials of the commissariat. Their numberless peculations, and short-comings at critical moments, had exasperated him into a conviction that they were necessary evils, and rascals to a man by right of office, and only to be dealt with as such. And Sir Rowland Hill, to whose division the brigade belonged, had learned this, among other lessons, from his great commander. Now L'Isle was known to have the ear of Sir Rowland, and the commissary was of opinion that, while Lord Strathern commanded the brigade, Lady Mabel commanded him, so that the good opinion and good word of those parties might avail him much on certain emergencies. If a friend at court be a good thing, two are still better; so he was all compliance, and let the ladies fix the next day but one for the journey.

Early on that morning, accordingly, the party assembled at headquarters, and their horses and mules crowded the little court of the monastic building. L'Isle had provided an *arriero* for a guide, with his three mules for their baggage. The kind, and quantity, too, of provision he had prepared for their journey, was a reflection on the resources and hospitality of the country they were to pass through. Nor had the commissary been negligent of creature comforts.

Lord Strathern placed his daughter in the saddle. "Remember, *ma belle*, your blood is not used to this feverous climate, and even your pretty neck may get broken in a mountain path.

Lady Mabel listened with dutiful attention to the warnings of experience against the dangers from the noonday sun, the chilly night wind, and fast riding over rough paths; but, full of anticipated pleasure, she perhaps did not remember them an hour after.

"You are much encumbered with baggage, L'Isle," said Lord Strathern; "and your party larger than I expected."

"My party, papa," said Lady Mabel, with an air of asserting her position. "I like to travel in good style. This is my retinue, and a very complete one it is. Colonel L'Isle is my dragoman, and interprets for me among the barbarous natives. The servants, armed to the teeth, are my guards. The commissary is my purveyor, and" she added, glancing at his rotund figure, "I have no fear of starving in his company. Mrs. Shortridge, though she does not look sour enough for the office, is my duenna, punctilious and watchful—" Here she suddenly broke off her discourse, and fixed her eyes on old Moodie, who now entered the court, leading in a powerful horse of her father's, with a pair of huge holsters at the saddle-bow. Being a small and an old man, he climbed stiffly and with some difficulty into the saddle; but, when seated there, his earnest face and resolute air made him look a hero of the covenant quitting the conventicle for the battle-field.

After watching him in silent surprise, she exclaimed: "Why, Moodie, are you going too? I did not know that you were so fond of traveling, and so inquisitive about these idolatrous foreigners and their country."

"I would gladly turn my back on them and their country; but my duty forbids it."

"But how will papa do without you?"

"Better than your ladyship can."

"But you have made yourself so useful, indeed necessary, as steward in this house, which needed one sadly."

"Perhaps, so, my lady. But I know where I am most needed. I do not mean to lose sight of you for twenty-four hours, until you are safe at Craiggyside."

Lady Mabel looked exceedingly provoked and much out of countenance at the *surveillance* he assumed over her. Did he think her still a child now, when she felt herself a woman? It was well she did not ask *him* that question, for Moodie thought this the time when she needed most watching. She was about to forbid his following her, but her father, laughing at her discomfiture, said, "Moodie told me last night that he would have to be of the party. He got his general orders before he left Scotland, and in this case my sister is commander-in-chief."

The party was now ready, and rode out of the court, L'Isle putting himself by Lady Mabel's side.

"What special part does this old man fill in your father's household?"

"Properly, none; though he has made himself steward by an act of usurpation. Just at this time he belongs to my household," said she, with mock dignity. "And, when at home, he is a very important person at Craiggyside, a place unknown to your geography, but a very important and delightful place, notwithstanding."

"I blush to acknowledge my ignorance. Pray put an end to it by telling me what sort of a place Craiggyside is."

"It is a villa and farm, the home of my aunt, with whom I live. There old Moodie fulfills his round of duties. He manages the farm, sells the crops, tasks the ploughmen, overlooks the shepherd, scolds the dairymaid, bullies the servants, and regulates all that come near him. He can be charged with no shortcomings, for he overdoes all he undertakes. Not content with controlling our secular concerns, he would gladly take upon him the cure of souls. But there he meets with stubborn resistance."

"He has a varied sphere of duty," said L'Isle, "and seems accustomed to have his own way. He does not wait for your orders, nor, indeed, seems to be very amenable to them. In short, notwithstanding the official title you have bestowed on Mrs. Shortridge, it is plain to me that the real duenna does not wear petticoats."

"His presumption is equal to any thing," said Lady Mabel, provoked at the suggestion. "But I will make him repent it shortly. He shall long remember this journey. But enough of him for the present. Let us make the most of this delightful morning hour. It will be hot enough by noon. I am now in the traveler's happiest mood, enjoying at once the feeling of adventure with the sense of security, which, you must admit, is a rare and difficult combination of emotions."

L'Isle was quite as well pleased as Lady Mabel with the prospect before him. He had, at Lord Strathern's request, assented to join a party, which he alone had gotten up, solely that he might put himself in the relation of companion and protector to Lady Mabel. The commissary and his wife were convenient screens, not at all in his way. Whether the part of guide, philosopher, and friend to such a pupil suited a man of four-and-twenty, he was yet to learn. No doubts of this kind troubled him, however, as the *arriero* led his mules down the hill, and the party followed the music of their bells, all in high spirits, except old Moodie, who, though a volunteer, continued to be a grumbler.

Two hours' riding carried them beyond the point to which the botanical excursions had led them in that direction. They were leaving the valley, and entering on the high and broken uplands, when Lady Mabel spied a low cross by the roadside. Though rudely formed, it was of stone, and not of wood, like most of those in such places, and a short inscription was carved upon it. Faintly cut, badly spelt, and with many abbreviations, it was an enigma to her scholarship, and L'Isle had to decipher it for her: "Andreo Savaro was murdered here. Pray for his soul." "It is only one of those monumental crosses," said he, "of which you see so many along the roads throughout the peninsula."

"Do they always add murder to robbery here?" she asked.

"Too often, but not always," answered L'Isle. "Nor is robbery the only motive which leads to the taking of life. A solitary cross by the roadside is usually in memory of the victim of robbers, or, occasionally, of fatal accident; but when you see crosses, two or three together, in villages or towns, or their immediate neighborhood, they oftener mark the scene of some deed of bloodshed prompted by revenge, not lucre."

"They are certainly very numerous," said she, "and form a shocking feature on the face of the country, indicating a dreadful state of society."

"I wonder these people persist in putting them up," said the commissary, "for they are of no manner of use."

"Use!" said Lady Mabel, "what is the use of a tomb-stone?"

"If you mean real use, I am sure I don't know," said Shortridge.

"I see that you are a thorough utilitarian," she replied; "and since these people will continue to commit murder on the high road, I suppose you would have them do it at regular intervals, so that by aid of these monumental crosses we might measure our journey by murders instead of miles. Come, Mrs. Shortridge, road-side murder is rife here, so the less we loiter on our way the better."

This remark had the effect mischievously intended. Mrs. Shortridge, turning somewhat pale, and twitching her bridle convulsively, urged her mule close up to the party.

They went on some miles across a desolate country, covered with heath, rosemary, and gum cistus, more fragrant than the many rank bulbous plants, which disputed possession of the soil with them. The road was rough with slaty rock, the air became beaming hot, and L'Isle told the guide to lead them to some place of shelter from the noon-day sun. Before them lay a high open plain, on which a large flock of sheep, dusky, and many of them black in hue, were feeding, and filling the air with their bleatings. On the right, beyond the plain, there was a grove of the *Quercus Ilex*, rugged, stunted, thirsty-looking trees, yet whose evergreen boughs gave promise of at least a partial shade. The *arriero* led the party toward it, but just as they approached the wood, several large and savage dogs flew out, and charged them with a ferocity that might have cost a solitary traveler his life. They were busy repelling this assault, when five or six men showed themselves from behind a thicket. Dark, sunburnt, smoke-dried fellows they were, with shaggy hair, and rudely clad, each man having a sheep-skin thrown over his shoulders, and most of them grasping long, rusty guns in their hands.

Mrs. Shortridge called out "robbers!" and entreated L'Isle to fire upon them. The commissary, too, but more coolly, pronounced them to be robbers, "when they find an opportunity to follow that calling; but, just now, they are watching their flocks."

"Shepherds! those ruffians, shepherds!" exclaimed Lady Mabel; "O! shades of Theocritus and Virgil, what a satire upon pastoral poetry!"

Shepherds, however, they were, who called off their dogs, after reconnoitring the party. The *arriero* inquired of them where water was to be found, and they pointed to a little hollow in the wood, an hundred yards off. He was leading the party that way, when L'Isle said to the ladies, "let us have a talk with these fellows."

"Certainly," said Lady Mabel, and she turned her horse's head toward them.

"Certainly not," said Mrs. Shortridge, and she reined her mule back, "I am too near them already. I will not dare to take my siesta with these fellows in the neighborhood, for fear of waking up in another place than Portugal." And she followed her melting husband, who was hastening out of the sun, in the hope of regaining his solidity in the shade at hand.

L'Isle and Lady Mabel rode close up to the shepherds. They had been resting under an oak, and the cooking utensils, some baggage, and two asses near at hand, looked as if they, too, were travelers. L'Isle addressed a tall, dark man, of middle age, who seemed to be the head of the party. As soon as these men heard their own language from the mouth of a foreigner, so fluently and correctly spoken, their faces lightened up with interest and intelligence. They gave ready answers to all inquiries, and L'Isle had to reply in turn to many a question as to himself, his companions, and the news of the war. The chief shepherd was particularly anxious to know the condition of the province of Beira, and what were the chances of a visit there from the French during the coming summer. His flock, he said, was one of those which winter on the heaths and plains of Alemtejo, and, to avoid the droughts which make them a desert in summer, are driven across the Tagus in the spring, into the *Serra Estrella*, when the snow has melted, and vegetation again covers that range of mountains.

One of his companions offered for sale two rabbits and some partridges he had shot on the moors, which L'Isle bought, like a provident traveler, who does not rely too much on the larder of the next inn.

Lady Mabel, with attentive ear, had gathered the sense of much that had been said, and L'Isle had interpreted what puzzled her. But being a woman, she was unwilling to remain a mere listener; so, elaborately framing a question in Portuguese, she addressed the head shepherd, seeking to know how far the migrations of these flocks resembled the Spanish *mesta*. The dark man gazed at her admiringly and attentively, repeating some of her words, but unable to make out her meaning. She bit her lip, while he, shaking his head, turned to L'Isle, and said, "what a pity so lovely a lady cannot speak Portuguese. She looks just like our 'Lady of Nazareth,' at Pederneira, only her hair is brighter, and her eyes are blue."

"What says he about my language and *Nossa Senhora de Nazareth?*" said Lady Mabel. "Tell him that I speak better Portuguese than she ever did, for all her black eyes and tawny skin."

"By no means," said L'Isle, smiling. "As you will have no opportunity to evangelize the man, it will do no good to outrage his idolatrous veneration for *Nossa Senhora de Nazareth?* You might shake his superstition, yet not purify his faith, but merely drive him to a choice between the church and infidelity.

They now left the shepherds to join the party. "I am provoked," said Lady Mabel, "to find how little progress I have made in speaking Portuguese. But it is not surprising what a complete mastery the rudest and most illiterate people here have over their tongue."

"And how polite and sociable they are," said L'Isle. "Unlike the unmannered and almost languageless English peasant, they are unembarrassed and social, fluent, and often eloquent."

"Yet these men," said she, "in habits, though not in race, are but nomadic Tartars at the western extremity of Europe."

"They differ too," said L'Isle, "from their immediate neighbors, the Spaniard, in being far more sociable and communicative. For instance, I have got much more out of my Portuguese shepherd than a certain French traveler got out of his shepherd of Castile."

"What do you allude to?" she asked.

"A French traveler, it is said, as he entered Castile, met a shepherd guiding his flock. Curious to know all the circumstances which give to the Spanish wool its inimitable qualities, he asked the shepherd an hundred questions: 'If his flock belonged to that district? What sort of food was given it? Whether he was on a journey? From whence he came? Whither he was going? When he would return?' In short, he asked every question a prying Frenchman could think of. The shepherd listened coldly to them all. Then, in the sententious style of a true Castilian, replied, '*aqui nacen, aqui pacen, aqui mueren,*' (here they breed, here they feed, here they die,) and went his way without a word more."

The party spent some time here, dining and resting under the shade of these prickly oaks, the tree that yields the famous *botolas*, so largely used for food by men and swine, and on tasting which we are less surprised that in "the primal age,"

"Hunger then
Made acorns tasteful, thirst each rivulet
Run nectar."

Mrs. Shortridge had contrived to snatch a short siesta,

in spite of her fears. Their horses were led up, ready for them to mount and proceed on their journey, when Lady Mabel, plucking a twig from a branch overhead, observed on it several specimens of the *kermes.* She could not resist this opportunity of displaying her scraps of scientific lore, and detained the party while she delivered a discourse on the *coccus arborum*, "which," she said, "infests this tree; the *quercus cocci.* This furnishes what the ignorant-learned long called grains of kermes, looking like dried currants, which they mistook for the fruit of a tree, while it is, in truth, the dried body of an insect. It affords a vermilion dye, not so brilliant, but far more durable than the cochineal of Mexico. There are in the Netherlands," she continued, "rich tapestries dyed with kermes, known to be three hundred years old, which still retain their pristine brilliancy of color. Only think, Mrs. Shortridge, of having carpets, shawls and cloaks of such unfading hues!"

"They would be of no use to me," yawned Mrs. Shortridge, "I would be even more tired of myself than of my cloak, before the end of three hundred years."

"Why," exclaimed L'Isle, "this indestructible dye must be the very stuff with which the old lady of Babylon dyed her petticoat; for it has not faded in the least since she first put it on, as we may see in this country, where she wears it openly, without even a decent piece of lawn over it, to suppress the brightness of its hues."

"As our lives are not so lasting as the dye Lady Mabel talks of," said the commissary, "let us make the most of them by taking horse at once, and hastening on, for we must pass through Villa Vicosa, and sleep several miles beyond it to-night."

Returning to the road, they presently reached a cultivated valley, and passed through a hamlet, scarcely seen before it was entered, so completely were the low stone walls of the houses hidden by the olive, orange, almond, and other fruit-trees surrounding them. The only inhabitants visible were two or three squalid children, playing in the road, and a woman lounging at her door, eyeing the party with mingled curiosity and suspicion, while a stout yearling calf pushed unceremoniously past her into the house, thus asserting his right as a member of the family.

L'Isle paused before the little church, just beyond the village, and pointed out to Lady Mabel a curious cross, the first of the kind she had met with, though common enough in the peninsula. It was composed of human skulls, on a pedestal of thigh bones, the whole let into the wall, and secured by a rough kind of stucco.

"Certainly these people have curious ways of exciting devotional fervor, and keeping death in memory," said Lady Mabel.

"One might suppose them to have remarked the grave-digger, who deals habitually with the moldering remains of humanity, to be the most God-fearing of men," said L'Isle; "so they seek to afford to every one the devotional incentives peculiar to the grave-digger. Yet their symbols serve rather to familiarize us with material death in this world, than to remind us of a spiritual life in the world to come. They often teach no better lesson than 'Eat, drink, and be merry, for to-morrow we die.' "

"I have been told," said Lady Mabel, "that in spite of these pious devices, the people have lost much of their devotional ardor and fullness of faith."

"Not the rustic population," said L'Isle; "the church still retains full sway over them."

"I cannot say," observed Lady Mabel, as they turned to proceed on their way, "that the Romish system is very attractive to me. But, viewing it as a sensuous worship, if ever I become a convert, it will be through the influence of its music." And dropping the reins on her horse's neck, she, with clasped hands and upturned eyes, began to chant:

"O Sanctissima! O Purissima!
Ora, Ora, pro nobis," etc.

Music at once so sweet and orthodox from a heretic mouth, attracted the muleteer's attention, and turning, he sat sideways in his saddle to listen. This exciting old Moodie's suspicion, he pushed his horse close up to Lady Mabel's, and as soon as she paused, said: "My lady, what is that you are singing?"

"A hymn to the Virgin."

"A hymn to the Virgin!" he repeated, horror-struck.

"Yes; it is in Latin, you know. Have you never been to any of the churches in Elvas, to 'assist' at the service and enjoy the music?"

"God forbid that I should countenance any of their idolatrous rites."

"Their music, however, is excellent, and has a grandeur suited to the worship of God." You lose much in not hearing it, and may, at least, let me amuse myself by singing a Popish hymn."

"You may amuse yourself by turning Papist in time. What begins in jest often ends in earnest; and yours, my lady, will not be the first soul that has been caught by such gear as the sweet sounds and glittering shows of idolatry."

"But," said Lady Mabel, coolly, with a provoking insensibility to her danger, "there are, not only in Latin, but in Spanish and Portuguese, many of these hymns to the Holy Virgin—for, doubtless, she was a holy virgin—exquisitely happy, both in words and music. A devout nation has poured its heart into them."

"They are all idolatrous, every one of them. There is not a word of authority for the worship of her in Scripture, and the texts of God's book are our only safe guide."

Lady Mabel, while fanning a fire that never went out, was gazing around on the landscape. Suddenly she said: "You are a great stickler, Moodie, for the words of Scripture, yet these idolatrous people often stick to it more closely than you do."

"I will trouble you, my lady, to name an instance," Moodie answered, in a defiant tone.

"Do you see those men in that field, with three yoke of oxen going round and round on one spot?"

"I see them. But what of them?"

"While you and other heretic Scots are racking your brains to devise how to thresh corn by machines, these pious people, in simple obedience to the injunction, 'Muzzle not the ox that treadeth out the corn,' are treading out their corn with unmuzzled oxen. What think you of that, Mr. Stick-to-the-text?"

"I think, my lady," he answered, doggedly, "that you had better read your Bible to profit by it; not to puzzle an old man less learned than yourself. But all things are ordered." Yet he loitered behind the party, to gaze with mingled curiosity and pity at these people, at once so benighted in theology and farming, the two points on which he felt himself strongest.

They had not ridden much further, when they drew near to the ruinous walls of a considerable town, situated in a fertile and delightful region, and retaining amidst its dilapidation many marks of grandeur. Entering through a ruinous gateway, they paused in the grand *praça*. "This," said L'Isle, "is Ville Viçosa, 'the delightful city.' What a pity we have but time to take a hasty glance at this ducal seat of the house of Braganza. Two sides of the *praça*, as you see, are occupied by the classic and imposing front of the palace in which the dukes of Braganza lived during the sixty years of the Spanish usurpation, before the heroism of the nation restored the royal line to the throne."

"Even in its declining fortunes," said Lady Mabel, "Villa Viçosa has not forgotten its connection with Portuguese royalty and nationality. Was it not the first place in Alemtejo to resist the French robbers, who were lording it over them?"

"Yes. But it was neither loyalty nor patriotism that spurred them on. You must not look to the royal palace before you, nor even to that ancient and noble church, founded by the illustrious Constable, Alvarez Pereira, which you see yonder, aspiring to heaven, nor to the associations immediately connected with them, for the impulse which at length stirred up these people to resist the oppressor. You must rather seek it in that chapel, devoted to '*Nossa senhora dos Remedios*,' and containing her miraculous image. They had submitted to robbery, insult, and outrage without stint. They had seen Portuguese soldiers seized on by regiments, and marched off to serve under French eagles. They had heard Junot's insolent order to their priests, commanding them to preach submission. They had witnessed the utter degradation of their country. They had just seen the plate of the churches, and the plunder of individuals, collected throughout the neighboring *comarcas*, escorted through the town, and, though groaning in spirit, they stood by with folded arms. But when the godless

French soldiers went so far as to offer insults and indignities to *Nossa Senhora dos Remedios* on her own holy day, on which she yearly displays her miraculous powers, it was more than Portuguese nature could bear. They broke out into open resistance, at first successful—but which here and elsewhere led to woful slaughter of the patriotic but half-armed mob."

"Heretic as you are," said Lady Mabel, "you must admit, that as 'Our Lady of the Pillar' proved a tower of strength to the Saragossans in their first siege, so here, either the patron saints of the Portuguese, or their faith in them, has often done them yeoman's service."

"And often brought disaster upon them," L'Isle replied. "For instance, St. Antony is the patron saint of Portugal. I am not going to deny that he may have done them good service at times. But when the archduke, Charles of Austria, commanded the army, about 1700, the soldiers became exceedingly unruly, and demanded a native general. The king sent them St. Antony, in the shape of a wooden image. He was received with all the honors due to his rank. By royal decree a regular commission was made out, appointing him generalissimo of all the forces of Portugal, and he continued long in command; but, though an excellent saint, Antony proved a very bad general, and repeatedly brought the kingdom to the brink of ruin. They have lately been compelled to displace him. Now that Beresford does their fighting, St. Antony has full leisure to devote himself to intercession on their behalf, and, between the two, with some help from us, they are getting on pretty well."

The commissary now hinted that they had before them all that was worth seeing in "this musty old place," and the party passing out of the opposite gate pushed on as fast as they could over a rough road, running across a succession of hills, the off-shoots of Serra d'Ossa.

"Traveling in this country," said Lady Mabel, as she paused with L'Isle, to let the rest of the party come up, "is like sailing over rough waters, a perpetual up and down, neither speedy nor safe."

Few countries exhibit a greater variety of surface than Portugal," said L'Isle; "it may be likened to the ocean the day after a storm, when a change of wind has intersected the mountain billows with every variety of little waves. The language, accordingly, is rich in terms expressive of these variations of surface. It has *Monte*, a mountain; *Montezhino*, a little mountain; *Outeiro*, a hill; *Outeirinho*, a hillock; *Serra*, a lofty mountain, with various inequalities of surface; *Serrania*, a cluster of mountains; *Penha*, a rocky precipice. So that you can hardly be at a loss for a word to express the character of any elevation. Meanwhile, let us hasten up this *Montezhino*, for both the sun and our night's quarters are on the other side of it, and the former will not wait for us there."

They presently caught sight of what seemed at first to be a very tall woman; but they soon perceived that it was a friar, who, with the hood of his black cloak thrown back on his shoulders, and the skirts of his dingy grey frock girded up under St. Francis' cord, was making such good time on his up-hill path, that they overtook him with difficulty at the top of the hill. He grasped in his hand what had a marvelous resemblance to the *cajado*, a seven-foot staff, pointed at one end, and with a heavy knob at the other, with which the Portuguese peasant always goes armed; and a formidable weapon it is in his skillful hands. The shortened skirt of the friar exposed a pair of muscular calves, that bore him well over the mountain road.

He turned to look at them as they drew near, and they saw that he was a young man, not much over twenty, tall and strong, and remarkably well made and good-looking.

Old Moodie cast a sinister look on him, and longed to strip him of his frock, and put him between the stilts of a plough.

"This is a noble specimen," the commissary remarked, "of that useless army the country maintains at free quarters. His ration would more than feed one English or two Portuguese soldiers for its defence."

"I would like to turn him loose on a Frenchman," said L'Isle, "armed, like himself, only with the *cajado*. What a recruit Beresford lost when this young fellow put on the uniform of St. Francis' brigade!"

L'Isle exchanged greetings with the young friar as he rode up abreast of him, and entered into conversation with him at the suggestion of Lady Mabel, who, partly to annoy her crusty watchman behind her, affected to be much interested in this young limb of the church.

The able-bodied servant of St. Francis proved intelligent and sociable, and, while he eyed the travelers, particularly Lady Mabel, with much interest, let them know that he had left his conventual home at Villa Viçosa, on a visit to his mother, who lived at a village near Ameixial, and that he would pass the night at the *venda* near the bottom of the hill. They being also bound thither, he joined them without ceremony, keeping up with them with ease, while he drew out the news by a number of questions, which showed that he was truly an active young friar, disposed to gather ideas as well as alms on his perambulations.

CHAPTER VIII.

When late arriving at our inn of rest,
  Whose roof exposed to many a winter sky,
Half shelters from the wind the shivering guest,
By the pale lamp's dreary gloom
I mark the miserable room,
And gaze with angry eye
On the hard lot of honest poverty,
And sickening at the monster brood
Who fill with wretchedness a world so good.
  *   *   *   *   *   *   *

SOUTHEY.

It was twilight when they reached the *venda*, a large but somewhat ruinous building, surrounded by a few scattered trees, on the sloping ground near the foot of the hill. The *arriero* led his mules through the archway which formed the only entrance, and the travelers following found themselves beside and almost in a large apartment, which served at once as kitchen, parlor and dining-room to this *house of refuge*, which betrayed by many signs, that if it had ever done a thriving business, that day had long gone by. Dismounting here, their horses were led on into the stable under the same roof, and imperfectly separated from the kitchen by a rude wall.

The people of the house, an old man and two women, sat staring at them without making any hos-

6*

pitable demonstrations. So L'Isle made the first advances, and, addressing them with a studied courtesy that seemed ironical to the ladies, awakened them somewhat to a sense of their duty to the wayfarers. Seats were got for the ladies on one side of the huge fire-place, in which some embers were smouldering, and L'Isle placed two cork stools to raise their feet above the damp pavement of flat stone. On the young friar's now coming forward (for with a modesty rare in his order he had hitherto kept in the background), L'Isle resumed his sociable conversation with him, and accepted the proffered pinch of snuff, that olive-branch of the Portuguese. This evidently had a good effect on their hosts; while Shortridge was surprised to see the colonel, whose *hauteur* he had himself felt, demean himself by familiarity with these low people. He did not know that a proud man, if his be generous pride, is apt to keep it for those who assume superiority, or at least equality, with himself.

That was not the commissary's way. So he began to question abruptly, in very bad Portuguese, as to the state of her larder, the elder woman, who, ugly and blear-eyed, with ragged, scanty dress, and bare feet, yet wore a necklace of beads and earrings of gold. She answered tartly, that it being a fast-day, there was no flesh in the house. They had *bacalhao* and *sardinhas*, and garlic, and pepper, and onions, and oil, and everything that Christians wanted on a fast-day. She forgot to say that the house was without flesh many more days than the church commands. L'Isle, with more address, applied to the younger woman with better success, inquiring after accommodations for the ladies. He so moved her that she snatched up the only lamp in the room, and, leaving the rest of the party in the growing darkness, ushered the ladies up the ladder, like stairs, to the only two chambers where they could be private.

Shortridge, meanwhile, finding out the desolate state of the larder, let the woman know that they had not come unprovided with a stock of edibles of their own. He urged her to make preparations for cooking it; so rousing the old man from his chimney corner, she carried him out with her, and they soon returned with no small part of a cork-tree; and when Lady Mabel and Mrs. Shortridge came down, a cheerful blaze had brought out more fully the desolation of the room in dispelling half its gloom.

"I trust you have found a habitable chamber over head," said L'Isle to Lady Mabel.

"I were a heretic to complain," she answered. "It is true the room has no window; but it has a square hole in the wall to let in the light and let out the foul air. The bed is hard and not over tidy. But what is wanting in cleanliness is made up in holiness; for the bedstead has an elaborate crucifix carved at its head, and I shall sleep under its immediate protection. On the slightest alarm, by merely throwing my arms upward, I can lay hold on the cross, and nothing will be wanting to the sense of security but faith in this material symbol of my faith. I shall have saintly company, too. On the wall to the right is a print of St. Christopher carrying the infant Christ over a river, and a bishop, in full canonicals, waiting on the other side, with outstretched arms, to receive him; on the left, is a picture of St. Antony, of Padua, preaching to the fishes. Religion is truly part and parcel of this people's every day life; and the reality of their devotion, and the falsehood and frivolity of many of its objects, make a contrast truly painful to me."

Old Moodie, the muleteer, and the servants, having seen after their horses and mules, now came straggling into this hall, common to all the inmates of the house. Here they accommodated themselves with such seats as they could find, or contrive out of the baggage; and one of L'Isle's servants produced the rabbits and partridges purchased on the road, with some other provisions brought from Elvas. These he gave to the woman of the house to cook for the travelers, and no objection was started as to cooking flesh, that other people might commit the sin of eating it on a fast day. The whole party sat in a large semi-circle around the fire, conversing and watching the cooking of their supper; but no sooner did the savory fumes diffuse themselves through the building than another personage joined them. A stout pig, evidently a denizen of the house, came trotting and grunting out of the stable, and pushed his way into the interior of the social circle. Though he received some rude buffets, he persisted in keeping within it, until, trenching on

Lady Mabel's precincts, she made such an application of her riding-wand that he was glad to seek refuge again among his four-legged companions.

"It would seem," Lady Mabel remarked, "that these *Vendas* are caravansaries, providing only shelter for the traveler, who is expected to bring his own food."

"This is so true, that it is a blessing there are no game laws in the peninsula," said L'Isle. "The traveler would often starve at the inn but for the game purchased on the road. And it is well to travel prepared to shoot *one's own* game, as you are perpetually threatened with famine or robbers. The cookery, too, of this country is peculiar, and if you ladies watch the process closely, you may carry home some valuable hints in what some people think the first of the arts."

They accordingly closely watched the cooking, of the rabbits particularly. Each was spitted on a little spit, which had four legs at the handle, the other end resting on a piece of the fuel. When one side was roasted, the other was turned to the fire. To know when they were done, the woman cracked the joints; laying them by until cool, she then tore them to pieces with her fingers; and afterward fried the already over-roasted meat with onions, garlic, red pepper, and oil, which is always rancid in Portugal, from the custom of never pressing the olives until they are stale.

The commissary knew too much about Portuguese cookery to trust to it. He had provided himself before leaving Elvas with the commissary's cut, which is always the best steak from the best bullock. He now produced from among his baggage that implement so truly indicative of the march of English civilization—the gridiron; and not until the large table, at the other side of the room, had been spread, and supper was ready, did his man proceed to dress it skillfully and quickly, under the vigilant superintendance of the commissary himself.

They were sitting down to supper when L'Isle, seeing that the young friar remained by the fire, pointed out a vacant seat, and asked him to join them. But he shook his head.

"You are eating flesh. I must fast to-day."

"Because the Scriptures bid you?" L'Isle inquired.

"Because the Church commands me."

"You are aware, then, that there is no absolute injunction in Scripture to fast on particular days."

"Yet the Church may have authority—it doubtless has authority to appoint such days," the young friar answered, seeming at once to stifle a doubt and his appetite.

Cookery must be judged of by the palate, and not by the eye. So Lady Mabel made a strong effort to try the rabbits by the latter test—having had ocular proof that they were not cats in disguise. But, after persevering through two or three mouthfuls, the garlic, red pepper, and rancid oil, and the fact of having witnessed the whole process of cooking and fingering the fricasseè, proved too much for her; and she was fain to be indebted to the commissary for a small piece of his steak, reeking hot, and dripping with its natural juices.

The woman of the house now placed on a bench before the friar, some *broa*, or maize bread, and a piece of *bacalhao*, fried in oil. From the size of the morsel, the stock in the larder seemed to have run low, even in this article, which is nothing but codfish salted by British heretics for the benefit of the souls and bodies of the true sons of the Church. The friar eat alone and in silence, less intent on his meal than in watching and listening to the party at the table.

"They are, every one of them, eating flesh, and this day is a fast," said the elder woman to the friar, in a tone of affected horror.

"And they eat it almost raw," answered the friar, as Shortridge thrust an ounce of red beef into his mouth. "But I know not that the Church has prohibited that."

The ladies and the commissary retired soon, fatigued with their long day's ride. The friar was devoutly telling his beads, and L'Isle sat musing by the fire, while the servants, in turn, took their places at the supper table. Presently the friar, having got through his devotions, rose as if about to retire for the night; but, as he passed L'Isle, he loitered, as if wishing to converse, perhaps for the last time, with this foreigner, whose position, character, and ideas, differed so much from his own, and who yet could make himself so well understood. As L'Isle looked up, he said:

"Men of your profession see a great deal of the world."

"Yes. A soldier is a traveler, even if he never goes out of his own country."

"But the soldiers of your country visit the remotest parts of the world, the Indies in the east and west, and now this, our country, and many a land besides."

"At one time the soldiers of Portugal did the same," said L'Isle.

"Yes; there was a time when we conquered and colonized many a remote land, where the banner of no other European nation had ever been seen. We still have our colonies, but, some how or other, they do not seem to do us any good."

"But men of your profession," said L'Isle, "have been as great or even greater travelers than soldiers. They are few regions, however remote or inaccessible, which the priests of the Church of Rome, and members of your own order, have not explored."

"The friar was silent and thoughtful for a moment, and then said: "What you say is true; yet it seems to me, that is no longer the case, or, at least, that our order here has been remiss in sending forth missionaries to foreign lands. Here most of us follow through life the same dull round. It is, however, the round of our duties. But, perhaps, to find one's self in a strange country, surrounded by new scenes, an unknown, perhaps heathen people, with difficulties to struggle with, obstacles to overcome, might awaken in a man powers that he did not know were slumbering in him, and enable him to do some good, perchance great work, he never would have accomplished at home." And the young friar drew himself up to his full height, while his frame seemed to expand with the struggling energies that were shut up unemployed within him.

Visions of travel, toil, adventure, perhaps martyrdom, seemed to float before his eyes, and without another word, he strode off with a step more like that of a soldier than a Franciscan.

L'Isle gazed after him with interest and pity, then ordering the table to be cleared, stretched himself on it for the night, wrapped in his cloak, rather than rely on the accommodations of the large room up stairs, common to wayfarers of every grade, and populous with vermin.

CHAPTER IX.

When at morn the muleteer,
With early call announces day,
Sorrowing that early call I hear
That scares the visions of delight away;
For dear to me the silent hour,
When sleep exerts its wizard power.
SOUTHEY.

"I trust you rested well last night, under the protection of your saintly guardians," L'Isle said to Lady Mabel, when she made her appearance down stairs, before the sun was yet up.

"Do not speak of last night," she said, throwing up her hands in a deprecatory manner, "let it be utterly forgotten, and not reckoned among the number of the nights. It was one of penance, not repose! Never will I speak lightly of the saints again. I can only hope that that and all my other sins are expiated, if I can infer any thing from the number of my tormentors."

"Were they so numerous?" L'Isle asked, in a tone of sympathy.

"And various!" emphasized Lady Mabel. "Whole legions of various orders, light and heavy armed. I could have forgiven the first, were it only for their magnanimous mode of making war, always sounding the trumpet, and giving fair warning before they charged; and the attack being openly made, I could revenge myself on some of them by the free use of my hands, and protect my face by covering it with my veil, at the risk of being smothered. But the next band were so minute and active, and secret in their movements, that I never knew where to expect them. But the last slow, heavy legion which came crawling insidiously on, were the most tormenting and sickening of all. To be tortured by such a crowd of little fiends was enough to produce delirium. But I will not recall the visions of the night. It was worse than dreaming of being in purgatory!"

"I am sorry to hear that you had such shocking dreams," said Mrs. Shortridge, who, as she came down the stairs, heard Lady Mabel's last words, "I would have been thankful to be able to dream; but the mule bells jingling under us all night were a trifling annoyance compared to the mosquitos, fleas, and bugs, which scarcely allowed me a wink of sleep."

"Sleep!" Lady Mabel exclaimed, "they murdered sleep, and mine were waking torments."

"It is all owing to the filthy habits of the nation," continued Mrs. Shortridge. "The very pigs and asses are as much a part of the family as the children of the house."

"The fraternization of the human race with brutes, which prevails here," L'Isle remarked, "certainly, promotes neither comfort nor cleanliness. Indeed, it is curious, that as you go from north to south, cleanliness should decline in the inverse ratio with the need of it. Compared with ourselves, the French are not a cleanly people, but become so when contrasted with their neighbors, the Spaniards, who are, in turn, less filthy than the Portuguese, whose climate renders cleanliness still more necessary."

"By that ratio, what standard of cleanliness will you find in Morocco?" asked Lady Mabel.

"Perhaps a prominent and redeeming feature in their religion," said L'Isle, "may exalt the standard there. Mahomedan ablutions may avail much in this world, though little in the next."

"I am afraid," said Lady Mabel, "that their cleanly superstition will make me almost regret the expulsion of the Moors."

The commissary was now bustling about, hurrying the preparations for breakfast, and L'Isle went to see if the servants were getting ready for the journey; but Mrs. Shortridge, full of the annoyances she had suffered, continued to denounce their small enemies. Her talk was of vermin.

Lady Mabel, thinking the subject had been sufficiently discussed, interrupted her, saying, "you do not take the most philosophical and poetical view of the subject. Is it not consolatory to reflect, that while men, on suffering a reverse of fortune, too often experience nothing but ingratitude and desertion from their fellows, and sadly learn that

"'Tis ever thus: Those shadows we call friends,
Attend us through the sunshine of success,
To vanish in adversity's dark hour."

Yet there are followers that adhere to them in their fallen fortunes with more than canine fidelity, sticking to them like their sins, clinging to their persons, cleaving to their garments, with an attachment and in numbers that grow with their patron's destitution."

"But I maintain," Mrs. Shortridge replied, "that it is not only the poor and destitute that here support such a retinue. I have repeatedly seen in Lisbon, and elsewhere, young ladies, and among others a young widow of high rank, the sister of the Bishop of Oporto, lying with her head in the lap of her friend, who parted the locks of her hair to search—"

"Stop!" said Lady Mabel, laying her hand on Mrs. Shortridge's mouth, "you need not chase those small deer any further through the wood. Leave that privileged sport to the natives."

Breakfast was now ready, and Shortridge called to the ladies to lose no time. L'Isle, seeing the young friar in front of the *venda*, brought him in and seated him beside him. He pressed upon him many good things, which the house did not furnish; and this being no fast-day, the friar eat a meal better proportioned to his youth, his bulk, and his health, than his last night's meagre fare. He showed his patriotism by his approval of one of those hams of marvelous flavor, the boast of Portugal, the product of her swine, not stuffed into obesity in prison, but gently swelling to rotundity while ranging the free forest, and selecting the *bolotas*, and other acorns, as they drop fresh from the boughs. The friar was not so busy with his meal but what he continued to observe his new friends closely, and while the servants were getting their breakfast, he seized the leisure afforded to converse with L'Isle, and with Lady Mabel through him. After many questions asked and answered, the friar became thoughtful and abstracted, as if he had been brought in contact with a new class of persons and ideas, which he could not at once comprehend.

L'Isle now asked him, "When and why he had put on St. Francis' frock?"

"I do not remember when I wore any other dress. I was not four years old when I was seized with a violent sickness, and soon at the point of death. My mother vowed that if St. Francis would hear her prayer, and spare me, her only son, she would devote me to his service. From that moment, as my mother has often told me, I began to mend. As soon as a dress of the order could be made for me, I put it on. From that day I grew and strengthened rapidly, and have not had a day's sickness since. When old enough I was sent to school, and then served my noviciate in the Franciscan convent in Villa Vicosa. I am now on leave to visit my mother and sisters, who live near Ameixial."

"If you had chosen for yourself," L'Isle suggested, "perhaps you would not have been a friar."

"Perhaps not," said the young friar, hesitating. "Indeed, I have been lately told, though I am loath to admit it, that, urgent as the necessity was that gave rise to our order, and great as its services have been, especially in former days, our holy mother, the Church, can be better served now, by servants who assume a more polished exterior, and obeying St. Paul's injunction to be all things to all men, mingle on a footing of equality with men of this world, although they are not of it."

"Who told you this?" asked L'Isle.

"A learned and traveled priest, whom I lately met with. He delighted me with his knowledge, while he startled me by the boldness of some of his opinions."

"But, perhaps," L'Isle persisted, "if left to your own unbiassed choice, you would not have taken orders at all."

The young man paused, evidently unable to shut out the thought, "Are there callings, which, without doing violence to my nature, are compatible with the service of God?" At length he answered, with a reserve not usual to him, "It is not every man whose way of life is, or can be, chosen by himself." Then, crossing himself earnestly, as if stifling the thought, and trampling down the tempting devil within him, he exclaimed, "I *must* believe that my instant recovery from deadly sickness as soon as I was devoted to St. Francis, proves that he has chosen me for his service and God's."

He said this eagerly and with an air of sincerity, and again made the sign of the cross. Yet the doubting devil seemed to linger about him, and he sunk into silence, seeming little satisfied with himself. Meanwhile, during his conference with L'Isle and Lady

Mabel, old Moodie stood near, eyeing him with sinister looks, as if he had been the inventor, not the victim, of the popish system, and all its corruptions rested on his head. The old man now urged them to take horse, and allowed them no respite from his bustling interference until the party was again on the road.

The friar watched their motions with interest; and when, after crossing the valley and ascending the hill before them, Lady Mabel turned to take a last look at the ruinous old venda, she saw him still standing like a statue in the archway, doubtless with eye and thought following their steps.

"I am afraid," said L'Isle, "that our young gownsman will have to undergo a ruinous conflict in the struggle between his nature and his fate. His is the worst possible condition for a man of vigorous character and inquiring mind. He has not arrived at his convictions, but had prematurely thrust upon him the convictions he is professedly bound to hold."

"And you have helped him into the conflict," said Lady Mabel, "without staying to see him through it."

"I trust not. But, anyhow, it would have come. Were he a monk even, seclusion and devotion might protect, study might withdraw him from many temptations. Were he a secular priest, the active and definite duties of a parish, fulfilling and inculcating the obligations of Christian morals, which are the same in every church, might have tasked his energies. But, to be all his life a wandering beggar, in the name of God and St. Francis! If enthusiasts are to be pitied, how much more those who, without being, are compelled to lead the life of enthusiasts! Is it wonderful that many of these men are apostles only of ignorance and profligacy?"

"But this young man has a mind too active and enquiring for contented ignorance," said Lady Mabel. "From his very nature he must go on adding fact to fact, and thought to thought."

"Until he has built up a system of his own," answered L'Isle. "And, a hundred chances to one, that will not coincide with the teachings of St. Francis and of Rome. What must he do, then? He, a professed Franciscan, has lost his faith in St. Francis, in Rome, perhaps in Christ!—known to him only through Rome. Must he persevere? or shall he abjure? Between hypocrisy and martyrdom, he now must choose. Think not, because the fires of the *auto da fe* are extinct, a churchman here can safely abjure his profession and his faith. A man may live a life of martyrdom, although he escape a martyr's death."

They had ridden on some miles, and new scenes had suggested other topics, when they heard a shout behind them, and, looking round, saw the old man of the *Venda* displaying unwonted energy. He was vigorously pummeling with his heels the vicious *burro* on which he followed them, while he held up some article of clothing, and shouted after them at the top of his voice.

They stopped for him to come up, and he handed to Lady Mabel a rich shawl, which she had left behind in her bed-room, and a scrap of dingy white paper. Refusing any reward for his trouble and honesty, he at once took leave and turned back, the ass showing a more willing spirit on his homeward path.

After trying in vain to decipher the scroll, Lady Mabel handed it to L'Isle. "*Cito, tute, jucunde peregrineris.*" "Swift, safe and pleasant may your journey be," said L'Isle, translating it. "This is, doubtless, from the young friar. He is anxious to show you at once his scholarship and his good-will. We must not find fault with his Latin, which is capital—for a friar!"

"Give it to me. I will keep it as a talisman of safety, and as a memorial of our friar. Poor fellow!" continued Lady Mabel, "I suppose the best wish I can return him is, that enthusiasm may carry him, in sincerity and purity, through the path others have chosen for him."

"He is an impudent fellow!" growled out old Moodie. "You set too great store, my lady, by this young vagabond!"

"Vagabond!" she exclaimed, with a look and tone of grave rebuke, "I am afraid, Moodie, if you had met St. Paul wandering through Macedonia without staff or scrip, or the cloak he left behind at Troas, you would have found no better title for him."

"Is this man like St. Paul?" asked Moodie, startled at the profane supposition.

"I do not say so. But the whole order of friars, renouncing worldly objects, devote themselves to the imitation of the seventy disciples in Scripture, who were sent out by two and two to evangelize the Jews."

"I never expected, my lady, to hear you liken these lazy monks to our Lord's disciples."

"They are not monks, but friars," said Lady Mabel quietly, "and, without answering for their practice, I cannot but approve of what they profess. They do not shut themselves up from the world, like the monks, under pretence of escaping contamination, but devote themselves to the mission of traveling about in apostolic poverty from house to house, and, by prayer and preaching, by inculcating charity, and receiving alms, sow every where the seeds of the faith they profess."

"The words old Chaucer puts into the mouth of his friar," said L'Isle, "well express the objects of the order:

"In shrift, in preaching is my diligence,
And study in Peter's words and in Paul's;
I walk and fish Christian men's souls,
To yield my Lord Jesu his proper rent;
To spread his word is set all mine intent."

"A truly apostolic aim!" Lady Mabel exclaimed, looking triumphantly round on her old follower.

The descending road here narrowed suddenly, and Moodie reined back his horse, silent in the sad conviction that Lady Mabel had already got beyond that half-way house between the region of evangelical purity and idolatrous Rome.

In the narrow valley, overgrown with shrubs and

brushwood at the foot of the hill, they came suddenly on a large number of swine luxuriating in the cool waters, or on the shady banks of a brook. The swine vanished instantly amidst the thickets, though hundreds were still heard grunting and squealing around them, and the travelers might have taken them for wild denizens of the wilderness, had not a fierce growl attracted their attention, and they saw on the opposite bank a man reclining under a *carob* tree, one hand resting on the neck of a huge dog, who yet showed two savage rows of teeth, and fixed his vigilant and angry eyes on the intruders. The wild air of the master delighted Lady Mabel, for there was mingled with it a savage dignity as he stretched his manly form on the wolf-skin spread out under him; and gazed calmly on the party drawing near. While their horses stopped to drink at the stream, they observed him narrowly—he receiving this attention with stoic indifference. A long gun lay on the ground beside him, and his garments, made chiefly of the dressed skins of animals, defied brier or thorn.

"Are we on the road to Evora?" L'Isle asked, by way of opening a parley; but the man merely waved his hand gently toward the hill and path before them. Resolved to make him speak, L'Isle asked, "What game have you killed to-day?"—for he saw some animal lying in the moss at the foot of the tree. The hunter silently held up a lynx and an otter, which he had lately snared, and seemed to forget the presence of strangers in contemplating his game. Despairing of extracting a word, the travelers rode on.

"What a silent, unsocial wretch!" Mrs. Shortridge exclaimed. "He seems to prefer the company of a savage hound, and his dead game, to that of living Christians."

"He thinks a heretic no Christian, if he thinks at all," said L'Isle; and he called to the guide, to ask what this wild man was.

"He is a swine-herd."

"Indeed!" said Lady Mabel. "I took him for a bandit, or a bold hunter, at least."

"But he is the swine-herd of the great monastery of the Paulists, who own half the lands on the southern slope of Serra d'Ossa. He is a matchless hunter too, spending fewer nights under a roof than on the mountain-side, where all the game is as much his, as the swine he keeps is the property of the good fathers. They have the best bacon in all Portugal, and plenty of it, as many a poor man can tell; and they know this man's value, for he were a bold thief that pinched the ear of his smallest pig."

"As soon as I get back to Elvas," said Lady Mabel, "I will send Major Warren to make his acquaintance. The major will be charmed with him. For his ambition is to take all sorts of game, in every possible way; and though I have, or might have had, the history of all his hunts by heart, neither lynx or otter has yet figured in the scene. You remember, Colonel L'Isle, how much satisfaction he expressed when you lately hinted at the probability of our brigade finding itself in the north of Portugal early in the coming campaign. I at first thought that the soldier saw some military advantage in the movement, but found it was only the sportsman's delight at the hope of visiting Truzos Montes, and killing one of the few Caucasian goats that yet linger on the most inaccessible heights there."

"No gamester," said L'Isle, "is more a slave to the dice. That at this time a soldier should be so little 'lost in the world's debate' as to be eager, above all things, to kill a goat!"

They had now reached a point which gave them a fine view of the southern side of Serra d'Ossa, so different from the northern, being fertile, and showing many a cultivated spot upon its lower slopes, while the light, fleecy clouds, gathering before the gentle western wind, now veiled and then revealed the overhanging dark blue ridge that crowned the scene. The guide pointed out the broad possessions of the great monastery of the Paulists. At a distance, on the right, rose Evora Monte, built like a watch-tower on a lofty hill; and, to the south, the monastic towers and Gothic spires of Evora, the city of monks, raised high above the plain, could be seen from afar.

"Why," asked Mrs. Shortridge, "do these people always build their towns on hills?"

"That is a true English question," answered L'Isle. "At home, in our bleak northern climate, we naturally seek sheltered situations. These people as naturally select an airy site, above the parching heat and poisoned air of the valleys. In founding colonies in tropical countries we English, and the Dutch, have constantly blundered, acting as if still at home; and choosing low and pestilential spots, establish only hospitals and graveyards where we meant to build towns; while the Spaniards and Portuguese, from the instinct of habit, select the most salubrious situations within their reach. Moreover, high points are safer from attack, and stronger to resist an enemy; and the Christians of the peninsula were taught by seven centuries of conflict with the Moors, that the safety of a man's house is the first point, its convenience the second. Now, we islanders have long been but a half military people. Content with incurring the guilt of war abroad, we have carefully abstained from bringing it home to our own doors."

"But we never wage any but just wars," said Lady Mabel.

"We, at least," said L'Isle, "always find some plausible grounds on which to justify our wars—to ourselves."

They were now on the outskirts of the undulating plain, on which a rich soil overlying the granite rocks extends from Evora southward to the city of Beja. The signs of cultivation and population multiplied as they went on. The fields became larger and more frequent; detached farm houses were seen on either hand, and they fell in on the road with many peasants riding large and spirited asses, or driving oxen all light bays with enormous horns, and so sleek and well grown, that the commissary gazed on them with admiring eye and watering mouth, and pronounced them equally fit for the yoke or the shambles.

It was a relief to find themselves once more in a cultivated country, and Lady Mabel gazed round, admiring the prospect. "There is," she observed, "one drawback to the landscape. At home, one of the most enlivening features in our rural scenes, are the white sheep scattered on the hills, but here they are almost black."

"But the goats you see are generally white," answered L'Isle. "It is, too, the more picturesque animal, and well supplies what is wanting in the sheep."

Evora was at hand. L'Isle launched out into an erudite discourse on the aqueduct of Sertorius, which, stretching its long line of arches from the neighboring hills, was converging with their road to the city. As they entered it he was giving Lady Mabel all the *pros* and *cons*, as to whether it was really the work of that redoubtable Roman. The commissary was luxuriously anticipating the shade and rest before him, when to his surprise and regret, L'Isle led the party another way, and halted them before a small but striking building, which here crowned the aqueduct at its termination in the city.

"Look, Lady Mabel. Observe it well, Mrs. Shortridge. This castellum is a miniature embodiment of Roman taste and skill in architecture. This is no ruin calling upon the imagination to play the hazardous part of filling up the gaps made by the hand of time. We see it as the Moor, the Goth, the Roman saw it, save the loss of a few vases which adorned the depressed parapet, and the scaling plaster which here and there betrays that the builder used that cheap but immortal material, the Roman brick."

Much did Lady Mabel admire this architectural gem, scarcely tarnished by the elements in nineteen centuries, and much more would L'Isle have found to say of it, when the commissary, impatiently fanning himself with his hat, ventured to ask, "how much longer shall we stay broiling in the noon-day sun, staring at this Roman sentry-box?"

"Sentry-box!" said Mrs. Shortridge, with a puzzled air, "were the Romans a gigantic people?"

"There were giants in those days," said Lady Mabel, gravely, gazing on the castellum. But a crowd of idlers and beggars began to collect around the cavalcade, and turning, they rode off, and were soon enjoying the shelter, if not the more substantial hospitality, of the *Estalagem de San Antonio.*

CHAPTER X.

Tell me, recluse Monastic, can it be
  A disadvantage to thy beams to shine?
A thousand tapers may gain light from thee:
  Is thy light less or worse for lighting mine?
If, wanting light, I stumble, shall
Thy darkness not be guilty of my fall?

Make not thyself a prisoner, thou art free:
  Why dost thou turn thy palace to a jail?
Thou art an eagle; and befits it thee
  To live immured like a cloister'd snail?
Let toys seek corners: things of cost
Gain worth by view; hid jewels are but lost.

FRANCIS QUARLES.

In the afternoon, the commissary going out in search of the objects of his journey, grain and bullocks for the troops, L'Isle strolled out with the ladies to survey the curiosities of Evora, and Moodie followed closely Lady Mabel's steps.

"If I am to play the part of *cicerone*," said L'Isle, "I will begin by reminding you that the history of many races and eras is indissolubly connected with the Peninsula, and especially the southern part of it. Here we find the land of *Tarshish* of Scripture, so well known to the Phœnicians, who, in an adjacent province of Spain, built another Sidon, and founded Cadiz before Hector and Achilles fought at Troy.

Yet they found the Celto-Iberian here before them—who after that built Evora, according to Portuguese historians, some eight or ten centuries before Christ. The Greeks, too, stretched their commerce and their colonies to this land. The Carthaginians made themselves masters of this country. The Romans turned them out, to give place in time to the Vandals; who were driven over into Africa by the Goths—whose dominion was, at the end of two centuries, overthrown by the Arabs; who, after a war of seven centuries, were expelled in turn by the descendants of their Gothic rivals. The land still shows many traces of these revolutions. In the neighborhood of this city the rude altar of the Druid still commemorates the early Celt. The majesty of the Roman temple here forms a singular contrast with the delicacy of the Arabian monuments, and the Gothic architecture with the simplicity of the modern edifices."

"A truly Ciceronian introduction to your duties as *cicerone*," said Lady Mabel. "But I have yet to see much that you describe so eloquently. To my eye the most striking feature of Evora at this day is its ecclesiastical aspect. It is full of churches, chapels, and monkish barracks, and seems to be held by a strong garrison of these soldiers of the Pope."

"Baal's prophets are four hundred and fifty men," said old Moodie, in loud soliloquy behind.

"I have often heard the Pope called Antichrist, but never knew him dubbed Baal before," said Lady Mabel. "Although not one of his flock, I cannot but feel a deep interest in the head of the Latin Church, now that the venerable old man is so shamefully treated; carried off and kept a prisoner in France, to be bullied, threatened, and cajoled, with a view to appropriate the papal influence to the furtherance of this Corsican's ambition."

"You had better leave all those feelings to his own flock, my lady."

"Is it possible, Moodie," Lady Mabel retorted, "that you do not know that we are on the Pope's side in this' quarrel? We are bound to sympathize with him, not only in politics but in religion, against his unbelieving enemies. We must forget all minor differences, and think only of the faith we hold in common. Even you must admit that it is better to see the Almighty dimly through mists and clouds, or even though our view be obstructed by a crowd of doubtful saints, than to turn our backs on the Christian Godhead, and deny his existence like these godless French. I assure you I have become a strong friend to the Pope."

"The more is the pity," groaned Moodie. "But what is written is written."

"I know, Moodie, that you believe that we who have deserted the Kirk of Scotland, and crossed the border in search of a church, have already traveled a long way toward Rome."

"About half-way, my lady. The church of England is no abiding place, but merely an inn on that road."

"Why," exclaimed Mrs. Shortridge, "is Moodie so much dissatisfied with our church? For my part it does not seem natural to me for genteel people to go any where else."

"You may find, madam," said Moodie, "a great many genteel people going some where else. Gentry is no election to grace."

Mrs. Shortridge resented the insinuation by indignant silence; but Lady Mabel, who had her own object in exasperating Moodie's sectarian zeal, now asked him: "What is the last symptom of backsliding you have seen in me?"

"It seems to me, my lady, that you are getting strangely intimate with the Romish faith and rites, for one who does not believe and practice them. It is a sinful curiosity, like that of the children of Israel, which first made them familiar with the abominations among their neighbors, then led them to practice the idolatries they had witnessed."

"But may there not be something sinful, Moodie, in denouncing the errors and corruptions of the Romanists, without having thoroughly searched them out?"

"We know the great heads of their offense—their perversion of gospel truth—their teaching for doctrine the commandments of men. There is no need to trace every error through all its dark and crooked windings. Truth is one: that God has allotted to his elect. Errors are manifold, and sown broadcast among the reprobate."

"Still it must matter much what degree and kind of error falls to our lot," Lady Mabel suggested.

"Perhaps so," Moodie answered, with doubting assent. "Yet if we are not in the one true path, it may matter little which wrong road we travel."

"Well, Moodie," said she, "however much you may narrow down your Christian faith, you shall not hedge in my Christian charity, and deprive me of all sympathy for the Pope in this his day of persecution."

"Whatever the holy father's errors may have been," said L'Isle, "we may now say of him, a prisoner in France, what was said of Clement the Seventh, when shut up in the Castle of St. Angelo, '*Papa non potest errare.*'"

"That is Latin, Moodie," said Lady Mabel, "and to enlighten your ignorance it may be rendered, 'The Pope cannot err.'"

"Why that is nothing but the doctrine of the Pope's infallibility," exclaimed Moodie, indignantly; "and saying it in Latin cannot make it true." And he dropped behind the party.

Gazing on the number of religious houses and habits around them, Lady Mabel said: "Monastic life must hold forth strong allurements. The monks seem to find it easy to recruit their ranks."

"Many motives combine to draw men into the church," L'Isle answered. "Devotion may be the chief; but, in this climate and country, the love of ease, and the want of hopeful prospects in secular life, exercise great influence. Moreover, one monk, like one soldier, serves as a decoy to another. Did you ever see a recruiting sergeant, in all his glory, among a party of rustics at a village alehouse? How skillfully he displays the bright side of a soldier's life, while hiding every dark spot. The church has many a recruiting sergeant, who can put the best of ours to shame. Many a recruit, too, like our young friar, is caught very young."

They had now turned into another street, and L'Isle, stopping the party, pointed out a large building opposite to them.

"What a curious mixture of styles it presents," said Mrs. Shortridge.

"What a barbarous mutilation of a work of art," exclaimed Lady Mabel.

"This is, or rather was," said L'Isle, "the temple of Diana, built before the Christian era, perhaps while Sertorius yet lorded it in the Peninsula, and made Evora his headquarters. The architect," continued he, looking at it with the eye of a connoisseur, "was doubtless a Greek. Time, and the mutilations and additions of the Moor, have not effaced all the beauty of this structure, planned by the genius and reared by the hands of men who lived nineteen centuries ago. The rubble work and plaster wall that fills the space between those columns, so requisite in their proportions—the pinnacles which crown the structure in place of the entablature which has been destroyed, are the work of the Moors, who strove in vain to unite in harmony their own style of building with that of their Roman predecessors. Enough remains to show the chaste, beautiful, and permanent character of the edifices of that classic age."

After gazing long with deep interest on this monument of the palmy days and wide-spread sway of the Roman, Lady Mabel said: "Let us see if there be not still left within the building some remains of a piece with so noble an exterior."

"Unhappily," answered L'Isle, "all is changed there. Moreover, though the sacrifices are continued, they are no longer conducted with the decorum of the heathen rites. The temple of the chaste goddess is now the public shambles of the city, defiled throughout by brutal butchers, with the blood and offals of the slaughtered herd."

"Is it possible!" Lady Mabel exclaimed. "Have these people sunk so low? Is so little taste, learning, and reverence for high art left among them, that they can find no better use for this rare memorial of the past."

"No people have proved themselves so destitute of taste, and of reverence for antiquity, as the Portuguese," replied L'Isle. "They seem to have found it a pleasure, or deemed it a duty, to erase the footprints of ancient art. Monuments of all kinds, beautiful and rare, and but lightly touched by the hand of time, have been ruthlessly destroyed here. To give you a single instance: A gentleman of the family of the Mascarenhas, who had traveled in Italy, and acquired a taste for the arts, collected from different parts about the town of Mertola, twelve ancient statues, with a view to place them on pedestals in his country-house. But he dying before completing his intention, these admirable productions of Roman art, the venerable representations of heroes and sages, were hurled into a lime kiln to make cement for the chapel of St. John. And such acts of Vandalism have been perpetrated throughout Portugal."

"The barbarians!" exclaimed Lady Mabel. "The ignorance they condemn themselves to, is scarce punishment enough for the offence."

"It is difficult to say how much they have destroyed," continued L'Isle. "But, beside the voice of history, proofs enough remain that Evora was, in the days of Sertorius, of Cæsar, and in after-times, a favorite spot with the Romans. This temple before us, mutilated as it is, and the aqueduct, though repaired in modern times, are still Roman; and no ancient monument in Italy is in better preservation than the beautiful little castellum which crowns its termination. Even where Roman buildings have been destroyed we still see around us the stones with ancient and classic inscriptions built into new walls. The plough, too, of the husbandman still at times turns up the coins of Sertorius, bearing a profile showing the wound he had received in his eye, while the reverse represents his favorite hind leaning against a tree."

"How completely do these things carry us back to

ancient times, and make even Plutarch's novels seem verities of real life," said Lady Mabel. "These same Romans, whom we read of and wonder at, have indeed left behind them, wherever they came, foot-prints indelibly stamped on the face of the country."

"They did more," said L'Isle, "wherever civilization extends, they still set their marks upon the minds of men."

"How barbarous seem the Moorish buildings, which we still see here and at Elvas," said Lady Mabel, "compared with these monuments of a yet earlier day."

"The Moors had a style of their own," said L'Isle. "Indifferent to external decoration, they reserved all their ingenuity for the interior of their edifices. Stimulated by a sensuous religion and a luxurious climate, they there lavished whatever was calculated to delight the senses, and accord with a sedentary and voluptuous life. They sought a shady privacy amidst sparkling fountains, artificial breezes, and sweet smelling plants; amidst brilliant colors and a profusion of ornaments, seen by a light sobered from the glare of a southern sun. Numberless were the luxurious palaces the Moors reared in Portugal and Spain. The Alhambra yet stands a model of their excellence in the arts; although many of its glories have departed, its walls have become desolate, and many of them fallen into ruin, though its gardens have been destroyed, and its fountains ceased to play. Charles V. commenced a palace within the enclosure of the Alhambra, in rivalry of what he found there. It stands but an arrogant intrusion, and is already in a state of dilapidation far beyond the work of the Arabs. In them the walls remain unaltered, except by injuries inflicted by the hand of man. The colors of the painting, in which there is no mixture of oil, preserve all their brightness—the beams and wood work of the ceilings show no signs of decay. The art of rendering timber and paints durable, and of making porcelain mosaics, arabesques, and other ornaments, began and ended in western Europe with the Spanish Arabs. But perhaps the most curious achievement attributed to them is, that spiders, flies, and other insects, shunned their apartments at all seasons."

"What!" exclaimed Lady Mabel, "had they attained that perfection in the art of building? Could they exercise those hordes of little demons, lay a spell upon them and turn them out of doors? Had you told me this yesterday I would have been less impressed by it. But, after last night's ordeal, I venerate the Moor. Almost I regret the expulsion of his cleanly superstition, since it has carried with it into exile so rare an art."

Mrs. Shortridge, too, seemed fully to appreciate the value of the lost art, and said, "these Moors must indeed have been a very comfortable people."

"And they crowned their comfort in this world," said L'Isle, "by inventing an equally comfortable system for the next."

"Is it not strange," said Lady Mabel, gazing on

the building before them, "that the production of two races, each so skillful, should be so utterly incompatible. Classic and Saracenic art, both beautiful, united make a monster."

"Not so strange," L'Isle answered, "as the simplicity of the Mohammedan faith, amidst all that is fantastic in arts and letters—a grotesque architecture, a wondrous alchemy, the extravagant in poetry and the supernatural in fiction; or the purity of classic art, characterized by simplicity and proportion, yet drawing its inspiration from a wild and copious mythology, made up of the sportive creations of fancy."

"They were a wonderful people, these Romans, as even this obscure corner of Europe can witness," said Lady Mabel, her eyes dwelling on the beautiful colonade, and tracing out the exquisite symmetry of the shafts, and the rich foliage of the Corinthian capitals.

"Were these Romans Christians?" asked Moodie, who had hitherto looked on in silence.

"No," she answered, "they worshipped many false gods."

"Then they were just like all the Romans I have known," said he dryly, and turned his back on the temple.

"Come," said Mrs. Shortridge, "let us take Moodie's hint, and look for something else worth seeing."

As they continued their walk, L'Isle remarked, "In many a place in the peninsula we find a Roman aqueduct, a Moorish castle, and a Gothic cathedral standing close together, yet ages apart. How much of history is embraced in this? We have just been gazing upon the mouldering remains of two phases of civilization, which were at their height, one, while our forefathers were yet heathen and almost savage, the other, while they were but emerging from a rude barbarism. We should never forget that this peninsula was the high road which arts and letters traveled on their progress into Western Europe, and to our own land."

"We are much indebted to letters and the arts for the unanimity with which they came on to us; for certainly," said Lady Mabel, looking round her, "little of either appears to have loitered behind. Every object around us makes the impression of a country and a people who have seen better days; and you cannot help wondering and fearing where this downward path may end."

"The history of humanity is not always the story of progress," said L'Isle; "one nation may be like a young barbarian, his face turned toward civilization, gazing on it with dazzled but admiring eyes; another, a scowling, hoary outlaw, turning his back on human culture and social order."

"Your young barbarian," said Lady Mabel, "makes the more pleasing picture of the two."

"Are there your hoary outlaws?" exclaimed Mrs. Shortridge, as a party of beggars from the door of the Franciscan church hobbled toward them, and beset them for alms.

"Oh, no!" said Lady Mabel, "they are angels in

disguise, tempting us to deeds of charity;" and with the devout air of a zealous daughter of the one true church, she distributed sundry small coin among them. "Come, Moodie," she exclaimed, "I know your pocket is never without a store of sixpences, those *canny* little dogs, that often do the work of shillings. Seize the occasion of doing good works, of appropriating to yourself a meritorious charity; for charity covers a multitude of sins. Lay up some treasure in heaven without loss of time."

The beggars, on this hint, surrounded Moodie; but he, repudiating such perversion of Scripture doctrine, shook them off with little ceremony. And the beggars' instinct saw, in his hard, indignant face, no hope of alms.

"If you will give nothing, at least buy something," said Lady Mabel; "that fellow bawling at you *pelas almas*, is offering snuff for sale; and the love of snuff, at least, is common ground to Scot and Portuguese."

Thus urged, Moodie paid liberally for a package, and was putting it in his pocket, when Lady Mabel exclaimed, "You do not know, Moodie, what a charitable and Christian deed you have done. Every thing is done in Portugal *pelo amor de Deos e pelas almas*. That fellow is employed by the priests to sell snuff *pelas almas*, and all the profits of the trade go to release souls from purgatory."

"Purgatory!" exclaimed Moodie, "I will not be tricked into countenancing that popish abomination;" and he hurled the package back to the man, who gladly picked it up, and turned to seek a second purchaser.

As they walked on toward the church of the Franciscans, Mrs. Shortridge said, "You need not fear a scarcity of objects of charity, Lady Mabel, for poverty seems rife in Evora."

"Yet, from the number of churches and monasteries, there must be much wealth," Lady Mabel answered. "Probably, most of the property is in their possession, and we may expect to see in their shrines and altars a gorgeous display of their riches."

"You will be disappointed in that," said L'Isle. "Evora has passed too lately through the hands of the French, too systematic a people to do things by halves. Their emperor is more systematic still. On taking possession of Portugal, his first edict from Milan imposed a war-contribution on the country of one hundred million of francs, as a ransom for private property of every kind. This being somewhat more than all the money in the country, allowed a sufficiently wide margin for spoliation, without making private property a whit the safer for it; the imperial coffers absorbed this public contribution, leaving the French officers and soldiers to fill their pockets and make their fortunes as they could."

"But what was there left to fill their pockets with?" Lady Mabel asked.

"There must have been a plenty left," said Mrs. Shortridge. "One does not know the wealth of a country till you plunder it. Even some of our fellows, though they came as friends, still continue occasionally to pocket a useful thing. The officers cannot put a stop to it altogether, do what they may."

"But, with some exceptions," said L'Isle, "each French general levied contributions on his own account. Some idea of the amount may be formed from the fact, that at the Convention of Cintra, Junot, who had probably not brought baggage enough into Portugal to load five mules, demanded five ships for the conveyance of his private property. Yet Soult's accumulations in Andalusia are said to exceed Junot's. Whatever may be the result of the war, many a French officer will have made his fortune here. Well did they obey the injunction—

> "'See thou shake the bags
> Of hoarding abbots; angels imprisoned
> Set thou at liberty.'

This last, though, in a sense different from the poets; in Lisbon alone, turning thousands of nuns into the streets, that their convents might be converted into barracks. In obedience to the imperial decree, all the gold and silver of the churches, chapels, and fraternities of the city were carried off to the mint; and, in this day of sweeping confiscation, individuals did not forget themselves. Indeed, throughout the country, the French soldier proved that he had the eye of a lynx, the scent of a hound, and the litheness of a ferret after booty, trained to it by the system which makes the war support the war. But Evora has been particularly unlucky. It not only bore its full share of the first burden imposed on the country, but the year after, when the Portuguese, rising too late in armed resistance, lost a battle before the town, the French, entering with the fugitives, massacred nearly a thousand persons, many of them women and children, including some forty priests, a class they made the especial objects of their vengeance; and they plundered the town so thoroughly, that the very cracks in the walls did not escape their search. The best excuse that can be made for their plunderings is, that in the confusion of their own revolution they so completely lost the idea of property, that though they have recovered the thing, they have not yet remastered the idea of it."

A number of friars now coming out of the church attracted Mrs. Shortridge's attention. But Lady Mabel had an English woman's ear for French atrocities, and continued the conversation:

"I can understand that a needy and ignorant soldiery may perpetrate such robberies amidst scenes of violence, and under the temptations of want; but we expect better things from the men who lead them."

"That supposes these men to be of a different class, with different education and habits from the common soldier. The revolution and conscription has leveled all those distinctions. Many a youth of good birth and education is made to bear his musket in the ranks, and does not elevate his comrades to his standard, but is soon degraded to the level of their sentiments and habits. Many a French general, for instance Junot, has been raised from the ranks. Military merit or accident has elevated them to command without a corresponding elevation of sentiment or principles. It is not easy to make a gentleman in one generation: somebody says, it takes three."

"What a moderate man that somebody was!" said Lady Mabel; "I thought that the gentry of a country were like its timber, the slow growth of centuries, and that the beginning of nobility must be lost in the dark ages, unless you can find some great statesman, warrior, or freebooter of later date to start from."

"But," said L'Isle, laughing, "we find men whose pedigree fulfills your requisitions, who are not gentlemen in their own persons. The son of a gentleman is too often one only in name."

"I think," said Lady Mabel, reflecting, "I have myself met with more than one gentleman rogue."

"That is impossible," said L'Isle, "for a gentleman is a superstructure which can be built on only one foundation—an honest man."

"We had better stop defining the gentleman," said Lady Mabel, "lest between us we narrow down the class, until there are not enough left to officer a regiment, or for any other useful purpose."

"This is a fine old building," said Mrs. Shortridge, peeping into the church, "and it will be a convenient time to look at it, for it seems quite empty."

"It is not much worth seeing," said L'Isle, "but there is something beyond it which I would like to show you."

They walked into it; but Moodie at first hung back, and hesitated to enter this idolatrous temple, until, luckily remembering the prophet's permission to Naaman the Syrian to accompany his master to the house of Rimmon, he swallowed his scruples, and followed Lady Mabel.

Passing through the church, they came to an archway, over which was inscribed—

Nos os ossos que aqui estamos
Pelos vossos esperamos.

Passing through it, they found themselves in a huge vault, its arched ceiling supported by large square piers, which, with the walls, were covered with human skulls, set in a hard cement. By the dim light they saw on all sides thousands of ghastly human heads, grinning at them in death; the only signs of life being a few crouching devotees, prostrate before an illuminated shrine at the extremity of this Golgotha.

Both ladies paused, awe-stricken. Lady Mabel turned pale, and Mrs. Shortridge, after gazing round her for a moment, uttered a little shriek, and covered her face with her hands. To face these objects was painful enough, but to have them grinning on her, as in mockery, behind her back, was more than she could stand. So seizing old Moodie by the arm, he being beside her, she rushed out of this charnel house, and impatiently called to the others to join her in the church.

With an effort Lady Mabel stifled her contagious

terror, and, advancing further into the gloomy repository, inspected it on all sides. There was little room left on the walls for more memorials of mortality. Having in silence sated her curiosity and her sense of the horrible, feeling all the while a strange reluctance to break the deathlike stillness of the place by uttering a word, she at length rejoined Mrs. Shortridge. After taking another look into this apartment of death, her eye rested on the inscription over the arch. L'Isle translated it:

> Our bones, which here are resting,
> Are expecting yours.

"God forbid that mine should find so gloomy a resting place," exclaimed Mrs. Shortridge, with a shudder.

"It is a weakness," said Lady Mabel; "yet we must shrink from this promiscuous mingling of our ashes, and are even choice in the selection of our last resting place. We hope even in death to rejoin our kindred dust in the ancestral vault, or at least to repose under some sunny spot, in the churchyard hallowed to us in life. Is not this your feeling?" she said, appealing to L'Isle.

L'Isle looked grave. "It is a natural feeling clinging to our mortal nature, and doubtless has its use. But I must not indulge it. The soldier is even less at liberty than other men to choose his own grave. The fosse of a beleaguered fortress, a shallow trench in a well-fought field, the ravine of a disputed mountain pass, the strand of some river to be crossed in the face of the enemy—all these have furnished, and will furnish graves for those who fall, and have the luck to find burial; the wolf and the vulture provide for the rest. We have a wide graveyard," he added, more cheerfully, "stretching from hence to the Pyrenees, and, perchance, beyond them. It embraces many a lovely and romantic spot, only the choice of our last resting place is not left to ourselves."

Lady Mabel shuddered at this gloomy picture, and his foreboding tone. She knew how many of her countrymen had fallen, and must fall, in this bloody war. Yet, some how or other, she had always thought of L'Isle as one who was to live, and not to die prematurely, cut off in youth, health, the pride of manhood, his hopes, powers, aspirations, just in their bloom. She looked at him with deep, painful interest, as if to read his fortune in his face. What special safeguard protected him? The next moment her conscience pricked her, when her father's image rose before her, grown gray in service, and seamed with scars, yet no safer by all his dangers past than the last recruit, and she walked slowly forth from the Franciscan church with sadder and more solemn impressions of the reality and imminence of death than could be generated by all that vast array of grinning skulls.

It was growing late, and they turned toward the *estalagem.* As they strolled on, L'Isle, in the same train of thought which had last occupied them, said: "War is essentially a greedy thing, a great and speedy consumer of what has been slowly produced in peace. We hear of veteran armies, but an army of veterans does not, perhaps never existed. We collect materials and munitions of war, expecting to expend them in military operations; but we are not aware, until we have tried it, how close a parallel there is between the fates of the inanimate and the living constituents that furnish forth an army for the field. It is not the sword chiefly that kills; the hospital swallows more than the battle-field. After a few campaigns, what has been falsely called the skeleton, but is, in truth, the soul of an army, the remnant of experienced officers and tried soldiers, only remains, and new flesh, blood, and bones must be provided for this soul, in the shape of new levies. When we see an old soldier glorying in his score of campaigns, we should call to mind the score of youths prematurely covered by the sod."

"Few, then," said Lady Mabel, "can enjoy Gonsalvo of Cordova's fortune. On retiring to a monastery, he avowed that every soldier needed for repentance an interval of some years between his life and his death."

"The great captain's conscience must have pricked him," said L'Isle, "when he made that speech. An unjust war, or a war unjustly waged, lay heavy on him. A soldier knows the likelihood of his dying in his vocation. If he think it criminal, let him abandon it. Up to this day my conscience has not troubled me on that score. War, always an evil, is often a necessity; and I wonder whether, after an hundred years of peace, we would not find nations worse and more worthless than they now are."

Mrs. Shortridge now called their attention to the number of storks in the air. The sun had set, and these grave birds were seeking their roosts; every tower of church and monastery affording a domicil to some feathered family, with the full sanction of the biped denizens below.

"The social position of these long-legged gentry all over the peninsula," said L'Isle, "is one of the characteristics of the country. It is astonishing what an amount of respect, and an immunity from harm, they enjoy. I am afraid they would fare worse at the hands of the more brutal part of our English populace. They are useful, too; but are more indebted for their safety, and the respect shown them here, to the clerical gravity of their demeanor."

They had now reached their lodgings, and were soon after joined by the commissary, who came in rubbing his hands, and exclaiming: "Capital bargains to be made here! Corn plenty, and bullocks that would make a figure in Smithfield. Some farmers have not threshed last year's crop. A curious country this: one province starving, and plenty in the next. It is all owing to the want of roads. But, luckily, Elvas is not far off."

"Yet the Romans," L'Isle remarked, "had once netted over the whole Peninsula with roads."

"When they went away," said the commissary,

"the first thing the people of the country did, I suppose, was to let them go to ruin in true Portuguese fashion."

Shortridge now said that he must spend some days in the neighborhood of Evora, and that the party would have to return to Elvas without him. This being agreed to, Lady Mabel suggested that they should find their way back by a different route, and, on consulting the muleteer, they found that it could be done without much lengthening their journey.

CHAPTER XI.

Led with delight they thus beguile the way
*　　*　　*　　*　　*　　*
When weening to return whence they did stray,
They cannot find that path, which first was showne,
But wander to and fro in ways unknown,
Furthest from end then, when they nearest weene,
That makes them doubt their wits be not their own,
So many paths, so many turning seene,
That which of them to take in diverse doubt they been.
FAERIE QUEENE.

THE party mustered early the next morning to continue their journey, and after breakfast L'Isle called for the innkeeper to pay him his bill. This worthy, acting on the natural supposition that the English had come into the country to indemnify the Portuguese for their losses at the hands of the French, at once named the round sum of sixty *crusados*. On L'Isle looking surprised, he began to run over so long a list of articles furnished, and items of trouble given, that L'Isle, who was annoyed at the interruption of an agreeable conversation with Lady Mabel, was about to pay him in full to get rid of him, when Shortridge peremptorily interfered. The demand was extortionate and aroused his indignation. Perhaps he looked upon the fellow as usurping a privilege be-

8*

longing peculiarly to the commissary's own brotherhood. He abused the man roundly in very bad Portuguese, and insisted that L'Isle should pay him but half the sum.

The innkeeper, a dark, sallow man, with a vindictive countenance, glared on him as if fear alone withheld him from replying with his knife. When he found his tongue, he began to answer with a bitterness that was fast changing into uncontrollable rage; but the commissary, who was a master in the art of bullying, cut him short.

"This fellow," said he, addressing L'Isle, but still speaking Portuguese, "has three fine mules in his stable. I shall need a great many beasts to carry corn to Elvas, and will apply to the *Juiz de Fora* to embargo them among the first."

The innkeeper turned as pale as his golden skin permitted at the bare suggestion. The French had made a similar requisition on him four years ago, and when he followed his cattle to reclaim them after the required service, he got only sore bones and a broken head for his pains.

"You may do as you please in that matter," said L'Isle, throwing on the table half the sum demanded, and leaving their host to swallow his anger, and take it up, if he pleased.

The muleteer, having come in for the baggage, on finding out the nature of the controversy, now poured out a flood of vociferous eloquence on the extortioner, denouncing him as a disgrace to the nation, and no true Portuguese, but a New Christian, as might be seen in his face; and he was urgent with Shortridge to let him show him the way to the house of the *Juiz de Fora* without loss of time.

L'Isle's commanding air and contemptuous indifference overawed the innkeeper quite as much as Shortridge's threats. So, sweeping the money into his pocket, he went out hastily to find a safe and secret hiding place for his mules.

"Pray," said Lady Mabel to L'Isle, while they were waiting for their horses, "what is a New Christian?"

"The explanation of the term does not tell well in the history of the country," said he. "When Ferdinand and Isabella expelled the Jews from Spain, many of them took refuge here, where John II. gave them shelter, on condition that they should quit the kingdom in a limited time. This king endeavored to keep faith with them. Nevertheless, in his and the following reign, they were subjected to unceasing persecutions, being required to become Christians, or leave the country; at the very time every obstacle was put in the way of their escape. At length their children were taken from them to be reared in the Christian faith, and numbers abjured Judaism in order to recover possession of their own offspring. But such a conversion failed not to furnish for many a generation a crowd of hapless inmates for the 'Tremendous House of the Inquisition' in every town. Even in the last century, no diversion delighted the

Lisbon mob like the burning of a relapsed Jew. The usage of them of old still influences the condition of the country, and the term New Christian is yet a by-word common in the mouths of people."

"We certainly see a great many Jewish faces among the Portuguese Christians," said Mrs. Shortridge.

"So the great Marquis de Pombul thought," L'Isle answered; "for when a great crowd had assembled to see him open a fountain he had erected in Lisbon, on a courtier's saying, 'See, my Lord, like Moses, you make water flow from the rock!' 'Yes,' replied the marquis, 'and here are the Jews looking at me.'"

"And our host," said Mrs. Shortridge, "is doubtless one of these New Christians."

"But has the commissary," Lady Mabel asked, "a right to make the requisition with which he threatens him?"

"Not on his own authority," said L'Isle, laughing. "But these people would well deserve that we should sweep off every mule and yoke of oxen around Evora. Last year when we were collecting materials for the siege of Badajoz, the ungrateful rascals would not send a single cart to help us."

"Why, were we not fighting their battles?" Lady Mabel exclaimed. "Would they not assist in their own defence?"

"Badajoz is not within sight of Evora, and that was enough for these short-sighted patriots."

"Has such blind selfishness a parallel?" asked Lady Mabel.

"Many," said L'Isle. "We may at times find one at home, in the wisdom of a whig ministry, which consists in taking a microscopic view of the wrong side of things just under their noses."

They now mounted their horses, and leaving the *praca*, had entered on a narrow and somewhat crooked street, where they suddenly met a funeral procession, with its priests, crucifix and tapers, the dead being carried by several persons on a bier, and followed by a few peasants. The travelers drew up their horses close to the adjacent wall, to leave room for the procession. The face of the dead was uncovered as usual, and the friar's dress which clothed the body, with the rosaries and other paraphernalia displayed about his person, led Lady Mabel to say, "I see that one of the good fathers is gone to his account."

"He will now find out," said Moodie, "the worth of his beads, crucifix and holy water."

"I am surprised," said Lady Mabel, "at so unpretending a funeral, in the case of a member of the great order of St. Francis."

L'Isle asked a question of a Portuguese standing near, and then said, "The cowl does not make the monk, nor must you infer from his dress that this man was a friar. He lived all his life a peasant in a neighboring village."

"Indeed!" exclaimed Lady Mabel.

"Almost every one," said L'Isle, as they turned to ride on their way, "here and throughout the Peninsula, is buried in a religious habit—the men in the uniform of friars, the women dressed like pilgrims, and the girls like nuns. They are loaded with a freight of rosaries, *agni dei*, and other saintly jewelry, fastened to the neck, hands and feet, and stuffed into the clothes. Convents have often a warehouse appropriated to this posthumous wardrobe, in the sale of which they drive a profitable trade. It was a most natural mistake made by a stranger, who, after being a few weeks at Madrid, and seeing so many Franciscans interred, expressed his astonishment at the prodigious number of them in the city, and asked if their order was not entirely carried off by this violent epidemic."

"I suppose," said Lady Mabel, "the custom originated in the propensity so strong in us all, to live sinners and die saints."

"Exactly so," L'Isle answered; "it is a fraudulent custom, old as the fifth century, and common in popish countries. It is nothing less than an attempt to cheat St. Peter, who, you know, keeps the keys of heaven, by knocking at the gate in the disguise of a monk or a friar."

"I have too much faith in St. Peter's vigilance and penetration," said Mrs. Shortridge, "to think he has ever been so taken in."

They presently got out of the city; but, to Moodie's displeasure, by a gate opposite to that by which they had entered it. He was still more annoyed, when, on coming to a place where the road branched into two, the commissary took a brief though kindly leave of his wife and friends, and, followed by his man, galloped off to the right, on a professional chase after grain and bullocks.

L'Isle was surprised to find himself regretting the loss of their fellow-traveler. He had found him, always remembering that he was a commissary, a very good fellow; for we can find some good in every man, if we take the trouble to look for it; and Shortridge was one who, after taking care of himself, was quite willing to take care of other people.

But L'Isle's regret was nothing to Moodie's, whose habits of life led him to appreciate the nature and importance of the commissary's official duties. He valued him as a practical, responsible man of business, with no foolish fancies about him. He admired the summary way in which he had disposed of the extortionate inn-keeper, and now looked after him almost in despair; for he did not think the party left behind by any means fit to take care of themselves or each other. L'Isle he did not understand and mistrusted, doubting whether he were merely idly rambling about the country, or harbored some covert design, the object of which was Lady Mabel, of course.

"My Lady," said he, riding up beside her, and speaking in an under tone, "this is not the road we traveled coming from Elvas. Where are you going to now?"

Remarking his dissatisfied air, and the look of suspicion he cast on L'Isle, she answered, with provoking coolness, "Oh, we are merely rambling about; any road is the right one, if it but leads to a new place."

"But now the commissary has left us, do you not mean to go back to Elvas?"

"In returning we will make a detour."

"And what is a detour?" asked Moodie, with a puzzled air.

"It means going back the longest way. We have plenty of leisure, for the campaign will not open directly."

"I would like to know what you, my Lady, have to do with the opening of the campaign?"

"A great deal, and so have you; for, as soon as it does open, you and I must march back to Scotland."

"I wish it were to-morrow," said Moodie.

"It will not be to-morrow, or to-morrow's morrow," Lady Mabel answered. "Meanwhile, we will see all that is to be seen, and learn all that is to be known. Even you, by crowding and packing more closely your old notions, may find room for some new ones."

"I am too old to learn," said Moodie, sullenly.

"Too wise, you mean," she said, breaking off from him. "Come, Mrs. Shortridge, let me tear you from this barren spot, to which grief has rooted you on parting from the commissary;" and, seizing that lady's mule by the rein, Lady Mabel led her, as if helpless from sorrow, after the guide, who had taken the left-hand road.

"Somewhere hereabouts," L'Isle remarked, as they rode on, "lies what is called the field of Sertorius. I know not why it is so named; but it figures largely in the tradition, and yet more in the superstitions, of the country. 'There exists in Portugal a strange superstition concerning King Sebastian, whose reappearance is as confidently expected by many of the Portuguese, as the coming of the Messiah by the Jews. The rise and progress of this belief forms a curious part of their history. It began in hope, when the return of that prince, after his hapless expedition to Morocco, and the fatal battle of *Alcaçar Quiber*, was not only possible, but might have been considered likely; it was fostered by the policy of the Braganzan party after all reasonable hope had ceased; and length of time only served to ripen it into a confirmed and rooted superstition, which even the intolerance of the Inquisition spared, for the sake of the loyal and patriotic feelings in which it had its birth. The holy office never interfered farther with the sect, than to prohibit the publication of its numerous prophecies, which were suffered to circulate in private. For many years the persons who held this strange opinion had been content to enjoy their dream in private, shrinking from observation and ridicule; but as the belief had begun in a time of deep calamity, so now, when a heavier evil had overwhelmed the kingdom, it spread beyond all former example. Their prophecies were triumphantly brought to light, for only in the promises which were there held out could the Portuguese find consolation; and proselytes increased so rapidly, that half Lisbon became Sebastianists. The delusion was not confined to the lower orders; it reached the educated classes; and men who had been graduated in theology became professors of a faith which announced that Portugal was soon to be the head of the Fifth and Universal Monarchy; Sebastian was speedily to come from the Secret Island; the Queen would resign the sceptre into his hands; he would give Bonaparte battle near Evora, on the field of Sertorius, slay the tyrant, and become monarch of the world.' "

"And this superstition now prevails?" Lady Mabel asked.

"So widely, that at least every other man you meet is a Sebastianist."

As they rode on they found the country dotted over with *quintas* and country-houses, here called *montes*, from being generally seated on hills. Around each homestead the meagre and tame-hued olive was mingled with the deep rich green of the orange-tree, which here produces its fruit in the greatest perfection of flavor, at least, if not of size, and a vineyard occasionally occupied the slope of the hill. The lower grounds were covered with extensive cornfields, bearing here a thriving growth of wheat, there a young crop of maize, which furnishes these people with more than half their food.

"The Portuguese," said L'Isle, "like their Spanish neighbors, are often charged with indolence; but here and elsewhere, under favorable circumstances, they show no want of industry. The husbandman of this part of Alemtejo has grown rich in spite of the greatest obstacle to thrift, which the church has raised up in devoting more than half the year to holy days. Good lands are apt to make good farmers, and labor and skill well repaid, leads to the outlay of more labor and greater skill."

"We see around us a people," said Lady Mabel, "reveling in the Scripture blessings of corn, wine, and oil. I think there must be no little resemblance between Portugal and Palestine."

"The Jews think so too," answered L'Isle. "The delights of Portugal can make a Jew forget Jerusalem. They clung, and still cling to it, as another promised land. Moreover, if their fathers of old longed after the leeks and onions of Egypt, their sons may satisfy that longing here."

"And stuff themselves with garlic to boot," like Portuguese sausage," said Mrs. Shortridge. "The quantity of these things in it leaves little room for the pork."

The travelers occasionally fell in with peasants singly, or in parties on the road; and L'Isle, prompted by the ladies, let few of them pass without exchanging some words, which were easily drawn out; for English uniforms, and ladies so evidently foreigners, excited much curiosity, especially in the women. Struck with the air of comfort common among these people, and the marks of fertility and cultivation in the country around them, Lady Mabel hoped that Moodie had at last met with something to please him; so she asked the opinion of that high authority on the rural prospect and the farming around them. But he at once condemned it as unskillful, wasteful, and slovenly; in short, just what was to be looked for in this benighted land.

"What a pity it is, Moodie, you cannot speak Portuguese," said Lady Mabel; "you might seize many a chance of giving these benighted people a valuable hint, particularly how to ferment their wine, and press their olives."

"I am sure," replied Moodie, "I could make as sour wine and rancid oil as the best of them, and they make no other."

"You are a fault-seeking traveler," said Lady Mabel; "and so will find nothing to please you, while I enjoy all around me, and see nothing to find fault with, except the abominable custom of the women riding astride on their *burras*, which I am glad to see is not universal."

"Nay, my lady, the country pleases me well enough. The pasturage is poor and parched, yet the oxen are fine in spite of their monstrous horns; and I see corn land that might yield good oats or barley in Scotland. The land is well enough; it is the people I find fault with."

"Moodie's verdict on Portugal," said L'Isle, "can be summed up in four little words: '*Bona terra, mala gens.*'"

"What pleasure," continued Moodie, not heeding the interruption, "can a Christian man find in traveling in a land where the people grovel in ignorance and a besotted superstition, which manifests that God has given them over to a reprobate heart. I cannot speak their language; I can only look on their wanderings in the dark, and think of the wrath to come."

"And so here is a missionary lost!" Mrs. Shortridge exclaimed.

"But, according to Moodie's favorite dogma," said L'Isle, "were he gifted with the purest and most eloquent Portuguese, or had he the gift of St. Francis Xavier, who, when thrown among any strange people, was soon found exhorting them in their own tongue, he could be to this people only a prophet of evil. You say that they are given over to a state of reprobation. Do you, like a great English philosopher, believe in election and reprobation by nature?"

"Not exactly; nor do I know any thing of your English philosopher; but since I have been among these people, I have seen much to lead my thoughts that way. And we have example for it. Had not God his chosen people of old? And the seven nations of Canaan, were they not swept off as utterly reprobate from the face of the earth?"

"And now," suggested L'Isle, wishing to know the old man's views, "election is for the Scotch nation, and reprobation for the Portuguese?"

"I do not say that all Scotchmen, even in the Kirk, are of the elect."

"No," interposed Lady Mabel. "You misconstrue Moodie. He holds a particular election within the Kirk, and a national reprobation outside of it."

"I am afraid, my lady, it is not given to you to understand that high doctrine. It is ordered that the blessing, and the comprehension of it, go hand in hand."

"I must despair then, for I certainly do not comprehend it. In truth, the tenor of your discourse calls up in my mind the involuntary doubt, did this people first desert God, or God them? But I trample it down as a snare laid by the evil one."

"We are in a land where the evil one bears full sway," said Moodie.

"Yet you have voluntarily put yourself in purgatory by coming to travel in it," said Lady Mabel. "But you have your consolation, and may give thankful utterance to the words of our Scotch poet:

'I bless and praise thy matchless might,
Whan thousands thou hast left in night,
That I am here afore thy sight,
For gifts an' grace,
A burning and a shining light,
To a' this place.'"

"I do not know that psalmist, if in truth he be a maker of spiritual songs," said Moodie, with a doubtful air.

"He did dabble a little in psalmody," said Lady Mabel; "but I doubt whether his attempts would satisfy you. How like you this sample:

'Orthodox, orthodox, who believe in John Knox,
Let me sound an alarm to your conscience;
There's a heretic blast has been blown in the Wast,
That what is not sense must be nonsense.

> Calvin's sons, Calvin's sons, load your spiritual guns,
> Ammunition you never can need;
> Your hearts are the stuff, will be powder enough,
> And your skulls are store-houses o' lead.' "

" 'Tis that profane, lewd fellow, Burns," exclaimed Moodie, angrily. " He did worse than hide his ten talents in a napkin. I wonder, my lady, you defile your mouth with his scurrilous words."

" I have done with him," said Lady Mabel, laughing. " He was a profane, lewd fellow, far better at pointing out other men's errors than amending his own."

Moodie now fell back among the servants; and L'Isle remarked, " your old squire, Lady Mabel, holds an austere belief. I never met a man so confident of his own salvation and of the damnation of others."

" He reminds me," Mrs. Shortridge said, " of a dissenting neighbor of ours, when we lived in London, who was always saying, ' I am called, but my wife is not,' much to the poor woman's disquiet in this world, if not to the hazard of her happiness in the next."

" The old man puzzles me sadly at times," said Lady Mabel; " and he has at hand many a text to sustain his dogmas."

" It is a pity said L'Isle, " that he will not bear in mind those that bid us ' Judge not that ye be not judged;' ' Let him that thinketh he standeth, take heed lest he fall; ' Unto whomsoever much is given, of him shall much be required;' and many others of the same tenor."

"Pray go on," said Lady Mabel, "and provide me with a refutation of Moodie's theology of destiny: not that I hope to silence him, for controversy is to him the breath of life."

Now L'Isle had acquired many things laboriously, but he had gotten his training in divinity somewhat incidentally, and hesitated, as well he might, to undertake the task imposed. But spurred on by the deference she showed to his opinions, he eagerly sought to satisfy, yet not mislead her. "Moodie is the type of a class," he said, "who are the most wilful men in the world, yet are even inculcating that man has no will of his own, but is the play thing of fate. Fatalism, indeed, is no modern invention, being as old as humanity itself, perhaps, older. We find it as strongly inculcated by the Greek tragic poet, as by the modern Calvinist. But the peculiar colors in which we see it dressed, are derived from the revolt of men's minds against the Romish doctrine as to good works. Among these, penance, fasting, alms, pilgrimages, bounty to the church and its servants, come first. This leads to the keeping of a debt and credit account with heaven; and to the saints is attributed the power of buying up a stock of works of supererogation, by which they acquire a mediatory power in themselves. Human reason has been likened to a drunken clown, who if you help him up on one side of his horse, falls over on the other. To deter men from the presumptuous sin of attributing merit to their actions, the reformers, and also individuals and even orders in the church, have labored to prove that man acts only in obedience to preordained decree, and can of himself do nothing good; yet their logic charges him freely with the *guilt* of sinning by necessity. I cannot for the life of me distinguish between fatalism and predestination. Either binds us with the same chain of necessity, in thought, word and deed, from the cradle to the grave. To escape this charge, fanaticism can only add a few links to the chain of necessitating cause, and tell you it is necessity no longer. Now, our most perfect conception of sin is found in a will which sets itself in opposition to God's will. This is the characteristic of the father of evil and his fallen hosts. Our highest idea of virtue is found in the creature's conforming his will to that of his Maker; this is the trait of the angels who were steadfast in their faith. How can you here couple fatality and will? If ours be a state of probation, it is only by a certain freedom of action, an originating power of causation in ourselves, that we can conceive of our being put to proof. Possibly, in fallen man, that freedom is limited to the power of rejecting or yielding to the influences of grace. Yet within that narrow range it may be still a perfect freedom. God said, 'let us make man in our image and after our likeness,' and this likeness between the 'cause of causes' and his creature, may well consist in man's being endowed with a spark from the Creator's nature, gifted with an originating will, and made a source of causes in himself. To say that this may not be, were to limit the power of God."

"Most assuredly," said Lady Mabel, who was on this point easily convinced. "I shall now be ready armed for Moodie, when next he broaches his dogma of predestination. But will he listen, much less understand?"

"If his dogma be a truth," continued L'Isle, encouraged by her approbation, "to know it, or any other revealed truth, can avail us nothing; for our knowledge, itself a predestined fact, cannot influence our preordained condition here or hereafter. On the other hand, if the doctrine be misunderstood or false, it is most dangerous; there being but a short step between believing it and applying it, presumptuously, in our own favor, and adversely to our neighbor. We are ever more successful in deceiving ourselves than others; and to indulge in the belief that we are the chosen of God, may be only less dangerous than a conviction of our utter reprobation."

"For my part," said Lady Mabel, "I can appeal yet more confidently to my feelings than my reason, for a refutation of the doctrine Moodie has so often urged upon me. I feel within me a capacity to be as wicked as I please, if fear and reverence did not withhold me."

"And I, as your duenna," said Mrs. Shortridge, "prohibit any such frank admission of propensity to evil in a young lady under my charge."

"Why, will you not let me make a Christian confession of the sinfulness of my nature? It were indeed heresy to claim an equal capacity for good. There I acknowledge the need of aid from above."

"And that aid is not compulsion," said L'Isle, "as every page of Scripture testifies. There is something strangely illogical in the reasoning of those who, starting from the point, that what has been decreed by God is as good as done, and the future as fixed as the past, thence exhort us to plead, because the decree has gone forth; to run in the race, because the victor has been chosen, and the prize adjudged; to strive, because the battle has been fought; and to repent and be saved, because our final destiny was decided before time was. Surely, if this life have any bearing on another, we are running a race, the issue of which is undecided until death; and ours is a real struggle, not merely the acting out of a foregone conclusion, not the dramatic representation of a past event. What would you think of a modern Greek praying zealously that Mohamed II. should not *have taken* Constantinople? Or of a Roman of to-day besieging heaven with prayers that Rome should not *have been* taken by the Goths, or sacked by the army of the Constable Bourbon? Yet what is commonly called Calvinist is nothing less than this; praying against past events, or the decrees of fate. Is the papist so absurd in offering his masses for the dead?"

The ladies were still complimenting L'Isle on his refutation of Moodie's tenets, so obnoxious to their own convictions, when they met a peasant trudging along, *cujado* in hand, with the small end of which he occasionally enlivened the motions of an ass toiling under a heavy sack of grain. The muleteer stopped him to enquire where they might find water for their animals in this thirsty land. The peasant pointed back to a thicket near the road, and said: "I would have watered my own beast there, but for the company I would have fallen among." He then went on his way, and they rode to the spot pointed out, where among the oleander and buckthorn bushes they found a puddle rather than a spring, so well had it been lately stirred up. A gang of eight or nine vagrants, who had been munching their crusts and *sardinhas* in the shade, now sprung up, and placing themselves between the travelers and the water, vociferously demanded alms. To rid themselves of this motley troop, L'Isle and Mrs. Shortridge threw each of them a small coin. They were not so easily satisfied, but thrusting themselves among the horses, continued to rival each other in whining petitions and adjurations of their favorite saints. Lady Mabel, who had emptied her purse of small coin the evening before, now entreated Moodie to let this second opportunity of alms-giving, so manifestly sent for his benefit, soften his stony heart. But he shook his head grimly, saying: "If they are strong enough to travel, they are strong enough to work; and work they shall, or starve, before they touch a penny of mine!"

L'Isle's short tempered groom, availing himself of

the impatience of a thirsty horse, now turned his about, at once spurring and reining him in, which made him lash out his heels at the intruders near him. The other steeds seemed to catch this infectious restiveness, and the beggars were driven to a safer distance. Their horses now could drink in peace of the water stirred up and muddied by their mendicant friends, whom they presently left behind them, without further heeding their continued and vociferous appeals. One stout ragged fellow put himself in their way, and displayed to their eyes a flaming picture, painted on a board, depicting the torments of the souls in purgatory. But the travelers were in a hurry, and unmoved at the sight, left the souls in unmitigated tortures there.

"What we have just seen," said L'Isle to the ladies, "may convince you that beggars are a formidable class in this country. They ramble about, and infest every place, not entreating charity, but demanding it. They often assemble at night in hordes, at the best country house they can find, and taking up their abode in one of the out-buildings, call for whatever they want, like travelers at an inn; and here they claim the right of tarrying three days, if they like it. When a gang of these sturdy fellows meets a traveler on the highway, he must offer them money; and it sometimes happens that the amount of the offering is not left to his own discretion. St. Anthony assails him on one side, St. Francis on the other. Having satisfied their clamor in behalf of these favorite saints, he is next attacked for the honor of the Virgin; and thus they rob him, for the love of God."

"I wonder," Mrs. Shortridge said, "the nation tolerates such a nuisance."

"There are laws for its abatement," answered L'Isle. "John III. and Sebastian both warred against the beggars. A law of the sixteenth century ordains that the lame should learn the trade of a tailor or shoemaker, the maimed serve for subsistence any who will employ them, and the blind, for food and raiment, give themselves to the labors of the forge, by blowing the bellows. But we see how the law is enforced. These men behind us are neither lame, halt, nor blind, but truly represent the sturdy vagrants with whom Queen Bess's statute dealt so roughly. With what result? It is but the ancestor of a long line of laws which load our statute-books, and have built up our poor-law system, merely substituting for one evil another which burdens the country like an incubus, and, vulture-like, is eating out its entrails."

"We have no such national institution for the breeding of beggars in Scotland," said Moodie, from behind.

"Is it because Scotland is too poor to maintain paupers?" inquired Mrs. Shortridge.

"It is because it is not natural for a Scotchman to be a beggar," replied Moodie, with patriotic pride.

"We cannot carry the system much further in England," said L'Isle; "the resources of the country, and the sturdy character of the people, are breaking down under it."

"Could our British population be brought down to as low a condition as these people?" Lady Mabel asked.

"Assuredly not," said Mrs. Shortridge.

"Have you ever been in Ireland?" asked L'Isle.

No, neither of the ladies had been there.

"Or in an English poor-house?"

That, too, was *terra incognita*, especially to Lady Mabel.

"Either of them might assist you in finding an answer to a very difficult question. Still, like Moodie, I have great faith in race, and in the fitness of climates to races. There is something enervating to a northern race in these subtropical climates. While the powers of enjoyment remain unimpaired, or are even stimulated, the energy of action is rapidly sapped. We know that the Gothic conquerors of this peninsula lost, in a few generations, their energy and enterprise. A war of seven centuries revived and sustained that of their descendants; but, after that stimulant was withdrawn, on the expulsion of the Moors, they gradually sunk to what we see them now. Some persons attribute the character and condition of these peninsular nations to the vices of government, others to the corruption of the church. I doubt the question's admitting of so simple a solution as either, or both of these. We may be putting effect for cause, and cause for effect. An inferior people may deteriorate government, and corrupt the church. The disciples of the apostles received Christianity in its purity. Whence originated the rapid degeneracy of the early Church? We see some portions of the human race betraying stronger downward tendencies than others. But the 'why' is too complex a question to admit of a simple solution. The Portuguese of this province especially are an inferior people. They are probably a degenerate people; and one cause of that degeneracy may be an intermixture of dissimilar races."

"It is evident," said Lady Mabel, "that the work Pelayo began was never finished by his successors; that in reconquering the country the Christians did not make thorough work in expelling the Moors."

"I know not how thoroughly they may have driven out the Moors," said Mrs. Shortridge, "but they certainly have not kept out the black-a-moors. The negroes now form no small part of the population of Lisbon."

"And the worst part," said L'Isle; "as will always happen when an inferior race is brought in contact and competition with one superior to it. A great part of the robbers, and other criminals there, are negroes. These are comparatively new-comers; but among the old population around us, though we meet with many specimens of men of pure and better breed, still, the great number of turned-up noses and projecting lips we see, gives us an idea of an intermixture with negroes. This mixture and deterioration of the people will control the condition of the country far more than revolutions in church and state. The presence of but one race in a country renders possible a real freedom, embracing the whole population, and it becomes more attainable if this people be a race of high caste; but an inferior people mingled with them, will be politically and socially subjected to them. This is the history of races all over the world."

They had now ridden many miles on the road to Murao, whither L'Isle would gladly have led the ladies, were it only for the pleasure of taking them across the Guadiana, so renowned in song; but he feared to prolong the fatigues of the journey beyond the next day, and bade the muleteer find the shortest way back to Elvas. On this their guide soon turned into a by-way, and they gradually left the cultivated country behind them. The heat of the day made them wish for shelter long before it could be found in so bare and desolate a region. At length they were cheered by the sight of a few pines of stunted growth, and seating themselves in the shade, prepared to dine, while the servants went in search of water, which proved scarce drinkable when brought. The sweet-smelling thyme, which abounded in this spot, now bruised under the horses' hoofs, gave a refreshing fragrance to the air, and they rested the longer, as Mrs. Shortridge seemed worn out with the heat. Lady Mabel seized the occasion to add some new plants to her *hortus siccus*, which, now swollen to a portentous bulk, occupied the highest place in the load of one of the mules. As she wandered from one cluster of plants to another, her voice rose into a tuneful strain.

L'Isle followed her with eye and ear, as imprisoned Palamon did Emilie, while

> "She gathered flowers, partly white and red,
> To make a subtle garland for her head,
> And as an angel, heaven-like she sang."

But she presently returned to her seat, and to her favorite diversion of exciting Moodie's controversial spirit, by asking him if there was not something exceedingly impressive in the external religion of the people they were among?

The term she used was enough to rouse him; but, checking himself, he sneeringly said, "I think these mummeries are well contrived for their purpose, to amuse a childish people, and keep them in a state of childhood."

"And why should they not be amused?" said Lady Mabel, "since you will view it in that light? The church, their nursing-mother, takes charge of them, body and soul, and strives to make religion part and parcel of the occupations of every hour of every day life. By spectacles, processions, pictures, music, by the lonely way-side cross, by the crucifix hidden in the bosom, by the neighboring convent bell, chiming the hour of prayer, the Romanist is reminded forty times a day that he does not live for this life alone. Does he seek amusement from books? she takes out of his hands the lewd tale or lying romance, and puts into it the more wonderful legend of a saint or a martyr. Does any son of the church neglect the practice of charity? she sends him an humble penniless friar to remind him of that duty. Does he strive to forget his sins? she startles his slumbering conscience by duly summoning him to the confessional. The youths and maidens, taking an evening walk, led by early habit, stroll toward some neighboring chapel, and suspend their thoughtless mirth, while they bend the knee to offer up a prayer, and make the sign of the cross, in emblem of their faith in Him who died upon it.'

Moodie shook his head. "You have well named its external religion. It is a whited sepulchre, full within of dead men's bones. The Kirk swept out all that rubbish long ago, and the less it is like Rome the nearer the pure faith."

"They would be odd Christians," said L'Isle, "who held nothing in common with Rome. I doubt, too, whether it be possible to preserve the substance with an utter disregard to form. When inspiration ceased, it was time to frame liturgies and creeds. But there is one material point in which the Kirk of Scotland and the Church of Rome still strongly resemble each other."

Moodie pricked up his ears at this astounding assertion, and scornfully asked: "What point is that, sir?"

"Their vicarious public worship," answered L'Isle. "They both pray by proxy. The Papists employ a priest to pray for them in a dead language which they do not understand, and the Presbyterians a minister to offer up petitions unknown to his people until after they are uttered, who stand listening, or seeming to listen, to this vicarious prayer, which may be, and often is, unfitted to the wants of their hearts, and the convictions of their consciences."

"And to escape these dangers, more possible than likely, you flee to those dead formularies you call your liturgy," retorted Moodie.

"To the formalist and the negligent," L'Isle replied, "the liturgy is but a form; but to the earnest churchman it is a thing of life. Using it, the Christian congregation, priest and layman, pastor and flock, join in an united confession of their sins, in the profession of their common faith, in prayer for mercies needed, in thanksgiving for blessings bestowed. God's praise is sung, his pardon to repentant sinners authoritatively pronounced, the sacraments ordained by Christ are reverently administered, and the whole body of revealed truth and sacred history sytematically recited to the people in the course of each year—a most profitable teaching to the young and ignorant, who cannot search the Scriptures for themselves. This is a true Christian public worship, complete in itself. Nor do we neglect preaching as a means of instruction and exhortation, without holding it to be an always essential accompaniment, much less, as you do, the right arm in the public worship of God."

"And to this form of words, made by man," objected Moodie, "you attribute a divine character, little, if at all, below that which belongs to the word of God."

"So far as it consists of the language of Scripture, rightly applied, it is divine," said L'Isle. "But it is an error to say that our liturgy, or any other worthy to be named, was made by a man, or the men of any one age. It has a more catholic origin than that. The spiritual experience of devout men of many centuries of Christianity, realizing the needs of sinful humanity in its intercourse with its Maker and Redeemer, and the comforting Spirit, have helped to build it up, and thus adapted it, in its parts of general application, to the spiritual wants, at all times, of every child of Adam."

"You speak up finely for your formal service, sir," said Moodie; "and I may not be scholar enough to answer you. But every spiritual minded man knows that it only fetters the spirit in prayer."

"Yet we might infer," said L'Isle, "from a passage in the Revelations of St. John, that a liturgy is used by the four and twenty elders who stand before the throne."

"You and Moodie do not seem to get any nearer to each other," said Mrs. Shortridge, "in your rambles through the mazes of controversy."

"We only need here a well-trained son of Rome," answered L'Isle, "to make confusion worse confounded. Luckily, Moodie and I can fight out our duel in quiet, without having a dexterous adversary come in as thirdsman, and kill us both."

The muleteer, who had shown signs of impatience unusual with him, now pointed to the sun; in a few minutes they were again on the road, which was but a bridle-path, and the country promised less and less as they rode on. Their guide looked around doubtingly, and at length turned aside to a half ruinous cottage, the only habitation they had seen for miles, where he closely questioned an old woman whom he found there as to the way before them. Little satisfied with her directions, he presently stopped an idiotic looking fellow, with a huge head, whom they met driving some milch goats toward the hovel, and questioned him. The goatherd stood staring at the party with open mouth, and gave little heed to him. But, at length, being pressed for an answer, he gave one in a harsh voice with great volubility, and much action, as if drawing in the air a map of the whole country around. The muleteer seemed satisfied, and they again moved on over a waste of low, rolling hills, without a tree upon them. Unlike the heaths of the north of Europe, it was covered with a false show of fertility, displaying a variety of plants; among them several species of heath, one six feet high, and entirely covered with large red flowers, another, smaller indeed, but with flowers of a yet more lively red. Here, too, were the yellow-flowered *cisti*, and many other plants with blossoms of many hues, perfuming the air while they delighted the eye. But the stunted juniper bushes, and the myrtles, not luxuriant and beautiful, like those growing on the banks of the rivulets, but dwarfish to the humble size of weeds, told of a land of starvation under this wilderness of sweets.

Lady Mabel, much as she loved flowers, was sated here, and owned that no profusion of them could make a landscape. "There is a dreary monotony in a scene like this, that words cannot express. The sky of brass over our heads, and this treeless, lifeless sea of sandy hillocks around us, excite a feeling of desolation and solitude, which forces me to look round on our party to convince myself that I am not alone in the world."

The muleteer, who was some way ahead, now stopped short. Riding up, they saw that the path here divided into two, and heard him heaping curses on the huge head of the simpleton, who had forgotten to tell him which to follow. But, on L'Isle's asking what they should do now, he dismounted, and stepped up to consult his wisest mule, which he did by slipping the bridle from his head. At once, sure instinct came to faltering reason's aid; the beast turned complacently into the right hand path, and moving briskly on, jingled his bells more cheerily than before, as if he already saw the open stable door, and snuffed his evening meal. Their path bending westward, they now saw clouds mustering on the heights before them, and one of April's sudden showers drawing near.

Within less then a mile, they came upon a hedge of American aloes, which, with their close array of massive leaves, each ending in a sharp point, protected an orchard. Following its course a few rods, they came to a rude gateway, which admitted them into a small cattle-yard, and a low, unpretending farm-house stood before them.

CHAPTER XII.

First, for thy bees a quiet station find,
And lodge them under covert from the wind;
For winds, when homeward they return, will drive
The loaded carriers from their evening hive;
Far from the cows' and goats' insulting crew,
That trample down the flowers and brush the dew,
The painted lizard and the bird of prey,
Foes to the frugal kind, be far away—
The titmouse and the pecker's hungry brood,
And Procne with her bosom stained with blood:
These rob the trading citizens, and bear
The trembling captives through the liquid air,
And for their callow young a cruel feast prepare.
* * * * * * * * *
Wild thyme and savory set around their cell,
Sweet to the taste and fragrant to the smell:
Set rows of rosemary with flowering stem,
And let the purple violet drink the stream.

DRYDEN'S *Virgil.*

THE building before them had low, thick walls, of undressed stones, and a heavy roof over it covered with tiles. The door was shut, and the travelers could see nothing of the household; but the sharp, angry challenge of the canine sentinels within, who did not pause to listen for an answer, proved that the place was not without a garrison. Some premonitory drops began to fall from the cloud, which now overhung them. Tired of waiting, L'Isle was about to complete the investment by sending the muleteer round to the other side of the house, when he perceived two young round faces peeping out at a square hole in the wall that served for a window; a man's voice was heard quieting the dogs, and a pair of sharp eyes were detected peering over the door, made too short for the doorway, perhaps for that purpose. The governor was evidently reconnoitering carefully the party outside. The result seemed, at length, to prove satisfactory, the presence of the ladies probably removing any fears of violence.

The door was thrown open, and one, who seemed to be the master of the house, stepped out with an air of frank hospitality to receive their request for shelter. Begging them to alight, he called out for "Manoel! Manoel!" who soon showed himself in the shape of a young clown, crawling out from behind a heap of straw in a neighboring shed, and who was ordered to assist in unloading the mules and taking care of the horses.

Tired and thirsty, and glad to find shelter, the ladies entered the house, where they were met by two young women, unmistakably the daughters of the host. Their sparkling eyes and coal-black hair, their round faces and regular features, were like his; and they were only less swarthy, from being less exposed to the sun. Their dress was in fashion, but commonly worn by the peasant women—the jacket and petticoat—but smarter, and of more costly stuffs than usual. Their feet, too, were bare, but small and well-formed, betraying little indurating familiarity with the rough paths around them.

Had they preserved their pedigree, this family would have found many an ancestor among the Lusitanian Moors, and afforded the most striking among the many proofs the travelers had met with, that many a Mohammedan, when the crescent waned before the cross, had preferred his country to his faith. The girls were for a while abashed at the presence of the strangers; but, with a hospitality spurred on by curiosity, soon recovered themselves, and encumbered the ladies with their attentions. Strangers they seldom saw, and these outlandish ladies were as strange to them as if they had dropped from the moon. Under pretence of assisting the travelers to rid themselves of their outer garment of dust, they examined the texture and fashion of their dresses, veils and gloves, spread out Lady Mabel's shawl to admire the pattern, and asked more questions than she could answer or understand. They were closely inspecting the rings on her fingers, and wondering at the whiteness of her hand, when their father coming in, rebuked their obtrusiveness. He made them gather up the pile of flax, with the spindles and distaffs now lying idle on the floor, and invited the ladies to take possession of the cushions, which, after a Moorish custom still lingering here, the girls had used as seats.

L'Isle coming in and finding father and daughters bestirring themselves to make their guests comfortable, suggested that their most urgent want was water.

One of the girls at once brought a cup, and one from among several jars, and, while the ladies were drinking, L'Isle called their attention to the peculiarities of the vessel, of so porous a nature, that the water, always oozing through it, kept the outside wet, the constant evaporation of a part cooling what remained within. He pointed out, too, the peculiar fashion of the jar—its beautiful and classic mould indicating that, amidst the corruption of taste and the loss of arts, in pottery at least, the antique type of form had been faithfully handed down from the time of the Roman. But the ladies were too busy with the water to bestow much thought on the jar, and L'Isle's lesson in *vertu* was pretty much lost on them.

The house consisted of several small rooms, besides the larger apartment, in which, after a while, the whole party was collected, including the servants and muleteer. The girls called in an old woman to assist them in their household duties, and she employed herself at the smoky fire-place in cooking some sausages, which, by the perfume they soon diffused through the room, proved that in stuffing them the genus *allium* had not been forgotten. To give a classic flavor to the fumes, L'Isle found himself quoting the lines:

> "*Thestylis et rapido fessis messoribus aestu*
> *Allia serpyllumque herbas contundit olentes.*"

But, if this sweetened the smell to him, it was lost on the ladies, and Thestylis was still to them a smoky old woman, frying, marvelously, ill-odored sausages. Their host disappeared for a few minutes, and then returned, no longer in dishabille, but in full dress, as if going to the next town on some high festival. This was evidently in honor of his guests. It was growing dark, and he now lit a lantern hanging against the wall. Within the lantern, and behind the lamp, a little image of some saint was seen shedding his benignant influence over the household. The hastily prepared meal was now ready. This was no time or place for nice distinctions of rank, and, urged by their host, the whole party sat down together. Besides the overpowering sausages, preserved fruits, honey, and black and white bread covered the table, with a pile of oranges just gathered from the boughs. These last vanished rapidly before the thirsty travelers. Their host seemed to think his more substantial fare neglected, and L'Isle took care to attribute it to their having dined too lately and heartily, to have yet recovered their appetites.

Lady Mabel, seeing Moodie at the end of the table, with his back to the dim light, eating almost in the dark, urged him to change his seat, and take one opposite to and close under the lamp. Moodie looked askance at the saint, who was bestowing a benediction on those before him, and grumbled out, "Better to eat in the dark, than by the light of Satan's lantern."

"You are over scrupulous," said Mrs. Shortridge: "if these illuminated saints be one of Satan's devices, I think it meritorious to turn them to a useful purpose, as was successfully done by a friend of mine residing in Lisbon. Finding the lamp he had put before his door repeatedly broken—for the Lisbon rabble love darkness better than light—he bought a little image of St. Antony, and put it up behind it, and the saint's presence seemed to paralyze the arms of the evil doers."

"There is an inward and an outward light," said Moodie, sententiously: "your friend, wanting that inward light, chose, for a little personal convenience, to countenance a shining idolatry." Their host, gathering from their looks and gestures that they wanted more light, now brought in another lamp, which the ladies soon used to light them to the chamber allotted to them. The girls went with them; and Lady Mabel, finding them loiter there, full of curiosity, and examining every article of dress and baggage with prying eyes, deliberately unpacked every thing she had with her, and induced Mrs. Shortridge, sleepy as she was, to do so too; then, giving them to understand that there was nothing more to be seen, politely turned them out of the room, that she might make more profitable use of the remaining hours of the night. A chamber and bed were found for L'Isle, but Moodie and the servants had no better accommodations than mats spread on the floor of the larger room. They had no sooner lain down than the rats overhead commenced their gambols, racing each other over the reeds which laid on the joists, formed the only ceiling to the room. Their gymnastic sports brought down showers of dust and soot on the would-be sleepers below, who were already beset by certain rejoicing tribes, which seized the occasion to hold their carnival.

The whole household were afoot early next morning and, while waiting for breakfast, Lady Mabel took the opportunity to survey the premises. Cleanliness is not essential to Portuguese comfort; but, within the house, there was not the squalor and poverty which here usually characterises the peasant's home. Without, a small orchard, and one narrow field, a few goats, and two or three stout asses, seemed to comprise the farmer's possessions.

On sitting down to an abundant breakfast, she expressed to L'Isle her wonder, how these people lived in such plenty, without flocks, or herds, or fields.

"You are mistaken," said L'Isle. "Our host has flocks so numerous, that it would startle you to hear their numbers told. The whole country for miles around is pastured by them. He is a farmer, or rather grazier, on a grand scale. Not to puzzle you longer, he is a bee-farmer, having many hundred hives. This land of flowers yields him two harvests a year. His income is derived from wax and honey, and his rustic talk is not of bullocks, but of bees. After breakfast, we will get him to show us something of the economic arrangements of his farm."

During this meal, the two girls seemed anxious to make the most of their guests, who were so soon to leave them. They had this morning put on their best clothes, and all their trinkets. Their animated and inquisitive conversation, addressed chiefly to L'Isle, as spokesman and interpreter, scarcely allowed him time to eat. Their restless, sparkling black eyes, excited the admiration of the ladies. "Do you think black eyes the most expressive?" said Lady Mabel to L'Isle; and, with a natural coquetry, she turned her own blue orbs full upon him. How else could he judge, but by a comparison?

"There is a liquid lustre in the full black eye," L'Isle answered, looking into those of the girl who was sitting, very sociably, close beside him, "which powerfully expresses languishing tenderness. It is capable, too, of an angry and fierce expression. But from its dark hues you cannot distinguish the pupil from the surrounding part, and lose all the varying beauty of its dilation and contraction. There are eyes of lighter and more heavenly hues," here he looked full in Lady Mabel's, while describing them, "which have an unlimited range of expression, embracing every shade of feeling, every variety of sentiment. They are tell-tale eyes, that would betray the owner in any attempt to play the hypocrite."

Lady Mabel, laughing and blushing, expressed great doubts whether any eyes exercised that controlling guardianship over the integrity of their owner.

As soon as the meal was over, the farmer, at their request, gladly undertook to show them some thing of his peculiar husbandry. A hive or two may be found any where—but a thousand hives! This was a great proprietor. Going out of the enclosure, he led them to a neighboring hill, on the south-eastern side of which, well sheltered from the northern blasts, many lanes, five or six feet wide, had been cut through the thickets, all leading to a central point, where, well sheltered by the natural hedge, he had formed one of his numerous colonies. Last night's shower had refreshed the thirsty vegetation, washing the dust from the leaves and deepening their green; some diamond drops still hung sparkling on the foliage; and numberless blossoms were opening to the early beams of the sun. The citizens of this thriving commonwealth were literally as busy as bees, and the region was vocal with their buzz. The ladies shrunk from the well armed but laborious crowd which surrounded them, going forth light or returning laden to their homes; but the farmer assured them that the busy multitude were perfectly tame, and as harmless as sheep, unless maliciously disturbed.

Though this was but one of several colonies, the hives were too numerous to be easily counted. They were all cylindrical in shape, being made of the bark of the cork-tree, which is an excellent non-conductor of heat, and were each covered with an inverted pan of earthenware, the edge of which overhung the hive like a cornice. Each hive was fastened together with pegs of hard wood, so that it could be easily taken to pieces, and the joints were stopped with peat.

Full of the economy of the industrious tribes, whose habits he had studied so profitably, the farmer talked long and well on the subject. From him they learned that the bees would range a league and more from the hive, if they could not gather honey nearer home.

That he gathered two harvests a year, spring and autumn each yielding one, while the cold winter and the parched and blossomless summer equally suspended the profitable labor of his winged workmen. He pointed out the plants whose blossoms were preferred by the bees, and professed to be able to distinguish the honey gathered in each month, varying as it did in qualities according to the succession of flowers which bloomed through the seasons, and he gave a preference to the product of the rosemary over all other plants.

Lady Mabel was delighted with the method and the scale of this branch of rural industry. "We have Moors enough in Scotland. Indeed, I wish so much of them had not fallen to papa's lot. But when I go home, I will endeavor to turn these wastes to better account, and rival our friend here, by establishing a bee farm on a grand scale."

"You must not forget to carry the rosemary and other choice plants with you," said Mrs. Shortridge, "and some beams of the Portuguese sun, to secure two seasons of flowers in the year."

While she was yet speaking, a snake glided slowly across her path. Starting back in terror, she uttered a little scream, and begged L'Isle to kill it without delay.

"How shall I kill it," he said, laughing at her alarm. "Shall I bruise the serpent's head with my heel, or shall I draw my sword on a reptile?"

"In any way you please, so you do kill it," she

exclaimed, seeing the snake stop and raise its head to look at them.

But the farmer now interfered: "Spare his life, this is one of my best friends. You see that he shows not the least fear. While providing for himself, he works too for me, destroying the frogs and lizards that make sad havoc among my bees."

Returning to the house, they found in front of it the mules laden and the horses saddled for the journey. Observing that Moodie looked particularly rueful this morning, Lady Mabel asked him what was the matter, and he admitted that he was very unwell. "But with bad food and worse water, loss of sleep and worry of mind, a man soon gets worn out in this unhappy country. You, my lady, look jaded enough, too."

"Oh, never mind my looks," she answered. "I feel perfectly well, and can travel on until I get tanned as brown as these Moorish girls. But I am afraid Moodie, you are paying the penalty for last night's insult to the patron saint of the house. Some saints are at times a little revengeful, and your troubled mind and aching body you may owe to him. Pray take the earliest opportunity to make amends."

"Who is the offended saint?" asked Mrs. Shortridge.

"I suppose," said Lady Mabel, "it is St. Meliboeus, the patron saint of bees and honey."

"Take care," said L'Isle, laughing. "You are usurping the Pope's function, and adding a new name to the calender."

"But what shall we do for Moodie?" she asked. "Whether stricken by the saint or not, something must be done to relieve him."

"Your saint had nothing to do with my sickness," said Moodie, angrily. "I was unwell yesterday, though I did not complain. I am sure I was poisoned by that rascally innkeeper at Evora, with some trash he called wine, which was nothing but drugged vinegar."

"If bad wine has poisoned you, good wine is the only antidote," said L'Isle, and bidding his servant bring a cup and bottle from the hamper, he persuaded Moodie to try the remedy.

Moodie tasted it with some hesitation, but the wine was excellent, and in truth, just what he stood in need of. On being urged, he took a good draught, and at L'Isle's suggestion, stowed away the bottle in his valise for future reference.

Their host would receive but a small remuneration for the well timed hospitality he had afforded the travelers. But the ladies had selected sundry spare articles from their wardrobe, and delighted his daughters with the gift of finery, such as they had never possessed before. As L'Isle was turning to ride off, the farmer said, with a courteous air: "When you or any friend of yours come this way, pray remember, sir, you have a poor house here, always at your command."

CHAPTER XIII.

Crabbed age and youth cannot live together,
Youth is full of pleasure, age is full of care;
Youth like summer morn, age like winter weather;
Youth like summer brave, age like winter bare.
Youth is full of sport, age's breath is short;
Youth is nimble, age is lame;
Youth is hot and bold, age is weak and cold;
Youth is wild, and age is tame.

SHAKSPEARE.

They had ridden but a short way, when Lady Mabel, reining in her horse, placed herself along side of Moodie, to ask how he felt now. She feared lest he might be too unwell to undergo the fatigues of the day. But, thanks to L'Isle's prescription, Moodie was already another man. He sat bolt upright in the saddle, with a martial air, and looked around as if ready for any emergency. She no longer felt any fears for him. His curiosity, too, seemed to be awakened, for he said: "You are a great botanist, my lady, and know every kind of plant. Pray, what were those two tall trees near the farmer's house, with bare trunks and feathery tops?"

"They are date palms," said Lady Mabel. "You see more and more of them the nearer you get to Africa."

"Indeed!" said Moodie, with more astonishment than the information seemed to warrant.

"Yes," she continued; "and they bear a luscious and nourishing fruit, which, in the deserts of Africa, is the chief food of the people. It is to them what oatmeal is to the Scot."

"And how far are we from Africa?" said Moodie, dreading the answer, but striving to put the question in an indifferent tone.

"Why some people say that Africa begins at the Pyrenees, but Colonel L'Isle, who knows the country thoroughly, says that the Sierra de Monchique is the true boundary. The kingdom of Algarve, lying beyond those mountains, is, in climate, soil, and vegetation, truly African; and it is only the strip of salt water that separates it from Morocco, that prevents its forming part of that country."

"I never heard of the kingdom of Algarve before," said Moodie, pondering the information he had received. "How far are we from it?"

"We will not find it a long day's journey to one of the chief towns," said Lady Mabel. "Its name—its name is Mauropolis, the city of the Moors. It lies on the border of Algarve, just like Berwick on the border of Scotland, only Algarve is a beautiful and fertile country, which poor Scotland is only to a Scot."

"It is an ill bird that fouls its own nest," growled Moodie in an undertone. "Have you forgot, my lady, that you are yourself a Scot!"

"A Scot!" said she, deliberately, as if now first considering that point. "My mother was an Englishwoman. So far, I am not a Scot."

"But your father! Your father, my lady!" Moodie angrily exclaimed. "He is a true Scot, and knows the worth of old Scotland well."

"He does," indeed," said she; "and has always thought it an excellent country—to come from; so he marched off at eighteen, and has seldom been back there since."

"So we are on the borders of Africa!" exclaimed Moodie, speaking to himself aloud.

"Why, do you not see Moodie, that the people grow darker, each day, as we travel on?"

"The innkeeper at Evora is dark enough," said he, that truth flashing on him; "but the farmer and his girls are browner still by many a shade."

"You will think them fair," said Lady Mabel, "when you have traveled far enough onward," and, leaving him confused and alarmed, she cantered on to join Mrs. Shortridge.

Now Moodie was a shrewd man, perhaps a little too shrewd, with an eye open to human depravity; he was learned, too, in his way; many a heavy tome of Scotch controversial divinity had been thumbed by him as carefully as his Bible; but he never dwelt on any thing he found there not sustaining his preconceived notions. He involuntarily slighted those parts even of Scripture that he could not wrest to his purpose. Many an historical and traditionary fact, too, floated loosely on his mind; but his geographical education had been sadly neglected. A topographical knowledge of half a dozen shires, a general notion of the shape of old Scotland, and a hazy outline of the sister kingdom, made up all he had attained to. Had you laid before him a chart of the sea coast of Bohemia, first discovered by our great dramatist, it would not have startled him in the least, and he was ready to look for Africa at any point of the compass.

He now saw clearly that this journey was part of a plot. L'Isle had first won the confidence of father and daughter; then availing himself of her love for botany, had habituated her to his presence and protection on short excursions around Elvas; he had used the commissary and his wife to beguile Lady Mabel from her father's protection, under pretence of a short journey to a neighboring town. Having now rid himself of the innocent commissary, he was leading her by devious paths far beyond pursuit. Lady Mabel seemed bewitched, and no longer saw with her own eyes. Was Mrs. Shortridge a simple gull or something worse? "Perhaps," thought Moodie, "Colonel Bradshawe is right;" for an eaves-dropping valet had given his scandal wings.

Moodie was not deeply read in romance; but he remembered the traditionary tale of the young Scotch heiress, who, while a party of her retainers were escorting her to the house of her guardian, was set upon by a neighboring chieftain at the head of his clan. Her followers, concealing the girl under a huge caldron, stood round it for her defence, and when the last man had fallen the victorious suitor carried off the girl, and married her for her lands. This, too, was a plain case of abducting an heiress, not indeed by violence, but with consummate art. Setting aside the rare attractions of the lady, in Moodie's estimation the prize was immense. L'Isle, with all his lofty airs, was but a commoner, with perhaps no fortune but his sword, a mere adventurer, and Lord Strathern's broad acres were an irresistible temptation; though, in truth, this coveted domain counted thousands of acres of sheep-walk to the hundreds of plough land.

Having made this matter clear to his own mind, Moodie cursed in his heart Lord Strathern's fatuity and the facile disposition Lady Mabel had so unexpectedly betrayed. But, though sorely troubled, he was not a man to despair. He resolved to watch L'Isle closely, and to rack his own invention for some way to foil his schemes, while taking care not to betray the least suspicion of them.

Meanwhile, Lady Mabel, as she could not herself visit Algarve, was extracting from L'Isle a full account of that delightful region. And he described well the picturesque and lofty mountains that cut off its narrow strip of maritime territory from the rest of Portugal; its tropical vegetation and its animal life, its perpetual summer, tempered alternately by the ocean and the mountain breeze. When he mentioned any fact which Lady Mabel thought might liken this region to Africa in Moodie's imagination, she would turn and repeat it for his benefit. Thus, the wolves and the wild boars abounding in the mountains, became to him nameless monsters infesting the country; the serpents were magnified in bulk, and the poisonous lizard redoubled its venom. The fevers common there grew more malignant; the plague broke out occasionally, and a few earthquakes were thrown in to enliven the narrative. She garbled it too, sadly, suppressing the fact that Algarve had furnished a large proportion of the adventurers who had discovered and conquered India and Brazil, and its mariners of this day, the best in Portugal, she converted into Barbary corsairs. She said nothing about Algarve having been the first province to rise against the French, or about the half-dozen adventurous seamen who had sailed boldly in a fishing-boat to Brazil, to inform the regent that Portugal still dared to struggle and to hope.

L'Isle overheard and wondered at her perversion of his account of Algarve, without detecting her motive, and Moodie thought her evident desire to visit this region proved her little less than mad, for only her version of select portions of L'Isle's remarks reached his ears.

"It is singular," said L'Isle, "that the Moors should have been more thoroughly driven out of Algarve, the most southern province, than out of others north of it. Its maritime position perhaps made it easy for them to escape to Morocco. But the people are not so dark as in Alemtejo, and many of the women are beautifully fair. In fact, I have seen as lovely faces there as in any country but our own."

Lady Mabel took care not to enlighten Moodie by

repeating to him this observation, and he remained convinced that L'Isle had been describing beforehand to the ladies the country he was leading them to.

The heat, fatigue, and discomfort of the last four days had almost worn out Mrs. Shortridge's strength, and now suggested to Lady Mabel some sage reflections on travel in general, as the result of her experience.

"Traveling is certainly one of the pleasures of life, with this peculiarity, that it affords most pleasure when the journey is over. With all the interest and excitement attending it, there are some drawbacks. We gratify our curiosity at times at no little cost. In the search after strange manners, the traveler may have to adopt them; in inspecting the various conditions under which men can live, we must often subject ourselves to these conditions, and thus acquire practical experience in place of theoretical knowledge. We cannot, like Don Cleofus, command the services of Asmodeus, to enable us to be lookers-on without becoming parties in the scenes we witness. To know how the Arab lives, we must for a time become an Arab; and to pry into the inner mysteries of Hottentot life, you must make yourself a Hottentot."

"And to estimate the prisoner's woes," L'Isle suggested, "you must try the virtues of a dungeon—musty straw, and bread and water."

"That would be buying the knowledge dearly," said she; "but I would like to try how the life of a nun would suit me."

"It would suit you the least of all women," said Mrs. Shortridge. "You might die in the cloister, but could not live there."

"Oh, I am sure I could stand a short novitiate, say three or six months," exclaimed Lady Mabel.

"Your novitiate, soon to end in freedom," said L'Isle, "would not help you to the experience of the true internal life of the nun. It is pleasant to walk, leading your horse by the rein, and at liberty to mount when you like; but the essence of monastic life lies in the conviction that you have turned your back forever on the world without, with all its trials, its hopes and fears, its passions and pursuits, and have given yourself religiously to tread through this life, the narrow path you have chosen, to the next."

"You have convinced me," said Lady Mabel. "In my longing after a varied experience of the conditions of life, I might sacrifice half a year to the trial of one, but I prefer ignorance on this point to the burden of a life-enduring vow."

"If our knowledge were limited by our own experience, we would know little indeed," said L'Isle. "Our capacity to bring home to ourselves other conditions than our own, depends more on the transferring and transforming faculties of the imagination, than on the observing powers of the eye. If, indeed, we had never felt bodily pain, we could not feel for a man on the rack. Had we never known anguish of mind, we might not estimate the mental agonies of others. But we have feelings, for the exercise of which sympathy and imagination can create conditions. We can feel with the captive in the dungeon, without going down there to take a place by his side."

"Still, there is nothing like experience in one's own person," said Mrs. Shortridge. "I can now sympathize fully with the toilworn traveler, across a parched and thirsty desert, under a broiling sun. I own that the pleasures of this journey far exceed its pains, thanks to your care and company; but, as Lady Mabel says, the chief pleasure comes afterward, and this journey will be still more pleasant next week than now."

"In spite of its hardships," said Lady Mabel, "it has been so agreeable to me, that I would have it last a week longer. As an escort, interpreter, and cicerone, Colonel L'Isle has no rival. He has, too, filled the commissary's place so well, that we have suffered nothing from your good man's desertion."

The pleasure Lady Mabel expressed, and her frank admission that she wished the journey longer, delighted L'Isle. He longed to tell her that he was ever at her command as companion, guardian, and guide on any journey, however long. But no—he must not say that. He had no thoughts of matrimony—at least, just now. A remote prospect did indeed float before his eyes, in which he saw himself having outlived this war, and attained the rank of Major-General, returning home to find Lady Mabel still lovely and still free to listen to a lover's suit. This was but a bright vista of the future, hemmed in and overhung by many a dark contingency, a glowing picture in an ebony frame.

The character of the country underwent a change as they rode on. Sloping downward toward the Guadiana, over a succession of hills which concealed the descent, the soil became more fertile, but was scarcely more cultivated than in the region which they had just left behind them. The heaths and broom plants now gave place to a variety of evergreen shrubs. Though the forest trees had vanished centuries ago, the prospect was often shut out by the thickets that overspread the country. An occasional spot of open ground indicated some attempts at cultivation, but they saw few peasants, and but one village seated on a hill, until passing a wretched hamlet, they reach the bank of a brook. The shade of some trees, already in full leaf, in this sheltered spot, tempted them to make here their noonday halt.

Seating herself on the fern and moss at the foot of an old mulberry-tree that overhung the little stream, Lady Mabel pointed out to her companions, that the trees around them were all of the same kind.

"They were doubtless planted here," said L'Isle, "when the silk culture throve in this country, a branch of industry, which, with too many others, has almost died out. Civil disorder and foreign war have been fatal to it. The Spaniards have made Alemtejo their highroad in every invasion of Portugal; and the disasters of late years have completed the ruins of this frontier, so long a debatable land. The country around, is, for the most part, a heath-covered waste, or a wilderness of brushwood; here the silk-worm has perished, the peasant's hand is idle, and the *amoreira* stands with unplucked leaves."

"The better for us," said Mrs. Shortridge; "we need its thickest shade."

A solitary stork, by the rivulet, was engaged in that gentle sport which Isaac Walton assures us, is so favorable to tranquil meditation. Deep in reverie, the philosopher seemed not to heed their presence. For a time, he stood gravely on one leg, then with a few stately strides, drew nearer to them. They were commenting on his sedate air, and disregard for man's presence, when Moodie came and sat down within ear-shot of them. The bird now raised his head and gave them a searching look. Then bending back his long neck, he uttered a dissatisfied chatter with his snapping beak, and taking wing, sought a sequestered part of the stream, remote from the intruders.

"The stork would not thus have shunned natives. He must have found out that we are foreigners and heretics," said Mrs. Shortridge.

"It is this arch-heretic, Moodie, that he shuns," said Lady Mabel. "His presence would drive away a whole congregation of storks, who are almost as good churchmen as the monks themselves."

"Perhaps quite as good," said Moodie. "My arch-heresy consists in protesting now and always against idolatrous Rome. Some here are not quite as good Protestants as I am."

"I never called myself a Protestant," said L'Isle.

"Do you not, sir?" exclaimed Moodie. "Pray what are you then?"

"I never called myself a Protestant in defining my faith."

"And why not, sir," asked Moodie, adding in an under tone. "Now he will show the cloven foot."

"Because mine is a positive creed, not to be expressed by negation. In defining it, I can admit no term not expressing some essential point. I would not mistake the accident for the essence. That God has given his revealed word to man, is an essential point in my belief. That Rome has misconstrued that word, may be true, but comes not within the scope of my creed. I believe that Christ by his Apostles founded a church to ramify through the world, like the fruitful vine running over the wall. Some branches may have rotted off, some may bear degenerate fruit, some in unpruned luxuriance may bring forth nothing but leaves. Be it so. My belief is that the branch I cleave to retains its vital vigor and produces life-sustaining fruit."

"But how does this prevent your protesting against Rome?" objected Moodie.

"It prevents my making that protest any part of the definition of my faith. Names are things, and he who is perpetually dubbing himself a Protestant, ends by making it the first article of his creed, that Rome errs, and his active religion becomes opposition to Rome. Now I find Voltaire quite as good a Protestant as you are.

"I can say nothing to that," answered Moodie, "never having met with that gentleman."

L'Isle smiled for a moment, but went on earnestly to say: "We believe that Christ not only gave us a father, but founded a church, and we will not let go our hold upon it, as some sects and nations have done, out of mere opposition to Rome. Our forefathers by God's providence, set earnestly to work reforming it where corrupted, repairing it when dilapidated, but did not pull it down, in the presumptuous hope of building up another. They purified the temple, but did not destroy it. They removed the idols, but did plough up and sow with salt the consecrated spot, because it had been defiled."

"I see" said Moodie warmly, "that you aim your anathema at the Kirks among other Christian bodies."

"Without anathematizing any one," L'Isle answered, "we take comfort to ourselves, in the conviction that our church is a continuous branch of that which the Apostles founded in Christ, and that it might have been in essentials what it now is, were its history as closely connected with the Greek church, as it is with that of Rome, or had it ever stood unconnected with either of them. Never having been rebuilt from its foundation, it has lost its apostolic character."

"You have given many branches to the vine planted by Christ," observed Moodie. "Perhaps you admit the Church of Rome, to be one that still bears fruit."

"To drop the figure of the vine, I will answer you by saying, that it is possible for a Romanist to be a Christian."

"Are Christianity and idolatry one and the same?" said Moodie, indignantly.

"Do you know how many dogmas the Kirk and Rome hold in common?" answered L'Isle. "If you set down each article of Christian doctrine in the order of its importance and certainty, you may travel the same road with the Romanist a long way; nor is it easy to prove that Rome does not hold to all Christian truths."

Moodie rose from where he sat and stretched forth a protesting hand. But he saw that protest was useless here, so he withdrew to the shade of another tree, and sat down to think what he should do for Lady Mabel's safety. To refresh himself and sharpen his wits, he took more than one draught from the bottle. The wine being old, mild and delicate in flavor, he classed it in the same category with small beer, far underrating its beguiling potency. This *vinho maduro*, the *vino generoso* of the Spaniard, was that which maketh glad the heart of man, being of a choice vintage from a famous vineyard. It was rich, oily and deceiving.

"Had Moodie not been too impatient to stay with us longer," said L'Isle, "he might have heard me admit, that though the Church of Rome has kept the truth, it has not been content with it, but has mingled with it so large a mass of falsehood, that the truth it teaches is no longer pure. It has not thrown away the God-given treasure, but it has piled over it such an ever accumulating heap of rubbish that it is not easily found. It may have guarded the fountain of life-giving waters, but has so hedged it in with a labyrinth of superstitions and ceremonial rites, that it is almost inaccessible to the flock."

"Call Moodie back, and redeem yourself in his opinion," said Mrs. Shortridge. "He is now mourning over your approaching conversion to Rome."

"It is useless," said Lady Mabel. "Moodie sets no value on half-truths."

"Moodie denies there being any Christianity left in Popery," said L'Isle. "I assert that there is many a thorough, though unconscious Papist among Protestants. Popery is not so much an accidental bundle of errors, as a spontaneous and necessary growth from corrupt human nature. Thus many a charity, with us, originates in the hope of atoning for sins; many seek salvation through vicarious but human means; many a sectarian, especially among women is not so much the member of a church, as the follower of an idolized man. There are Protestant popes, whose words are bulls in their little popedoms, and Protestant saints who, unlike those of Rome, are canonized in life by their handful of followers."

"I think I could find a patron saint for Moodie," said Lady Mabel. "At least I do not think he would have been startled as I was, on hearing a minister of the Kirk, after exhausting his powers of eulogy on the great Apostle of the Gentiles, crown his praise by likening the prisoner Paul preaching boldly in bonds before the Roman governor, in whose hand was his life, to John Knox, the mouth-piece of the dominant faction, bullying a lady and his queen, a capture in their hands. This was a strange canonization of John Knox, or a singular degradation of St. Paul. But I see that our dinner waits us; and though this is a charming spot, we must not linger here too long. I am sure," she added, "that the shy and meditative stork, who left us so abruptly, must be a deep theologian, for it was he who suggested this learned discertation on the church."

The travelers dined here under the shade of the trees, and soon after took horse again. Moodie threw himself into the saddle with a spirit and activity which led Lady Mabel to say: "Your good wine, Colonel L'Isle, has done wonders for Moodie. It carries him well through the labors of the day."

"It seems to have cured his ailing body," said L'Isle, "but has not mellowed his temper. He grows more crusty than ever."

"In him," said Lady Mabel, "crustiness is the natural condition, and betokens health."

They had ridden but a little way, when she heard Moodie call to her, and reining in her horse, she let him come up alongside of her. He evidently wished to speak to her in private, for he kept silence until L'Isle and Mrs. Shortridge were out of hearing, and looked cautiously round to see that the servants were not too near.

"My lady," said he, in a solemn manner, "I have been looking at you, wondering if you are the same girl I have seen for years growing up under my eye."

"Another, yet the same," said she. "I have not yet quite lost my personal identity."

"And how many months is it since we left Scotland?"

"Weeks you mean, Moodie, it is scarcely yet time to count by months."

"Weeks, then, have made a wondrous change in you."

"I suspect that often happens in the progress of life," said Lady Mabel. "We seem to stand still for a while at a monotonous stage of our existence; a sudden change of condition comes, and we leap forward toward maturity." So, too, we may for years continue young in heart and health; some heavy trouble or deep grief overtakes us, and we at once are old."

"It is not a leap forward in life that you have made, but a leap aside, out of your own character. It amazes me to see you galloping wildly over this outlandish country, without a thought but flowers, soldiers, and sightseeing. I sometimes think you bewitched."

"What is more likely?" said Lady Mabel. "To us silly women, flowers, soldiers, and sightseeing, are the most bewitching things in the world."

"But you have lost all caution, all fear, and let these friends of yesterday lead you you know not whither."

"Traveling is one way to grow wise; and as to danger, what did you leave Craiggyside for, if it was not to take care of me?"

"Heaven knows I knew not what I undertook. I find one young lady harder to look after than twelve score of ewes, the kine, and the crops, with the ploughmen, shepherd, and dairy-maid to boot."

"Pray do not tell that to any but myself. With such a character, so far from passing for a lady, I could not get a place as lady's maid."

"You may laugh, my lady, but the danger is real and near. I do not trust your new friends," and Moodie shook his finger at them before him. "I know what is ordered must come to pass, and it is sinful to repine at it. But I have known you from a girl, a child, for you are a girl still, my lady, and it grieves my heart to see you galloping on to Rome and ruin."

"Is that my predestined road?" said Lady Mabel. "Then I suppose I must ride it, but it will be at a spanking pace," and giving her horse a cut she dashed off to the head of the party, while Moodie gazed after her in despair.

Hearing the tread of horses close behind him, he looked round and saw L'Isle's servants at his heels, watching him closely. The thought struck him, that he might find these men useful. So, falling back alongside of them, he said to L'Isle's man: "Do you know any thing of the strange country we are going to now?"

The man looked around for a moment with a puzzled air, but perceiving that Moodie was under some strange mistake, he merely said: "I am following my master, and leave him to choose his own road."

"We are playing the game of follow your leader, Mr. Moodie," said the groom, dipping into the dialogue. "The Colonel leads, and we are to follow you know; and d——t, we will play out the game."

"But do you know that he is leading you to the land of the Moors?"

"If he is going to the land of the great Black-a-moor himself, we must shut our eyes and gallop down hill. His country is said to lie in that way."

Moodie muttered something about a son of Belial, but he wished to use these men, and not offend them. So, turning to the groom, with grim sociability, he asked: "Can you speak the language of the people hereabouts?"

"I can call lustily for meat and drink, and make my wants known at a pinch."

"Can you hire me a messenger at the next place we stop at? You must know," said he, in a confidential tone, "I left an important matter sadly neglected in Elvas. It is my lord's business, and I would be sorry to come to blame in it. Whatever it cost, I must send a letter there without delay, and while I write, you must find man and horse. He shall have two guineas the minute the job is done. Is that enough.

"Quite enough," the groom answered, gravely, while his companion turned away his head to conceal a grin. "I know something about riding express, and for two guineas I will find you a man to ride to Elvas and back in double quick time."

"You shall have a guinea for yourself, if you prove a man of your word, and send my letter in time."

"If I fail you, may your guinea choke me, for I mean to melt it down into good liquor," said the groom.

"And I'll help him to drink your health in it, Mr. Moodie," said the other man. "For a guinea's worth of liquor might choke a better man than Tom."

With hope renewed, Moodie rode on after his mistress. On coming up with them, he heard L'Isle and Lady Mabel talking Portuguese. To while away an idle hour, she was taking a lesson in that tongue. This annoyed Moodie, who suspected some plot, when they thus kept him in the dark. But he consoled himself with the hope that his important dispatch would yet be in time to prevent mischief, and he once more refreshed himself with his bottle, being now well convinced of its medicinal virtue.

Lady Mabel was in high spirits, talking and laughing, and occasionally looking round at Moodie, enjoying the deception she had put upon him. Her success in bewildering him, now tempted her to quiz L'Isle, and she abruptly said: "It must have been a violent fit of patriotism and martial ardor that made you abandon the thought of taking orders, and quit Oxford for the camp."

"I never had any thought of taking orders," answered L'Isle, surprised and annoyed, he knew not exactly why. "I only lived with those who had."

"You lived with them to some purpose, then, and have, too, a great aptitude for the church."

"It is not my vocation," said L'Isle, laconically.

"You have only not yet found it out. But it is not too late," she persisted. "Your case, my good man-slaying Christian, is not like Gonsalvo's of Cordova, who had but a remnant of his days in which to play the penitent monk. These wars will soon be over, and you are still young. If you cannot make a general, you may be a bishop in time. Indeed, I already see in you a pillar of our church."

It was not flattering to an ambitious young soldier to hint that he had so mistaken his calling. L'Isle was almost angry, at which Lady Mabel felt a mischievous delight; and Mrs. Shortridge was highly amused.

"It is but a small inducement I can offer you, among so many higher motives," Lady Mabel continued. "But I promise you, that, whenever you preach your first sermon, I will travel even to Land's-end to hear it."

"Lady Mabel shall offer a greater bribe," said Mrs. Shortridge, with an arch look. "If you will only exchange the sword for the surplice, Colonel L'Isle, whenever she commits matrimony, no one but you shall solemnize the rite."

Far from being tempted, L'Isle seemed utterly disgusted at the inducement.

Lady Mabel blushed to the crown of her head, and exclaimed, "I am too fond of my liberty to offer that bribe. That is a high and bare hill," she said, seeking to divert their attention. "Let us ride to the top of it, and survey the country around."

"You may do so, if you like," said Mrs. Shortridge, composedly; "but I have made a vow to do no extra riding to-day. This road is long enough and rough enough for me."

Lady Mabel turned from the path, and, followed by L'Isle, was soon ascending the hill. Moodie, somewhat under the influence of his soporific draughts, was in a reverie, wondering whether Lord Strathern would get his letter in time to send a troop of horse after the fugitives, and whether it might not come within the provisions of the military code to have L'Isle court-martialed and shot for running off with his General's daughter, when, looking up, he missed Lady Mabel, and then discovered her with L'Isle, scampering over the hill. In great confusion, he rode up to Mrs. Shortridge, and asked, "Where are they going now?"

"I scarcely know," she answered; "but Colonel L'Isle will take care of Lady Mabel, so you can stay and take care of me."

Moodie cast on her a look of angry suspicion, which scanned her from head to foot, and plainly pronounced her no sufficient pledge for his mistress. Spurring his horse, he followed Lady Mabel at a run. The animal he rode had often carried fifteen stone, in Lord Strathern's person, over as rough ground as this, and made light of Moodie's weight, which was scarcely more than nine. Without picking his way, he made directly for his companions ahead; and the clatter of his hoofs soon making Lady Mabel look round, she drew up her horse in haste, and anxiously watched Moodie's career. A deep chasm, washed out by the winter rains, was cleared by the horse in capital style, but Moodie lit on his valise, and with difficulty recovered the saddle. Just between him and Lady Mabel the last tree on the hill-side, torn from the shallow soil by some heavy blast, lay horizontally on its decaying roots and branches. Moodie rode at it with unquailing eye, and, while Lady Mabel uttered an exclamation of alarm, the horse cleared it in a bucking leap, throwing Moodie against the holsters; but he fell back into his seat, and rode up triumphantly to his mistress. This energetic demonstration seemed to overawe Lady Mabel. Turning from the hill-top before them, she rode demurely back to the party, resolved not to wander from the beaten path, or go faster than a foot-pace, until Moodie had dismounted, and his neck was safe.

A peasant on an ass, coming down the road, had stopped and stood at gaze at a distance, watching these equestrian manœuvres. But when he saw the party, now united, coming toward him, he turned short to the left, and hastened away at a pace that proved that his *burro* had four nimble legs.

"That must be a thief," said Mrs. Shortridge, "afraid of falling in with honest folks."

"Or an honest man," suggested L'Isle, "afraid of falling among thieves. I have observed a growing dislike in the peasantry to meeting small parties of our people in out of the way places. I suspect that they are sometimes made to pay toll for traveling their own roads."

Their road was winding round the side of the hill, and they presently got a glimpse of a cultivated valley before them. The spirit of mischief suddenly revived in Lady Mabel's bosom. She fell back alongside of Moodie, and said: "This way seems much traveled. It is no longer a by-path; we may call it a high road in this country. We must be drawing near to the city of Mauropolis. I wonder we have yet met none of these turbaned Moors."

Moodie roused himself, and looked anxiously ahead. The mountain shadows already fell upon the valley; but the evening sun still shone upon a city opposite to them. It was seated high above the valley, and flanked by two fortresses of unequal elevation, which partly hid it. The Serra de Portalagre rising behind, overhung it, and the city seemed nestled in a nook in the steep mountain side. Moodie from this point did not recognize the place, but gazed on it steadfastly, with no kindly feeling. "Edom is exalted. He hath made his habitation in the clefts of the rock. He sayeth in his heart, who shall bring me down?" But presently he distinguished the peculiar aqueduct, and his eye roving westward, was struck by the familiar outline of *Serra D'Ossa.*

"We have lost our road," said Lady Mabel, "and found our way back to Elvas;" and, laughing merrily, she shot ahead, leaving Moodie too much angered and mortified to enjoy the relief of his anxieties.

On reaching his quarters he went straight to his bed, to sleep off his fatigue, his chagrin, and the good wine which had befriended yet beguiled him.

CHAPTER XIV.

It snowed in his house of meat and drink,
Of all dainties that men could of think;
After the sundry seasons of the year,
So changed he his meat and soupere.
Full many a fat patriarch had he in mew,
And many a breme and many a luce in stew;
Wo was his cook, but if his sauce were
Poignant and sharp, and ready all his gere,
His table dormant in his hall alway,
Stood ready covered all the long day.
Prologue to Canterbury Tales.

Three days had gone by since the return of the party from Evora. The ladies had gotten over their fatigue, talked over their travels, and wondered at seeing nothing of L'Isle. He had merely sent to inquire after their health, instead of coming himself, as in duty bound. Lady Mabel had confidently looked for him the first day, asked about him the next, and on the third, feeling hurt at this continued neglect, concluded that she had had enough of his company of late, and it did not matter should she not see him for a month.

Meanwhile, what was L'Isle doing? He was busy reforming himself and his regiment. On his return to Elvas he had met with several little indications of relaxed discipline, and somewhat suddenly remembered that he had not come out to Portugal to ride about the country, escorting young ladies in search of botanical specimens, picturesque scenes, and fragments of antiquity. He, the most punctilious of martinets, had been sadly neglecting his duties, and had used the invalid's plea until it was worn threadbare long ago. He was dissatisfied with himself, and, of course, more dissatisfied with other people."

From the day he came back he was constantly in the midst of his regiment. He showed himself, too, at the head of the mess table at every meal, taking that, as well as other opportunities, to inculcate rigid precept and sound doctrine on military matters, and lecture his officers on the subject of discipline. Nor did he confine himself to generalities. He was exacting with his major, hard on his adjutant; he gave Captain A—— to understand that the days and nights spent in the mountains in pursuit of his game tended little to promote the King's service, and that leave would be refused in future, and he suggested to Captain B—— that the best way to ascertain the state of his company was not to send for his orderly sergeant, but to inspect it himself. He spoiled more than one party of pleasure for some of these gentlemen by finding very inopportunely something else for them to do than following the ladies of Elvas and other game of the vicinage.

Many of the officers grumbled, and voted the colonel a bore. They even talked of sending him to Coventry. But Adjutant Meynell excused him by whispering it about that the colonel had just met with a rude rebuff from a certain person at headquarters, and as the rank and sex of the offender hindered his showing his resentment in that direction, on whom could he vent his ill-humor but on those under his command? Meynell advised that they should all unite in sending a round robbin to Lady Mabel, begging her to smile upon their colonel, and put him in an amiable mood.

With the little festive skirmishes, ot almost daily occurrences at headquarters, Lord Strathern loved to mingle occasionally more serious affairs, in the shape of grander feasts; and on the fourth day after Lady Mabel's return, the guests assembled in force. Among them were three ladies of Elvas, who had established a social intercourse with Lady Mabel, and a greater, though less ostensible intimacy with some gentlemen of the brigade. Dinner company is a phase of social life almost unknown in Portugal, and Lady Mabel, aware of this, was needlessly anxious to put her female guests at their ease. Her smattering of their tongue proved inadequate, and even her Spanish but poorly served the purposes of conversation. Dona Carlotta Sequiera, indeed, despising the peninsular tongues, would speak only French—but such French! She had picked up most of it among Kellerman's officers, when he held Elvas with a French garrison in 1808. This lady, like some other renegade Portuguese, at that time assiduously courted the Gaul; and she was anxious now to wipe out this blot, in the eyes of her countrymen, by making much of their British allies. Lady Mabel, tired of her efforts to converse with the other ladies, and sick of Dona Carlotta's French,

"After the school of Stratford at bow,
For French of Paris was to her unknow"—

longed to see her self-appointed dragoman enter the room.

L'Isle had ridden out in the morning to a place on the borders, equi-distant between Elvas and Badajoz, the scene of a serious outrage by a party of marauders two nights before. A peasant, guilty of being richer than his neighbors, had been punished by having his house forced, his head broken, his premises sacked, and his family ill-treated. Though there had been but little blood shed, there had been much wine spilt, besides several plump goat-skins carried off with the rest of the plunder. The English in Elvas laid this achievement at the door of the irregular Spanish force at Badajoz. The Spanish officers were quite as sure that it was the exploit of volunteer foragers from the English cantonments. L'Isle, seeing nobody disposed to inquire into the matter, went and made an examination on the spot, which inclined him to believe that the Spanish version was the true history of this little military operation. After a hot ride he returned in time to make his bow to Lady Mabel among the latest of her guests.

Mrs. Shortridge was very glad to see him, but reproached him with his late neglect of his friends; and turned toward Lady Mabel, expecting her concurrence in this censure. But my lady said, with sublime indifference: "What matters Colonel L'Isle's absence hitherto, since he has now come in time to interpret between us and our Portuguese friends? I have exhausted my stock of Portuguese," she continued, addressing L'Isle; "and find that they do not always comprehend my Spanish. Major Warren, indeed, has been lending me his aid; but I think the interpreter the harder to be understood of the two. Is it not strange these ladies do not understand me better; for their language is but bad Spanish, and mine is surely bad enough."

"Do not say that to the Portuguese," said L'Isle. "They will be justly offended; for their tongue is rather the elder sister of the Spanish than a corruption of it."

"Pray, lend me your tongue, Colonel L'Isle," said Mrs. Shortridge. "Here Dona Carlotta Sequiera has been jabbering at me in what I now find out to be French; but I am ashamed to say, I do not know thirty words of the language."

"Better to be ignorant of it," said L'Isle with a sneer, "than learn it as Dona Carlotta did."

"I know not how she acquired it," said Mrs. Shortridge, "but I am told that here on the continent every educated person speaks French. We English are far behind them in that."

"Be proud rather than ashamed of that," said

L'Isle. "Monsieur has taught all Europe his language except ourselves. Flagellation is a necessary part of schooling. As he has never been able to thrash us, we are the worst French scholars in Europe, and those he has thrashed oftenest, are the best. They should blush at their knowledge; we plume ourselves on our ignorance. Thank God you have an English tongue in your head, and never mar a better language with a Gallic phrase. There is in every country a class who are prone to denationalize themselves; at this day, they generally ape the Frenchman. Now, I can tolerate a genuine Frenchman, without having any great liking for him; but if there is any one whom I feel at liberty to despise and distrust, it is a German, Spaniard or Englishman, who is trying to Frenchify himself. Such people are much akin to the self-styled citizen of the world, who professes to have rid himself of all local and national prejudice. I have usually met *no-prejudice* and *no-principle* walking hand in hand together. The French," he continued, "have the impudence to call theirs the universal language; and in diplomacy and war, they have been long too much encouraged in this. My Lord Wellington here is much to blame in giving way to their pretensions on this point. Whenever I have an independent command," said L'Isle laughing, "I will not let a Frenchman capitulate but in good English, or for want of it, in some other language than his own. I have already put that in practice in a small way," said he, as he handed Mrs. Shortridge down to dinner. "I once waylaid a foraging, *anglice*, a plundering party, returning laden to Merida. They showed fight, but we soon tumbled them into a *barranca*, where we had them quite in our power. But I would not listen to a word of their French, or let them surrender, until they found a renegade Spaniard to act as interpreter. When I want anything of them, I may speak French; but when they want anything of me, they must ask it in another tongue."

The dinner went off as large dinners usually do. The wrong parties got seated together, and suitable companions were separated by half the length of the board. Lady Mabel had Colonel Bradshawe, whom she did not want, close at hand; and her dragoman was out of hearing, which she felt to be not only inconvenient, but a grievance; for without entertaining any definite designs upon him, habit had already given her a sort of property in him, and a right to his services. But the Elvas ladies had no such ground of complaint. Each had her favorite by her side, and Dona Carlotta one on either hand.

It was a relief to Lady Mabel when the time came to lead the ladies back to her drawing-room. There she labored to entertain them until some of the gentlemen found leisure to come to her aid. She expected to see L'Isle among the first; but one after another came in without him; the Portuguese ladies were taken off her hands by their more intimate male friends, and she had leisure to wonder what could keep L'Isle down stairs so long, and to get out of humor at his sticking to the bottle, and neglecting better company for it.

Meanwhile, a great controversy was waging below. The more the disputants drank, the more strenuously they discussed the point at issue; and the more they exhausted themselves in argument, the oftener they refreshed themselves by drinking; swallowing many a glass unconsciously in the heat of the debate.

The farmer talks of seasons and his crops; the merchant of traffic and his gains; and the soldier, though less narrow in his range of topics, often dwells on the incidents and characteristics of military life. In answer to some very loose notions on the subject of discipline, L'Isle mounted his hobby, and said that he had pretty much come into the mechanical theory on military matters. "An army is a machine; the men composing it, parts of that machine; and the more their personal and individual characters are obliterated, by assimilating them to the nature of precise and definite parts of one complicated organization, the better will they serve their purpose. Now, a machine should be kept always in perfect order and readiness for instant application to the purpose of its construction. An army is a machine contrived for fighting battles; and if at any time it is not in a condition to fight to the best advantage, it is in a state of deterioration and partial disorganization. Troops, therefore, should be kept, at all times and under all circumstances, under the same rigid discipline, and in the full exercise of their functions, equally ready at all seasons for action."

Lord Strathern took up the cudgels and maintained that though an army might be called a machine, its component parts were men, who necessarily had some perception of the contingencies and emergencies incident to military life, and that great as were sacrifices they might make, and the restrictions they might bear with when there was obvious necessity for them, should the same exacting course be pursued as a system, it would only break their spirits, freeze their zeal, and disgust them with the service. "We have seen enough of your mechanical armies, drilled and regulated to perfection, as soulless mechanism. We have seen how, on the dislocation of this machine, the parts became useless and helpless, without resource in themselves. In short, it is the Prussian and Austrian system which has given half Europe to the French. No; if the bow need unbending, still more does the soldier need relaxation, to give vigor and elasticity to body and mind. A little ease and pleasure chequering his career only beget desire and the motives for new adventure and fresh exertions. How is it with our horses," exclaimed his lordship, who was a jockey of the old school. "Do we not give them a run at grass, to refresh their constitutions and renew their youth?"

But L'Isle unshaken maintained his opinion, "With such materials as make up a large part of our army, for his majesty gets the services of many a fellow who can be put to no good use at home, your lordship's relaxation system would only tend to sap its moral and physical strength, and make it a curse to the country in which it is quartered, whether at home or abroad."

It would have been well had the discussion stopped here. In the heat of debate each pushed his argument beyond his own convictions. Colonel Bradshawe sat sipping his wine, listening with mock gravity and seeming to oscillate between the opinions of the disputants, but most of the company agreed with Lord Strathern; still L'Isle found several staunch backers for his mechanical theory. But when quoting facts in support of his views, he referred to the conduct of their own men on sundry late occasions, and stated the result of the inquiries he that morning had made into the last outrage, he brought the whole company down upon him. They were all sure that the English soldiers had nothing to do with it. His lordship professed to detect, not only in the act itself, but in the *modus operandi*, infallible marks that fathered it on the Spaniard. The quiet, stealthy manner, the place, just on the border, yet out of Spain. "Besides," he urged, "you yourself say, that the few words the marauders were heard to utter were all Spanish."

"But the same testimony proves them to have been bad Spanish, even to the ears of a Portuguese borderer, and evidently used by foreigners for the purpose of disguise, like the dresses they wore. Who ever heard of a Spaniard breaking a man's head, when he could give him the blade of his knife? The farmer's bloody crown was a plain piece of English handicraft. Spaniards would have rummaged the house for *la plata*, and have snatched the earrings from the women's ears; the robbers, a more thirsty race, thought chiefly of carrying off the liquor."

The number and loud voices of those opposed to him only made L'Isle more stubborn in maintaining his views. He seemed rather to like being in a minority of one. On the other hand, Lord Strathern construed his remarks into an undisguised censure of his lax discipline. Luckily he was a truly hospitable man: nowhere, but at his own board, could he have kept his temper under control. Between the fumes of wine and smoke of cigars, the matter only became more and more cloudy. It was late when L'Isle left the table and entered the drawing-room, with a brow still ruffled by the controversy.

Striving to resume his equanimity, he took a seat by Lady Mabel. But she, by no means pleased at the long absence of her interpreter, and his late neglect in attending on her, pushed her chair back, and said something about "falling into bad habits."

"Do you think so?" said L'Isle, looking surprised, then reflecting a moment. "Why, Lady Mabel, I am not aware of having committed any excess, at least of the kind you suspect."

"Why, then, do you come from below so much heated and excited?"

"I have been engaged in a hot argument with my Lord, and others."

"Coolness would be more appropriate to argument than heat. But this was plainly an after-dinner discussion. The subject should be handled a second time, in imitation of those wise barbarians, who resolved on nothing until they had twice taken counsel, once of their cups, and then of cool sobriety the morning after."

"I feel no need of appealing to the cool reflecting morning hours."

"Of course you do not feel it now; that, too, will come with the sober morning."

L'Isle, a good deal nettled, was about to reply, when she exclaimed, "Why, you have been smoking!"

"No, I have only been smoked."

"That is just as unpleasant," she said, pushing her chair farther off. "The Portuguese snuff-taking is offensive enough, but this Spanish habit of smoking perpetually is intolerable. Wherever our officers go they pick up the small vices of the country, without abandoning any of their own. Here they add smoking to their native wine-bibbing propensities. They spoil a man utterly."

"Not utterly," said L'Isle; "there is Warren now, a capital fellow, a delightful companion, and an inveterate smoker."

"For that I cannot abide him," said Lady Mabel, out of humor with everybody.

"There is your friend, Colonel Bradshawe, who sets no little store by his wine and cigar."

"He is intolerable with them, and would be a bore without them."

"But my Lord himself smokes. Will you not tolerate him?"

"He is an old man, a general officer, and my father," said Lady Mabel. "After a life of hard service in the worst climates in the world, he may need indulgences not necessary to younger men. Besides, he is obliged to see so much of his officers. If he could choose his companions, he would lead a very different life. When we happen to be alone here," continued Lady Mabel, "he never sits long after dinner, seldom touches a cigar, and it is evidently only his position, and the habits forced upon him in a long military career, which interfere with his quiet tastes and love of domestic life."

L'Isle looked at Lady Mabel to see if she was in earnest. She had only said what she willingly believed on rather slight foundations. In truth, the novelty of having his daughter with him on the few occasions on which they were here left alone together, had proved of quite sufficient interest to enable Lord Strathern to dispense with other society and excitements, and led him to look back and to speak much of his short married life, and far beyond that, the days of his boyhood. L'Isle found himself convicted of contributing, with others, to mar the comfort and spoil the habits of the most abstemious and domestic old gentleman in the king's service. This was plainly a point on which it was not safe to contradict Lady

Mabel, if he would keep in her good graces—so he gladly waved the discussion.

Mrs. Shortridge, under the reviving influence of her love of sight-seeing, now asked L'Isle to suggest some excursion for them, on which they might see something new. But she begged that it might be within a reasonable distance, for she had been so thoroughly shaken on the rough paths to and from Evora, that she was not yet up to another long ride.

"Cranfield has just been talking of Fort la Lippe,' said L'Isle, "which overlooks us from the North. Let us make up a party to visit it to-morrow. Cranfield can entertain and instruct us by discoursing on this masterpiece of the Count de Lippe, and unveil the mysteries of the engineer's art. In the intervals, we can, from that high point, survey the country around us."

Cranfield eagerly seconded the proposal. Anything that looked like diversion was welcome to the ladies and the idlers about them, and Lady Mabel, somewhat mollified, condescended to approve of it.

Accordingly, the next morning she met, by appointment, Mrs. Shortridge and the three Portuguese ladies at the foot of the long flight of steps that lead up to the cathedral of Elvas. They were accompanied by L'Isle, Cranfield, and half a dozen gentlemen more, including the young surgeon of the —— regiment, who was always imagining that Lady Mabel had a cold, headache, or some other little ailment, that he might have the pleasure of prescribing for it. Irreverently turning their backs on the old church, without one prayer to the saints within, or those depicted on its windows of stained glass, they walked out of town down into the narrow valley lying north of the city, and crossing the brook which runs at the bottom (the Portuguese, making a river of it, have christened it the Seto), on the few stepping-stones which well supply the place af a foot-bridge, they toiled up the opposite hill, the lower part of which is covered with a grove of prickly oaks.

On reaching the gate Captain Cranfield stepped forward to the head of the party, and entered zealously on his duties as *cicerone.* He led them through the spacious barracks, in which the scanty garrison seemed buried in monastic seclusion; through the huge store-houses and bomb-proof kitchens and bakeries; showed them the vast tank containing water for a full garrison for a year; and what was better, a natural spring, welling out mysteriously within the circuit of the works. From the ramparts of this huge coronet that crowned the head of this eminence, he pointed out the strength of the position, the efficiency of the works, and their importance to the safety of Elvas. From this stronghold, with the works of the city and Fort St. Lucia on the other side of it, lying before them, Cranfield discoursed at length on his art, dealing largely in its technical terms: bastions, and curtains, covered ways, scarps and counter scarps, with ravelins thrown out in front of them, until Mrs. Shortridge, who listened with open-mouthed admiration, got so confused that she imagined that a ravelin was some kind of missile to be hurled at the French. Dona Carlotta and the other Portuguese ladies were not so attentive, not understanding the language of the lecturer, and feeling less interest in the defence of their country than in the attentions of the foreign officers, who were devoting themselves to their special service. But Lady Mabel, who prided herself on being a soldier's daughter, lent a willing ear to Cranfield, asked many questions, and even contrived to understand much that he had to say.

L'Isle now thought that the engineer had held the first place in Lady Mabel's attention long enough; so he broke in upon his eulogy on this inland Gibraltar, the master-piece of "*o gran Conde de Lippe.*"

"The whole thing is certainly grand and complete in itself," said he, looking around; "and is a monument to the engineering talents of the Count de Lippe. But, after all, constructing a great fortress in Portugal is like building a ducal palace on a dairy farm; the thing may be very fine in itself, but is altogether out of place. Half a dozen such strongholds as Elvas, with its forts, would swallow up the Portuguese army, yet be but half garrisoned, and leave not a man to take the field. See the extent of the works between this and St. Lucia, that other sentinel standing guard over Elvas on the south. It would need twelve thousand men to garrison the city and the forts. I never heard that this fortress was of use to any but the French, who got it without fighting; and the possession of it helped them to obtain the convention of Cintra; but for which we would have tumbled Junot and his fellows into the Tagus. The Count de Lippe was wonderfully successful in regenerating the army, and restoring the military character of Portugal in the last century; but his countryman, Schomberg, in the century before, showed how Portugal could be better defended, and we have now in the country one who understands it better than the Duke de Schomberg himself."

There was so much truth in what L'Isle said, that Cranfield was obliged to yield up his impregnable fortress as a very fine thing in itself, but quite out of place.

"I gather from your remarks," said Lady Mabel, "that Portugal has often had a foreigner at the head of its army."

"Very often, indeed," answered L'Isle. "This same kingdom, which, in spite of its narrow territory and small population, had, through the enterprise of its rulers and the energy of the people, extended its conquests in the East and the West; which, in the sixteenth century had thirty-two foreign kingdoms and four hundred and thirty garrisoned towns tributary to it—has now so much degenerated in its institutions, that for two centuries it has never been able to defend itself, or even make a decent showing in the field, but by foreign aid and under a foreign leader. The Duke of Schomberg, Archduke Charles, the Count de Lippe the Prince of Waldeck, and other Germans, have in turn led the army, and each had to reorganize it, and revive its discipline. Now, they rely on Beresford to train them for battle, and Wellington to lead them to victory. The Count de Lippe found the military character so sunk, that officers were often seen waiting at the tables of their colonels; and the sense of individual honor was so lost, that one of his first reforms was to insist on his officers fighting when insulted, if they would not be cashiered."

"The former greatness of Portugal," said Lady Mabel, "is even more wonderful than its present decay. Yet that is lamentable, indeed, when the government, without striking a blow, could run away from the country on the approach of the invader."

"That might have been called an act of deliberate wisdom," said L'Isle, "had it not been stamped with feebleness and cowardice in the execution. Resistance was hopeless against France united with Spain, its tool, and soon to be its victim. Yielding to the storm left the invaders without apology for the plunder and atrocities the French have since perpetrated on the people. Nor was it a sudden thought. As long ago as the beginning of the last century, a Portuguese Secretary of State, seeing the defenceless condition of his country, urged that the King should remove to Brazil, and fix his court at Rio Janeiro. He points out the dependent state of his country in Europe, and asks: 'What is Portugal?' A corner of land divided into three parts; one barren, one belonging to the church, and the other part not even producing grain enough for the inhabitants. Look now at Brazil, and see what is wanting! The soil is rich, the climate delightful, the territory boundless, and the city would soon become more flourishing than Lisbon. Here he might extend his commerce, make discoveries in the interior, and take the title of Emperor of the West.' In truth, the behavior of the house of Braganza in this migration, contrasts well with the infamous conduct of the Spanish Bourbons.

They had strolled on to the foot of a tower within the fort, and Cranfield led the party to the top to survey the panorama around them. The horizon was pretty equally divided between Portugal and Spain. On the North, close at hand, rose the rugged Serra de Portalegre, famous for its chesnut forests; to the west was the fertile plain of Eastern Alemtejo, crossed by the enormous pile of the aqueduct, and backed by the heights of Serra D'Ossa; to the south and east, the valley of the Guadiana lay before them, with few marks of culture on the Spanish side; and the eye could range over the sheep pastured plains of Estremadura to the misty sides and blue tops of the sierras that shut them in on either hand.

In the East, nine miles off, by the straight path the vulture makes, rose Badajoz, capped by its castle, and over-looked by fort San Christoval on a high hill across the river. The fame of its sieges during this war, its stubborn defence and bloody fall within the year, drew the eyes of the ladies on it. L'Isle pulled out a field glass to aid them in inspecting it. When the Portuguese ladies got hold of it, they were as much delighted as children with a new toy, snatching it out of each other's hands, without allowing time for its deliberate use, and protesting against their Spanish neighbors being brought so near to them.

"If they are so delighted at the powers of this little thing," said L'Isle, "what would they think of the glass Lord Wellington had put up in this tower during the siege of Badajoz?"

"Were its powers so great?" Mrs. Shortridge asked.

"Wonderful, according to rumor," answered L'Isle, "But I never had time to come from the trenches to prove them. It is said to have brought Badajoz so near, that you saw how the French soldiers made their soup, and even smell the garlic they put into it. Once, when my Lord saw Philipon leaning against the parapet of the castle, sneering at the besieger's clumsy approaches, he so far forgot himself, as to call for his holsters, that he might pistol the contemptuous Frenchmen on the spot."

"Did he, indeed?" exclaimed Mrs. Shortridge; then laughing at herself for being quizzed for the moment, begged L'Isle to tell this to the Portuguese ladies, and see if they would not believe it.

Meanwhile, Lady Mabel was gazing thoughtfully over the winding valley, which running toward them from the East, turned abruptly to the South, indicating the course of the Guadiana, and on the wide plains of Estremadura *baja*, or the lower, to the blue sierras that walled it round. "This, then, is Spain," said she; "the land I have read of, dreamed of, and for the last four years, thought of more even than of my own."

"And yet," said L'Isle, "you calling yourself a traveler, have been for months within sight of it, and have never set your foot on Spanish ground."

"I blush to own it. But you, my self-appointed guide, should blush, too, at never having led me thither. Come, Mrs. Shortridge: these soldiers are too slow for us; let us take horse to-morrow, and make an inroad into Spain."

"Willingly," said Mrs. Shortridge. "But let us take a strong party with us. We do not know how we might be received, should the Spaniards mistake us for Portuguese!"

"If a visit to Badajoz is your object," said Cranfield, "I offer myself as a guide. As I have been lately engaged in repairing its shattered walls, I may be useful in showing you how to get in. Knowing, too, some of the Spanish officers there, I may in a parley induce them to come to terms."

They now descended from the tower, and on leaving the fort, Lady Mabel led the party to head-quarters, to take their luncheon there, while they planned their measure for to-morrow's expedition to Badajoz.

CHAPTER XV.

"Where Lusitania and her sister meet,
Deem ye what bounds the rival realms divide?
Or ere the jealous queens of nations greet,
Doth Tayo interpose his mighty tide?
Or dark Sierras rise in craggy pride?
Or fence of art, like China's vasty wall?
No barrier wall, no river deep and wide,
No horrid crags, nor mountains dark and tall,
Rise like the rocks that part Hispania's land from Gaul.

But these between, a silver streamlet glides,
And scarce a name distinguisheth the brook;
Though rival kingdoms press its verdant sides,
Here leans the idle shepherd on his crook,
And vacant on the rippling waves doth look,
That peaceful still 'twixt bitterest foemen flow,
For proud each peasant as the noblest duke;
Well doth the Spanish hind the difference know
'Twixt him and Lusian slave, the lowest of the low."

Childe Harold's Pilgrimage.

THE next morning early a numerous party issued from the eastern gate of Elvas. The descending road led them between groves of olives, whose sad colored foliage was relieved by the bright hues of the almond tree, clothed with pink blossoms, the scarlet flowering pomegranate, the dark, rich green of the orange-tree, already spangled over with small white blossoms, yet still laden with its golden fruit, and the prune trees of Elvas, favorites through the world, leafless as yet, but conspicuous by the clouds of white flowerets which covered them. The roofs of the suburban quintas showed themselves here and there above the orchards, and by the roadside the *iris alata* bloomed on every bank.

The air is balmy, the scene lovely, and all nature smiling with the sweet promises of Spring. Is this the goddess Flora leading down a joyous train to the fields below? It is only Lady Mabel cantering somewhat recklessly down hill. When she reached the more level ground, she so far out-rode the ladies of her party, who were mounted on mules, that, tired of loitering for them to come up, she proposed to L'Isle, who had kept by her side, to employ their leisure in ascending the bare hill on their left, to examine the old tower, that stood solitary and conspicuous on its top. From the clearness of the atmosphere it seemed nearer than it was, and the broken ground compelled them to make a circuit before they reached it. Hence they looked down upon their friends, crawling at a snail's pace along the road to Badajoz. They rode round the weather-beaten, ruinous tower. It was square, with only one small entrance, many feet above the ground, and leading into a small room amidst the thick walls.

"What could this have been built for?" Lady Mabel asked.

"It is one of those watch-towers called *atalaias*," answered L'Isle. "Many of them are scattered along the heights on the border. They are memorials of an age in which one of people's chief occupations was watching against the approach of their neighbors."

"Stirring times, those," said Lady Mabel. "People could not then complain that their vigilance was lulled to sleep by too great security; but this is, perhaps, a more comfortable age."

"To us in our island home," said L'Isle. "The improvement is more doubtful here. There was a time when your forefathers and mine thus kept watch against each other; when our own border hills were crowned with similar watch-towers; but never did any country continue so long a debatable land, and need, for so many centuries, the watch-tower and the signal fire on its hills, as this peninsula during the slow process of its redemption from the crescent to the cross."

"From this point," said Lady Mabel, "Elvas and Badajoz look like two giant champions facing each other, in arms, each, for the defence of his own border, yet one does not see here any of those great natural barriers that should divide nations."

"They are wanting, not only here," said L'Isle, "but on other parts of the frontier. The great rivers, the Duoro, the Tagus and the Guadiana, and the mountain chains separating their valleys, instead of dividing the two kingdoms, run into Portugal from Spain. The division of these countries is not natural, but accidental; and in spite of some points of contrast, the Portuguese are almost as much like the Spaniards, as these last are like each other—for Spain is in truth a variety of countries, the Spaniards a variety of nations."

"At length, however," said she, "Spain and Portugal are united in one cause."

"Yet the Portuguese still hates the Spaniards," said L'Isle, "and the Spaniard contemns the Portuguese."

"And we despise both," said Lady Mabel."

"Perhaps unjustly," said he.

"Why, to look no further into their short-comings and back-slidings," to use Moodie's terms, have they not signally failed in the first duty of a nation, defending itself?"

"Remember the combination of fatalities that beset them," said L'Isle, "and the atrocious perfidy that aggravated their misfortunes. Both countries were left suddenly without rulers, distracted by a score of contending *juntas*, to resist a great nation, under a government of matchless energy, the most perfectly organized for the attainment of its object, which is not the good of its subjects, but solely the developement, to the uttermost, of its military power. They at once sunk before it, showing us how completely the vices of governments, and yet more, the sudden absence of all government, can paralyze a nation. But they have since somewhat redeemed their reputation, by many an example of heroism."

"Why did not the nation, as one man, imitate the heroes of Zaragoza and Gerona, and wage, like them, war to the knife's point against the infidel and murderous horde of invaders?" exclaimed Lady Mabel, with a flushed cheek and flashing eye, that would have become Augustina Zaragoza herself.

"Because every man is not a hero, nor in a position to play a hero's part. Spain was betrayed and surprised. The invaders came in the guise of friends, under the faith of treaties, by which the flower of the Spanish army had been marched into remote parts of Europe as allies to the French; nor was the mask thrown off until long after it was useless to wear it."

"Did the world ever before witness such complicated perfidy?"

"Perhaps not. But I trust it is about to witness its failure and punishment."

"*We* and the Czar will have to administer it," said Lady Mabel, with the air of an arbitress of nations. "We cannot look for much help from our besotted allies here."

"It must be confessed," said L'Isle, "that an unhappy fatality in council and in action, has beset the Portuguese and Spaniards, throughout the war. They have too often shown their patriotism by murdering their generals, underrating their enemies and slighting their friends. They have, too, attained the very acme of blundering; doing the wrong thing at the wrong time, and choosing the wrong man to do it."

"Say no more," exclaimed Lady Mabel. "If that be the verdict you find against our allies, I will not accuse you of blindness to their faults. They are unworthy of the lovely and romantic land they live in," she added, gazing on the scene before her. "What beautiful mountain is that which trenches so close upon the border, as if it would join itself to the Serra de Portalegre?"

"It is the mountain of Albuquerque, so called from a town at its foot."

"That was the title of the Spanish duke, who died lately in London," Lady Mabel remarked.

"And in one sense the most unfortunate Spaniard of our day," added L'Isle. "Of the highest rank among subjects, uniting in his person names famous in Spanish history; he was brave and patriotic, and though still young, one of the few Spanish leaders whose enterprize did not lead to disaster. But the Supreme Junta, in its jealousy would never entrust him with any but subordinate commands, subjecting him to the orders of Castanos Cuesta, and other inefficient leaders whose blunders his good conduct often covered. When, at length Andalusia was lost by the folly and cowardice of others, he only had his wits about him, and by a speedy march saved Cadiz. The rabid democrats of the city repaid him with ingratitude and insults, which drove him into exile; and, denied the privilege of falling in defence of his country, he died broken-hearted in a foreign land."

"Are these people worth fighting for?" exclaimed Lady Mabel, indignantly, reining back her horse, as if about to abandon her Spanish allies to their own folly.

"Perhaps not," said L'Isle, "if we were not also

fighting for ourselves. Spain is a convenient field on which to drub the French. But it is time to follow our party."

They now left the hill and getting back into the road, galloped after their friends, but did not overtake them until they had reached the little river Cayo, which here divides Portugal from Spain. The ladies, on their mules, were grouped together in doubt and hesitation on this bank, while several of the gentlemen were riding about in the water, searching for holes in the bed of the stream, which was swollen and turbid from the late rains.

"You hesitate too long to pass the Rubicon," said Lady Mabel, "just let me tuck up the skirt of my riding dress, from the muddy waters, and I will lead you over into Spain."

She was soon on the other bank, and her companions followed her. The road now led them across a sandy plain, which, treeless and desolate, contrasted strikingly with the fertility and cultivation around Elvas.

Looking at the fortress they were approaching, L'Isle remarked: "From the times of Saguntum, Numantia, and Astapa, Spain has been noted for cities that perished utterly rather than yield in submission to their foes—Zaragoza, Gerona, and other places have in our day maintained the old national fame. But Badajoz," he added, shaking his finger at the towers before him, "is not one of them. It cannot be denied that in this struggle the Spaniards have proved themselves a nation. 'Every Spaniard remembers that his country was once great, and is familiar with the names of its heroes; speaks with enthusiasm of the Cid, of Ferdinand Cortes, and a host of others.' When the hour of trial come, 'the nation instinctively felt, to use the language of one of their own *juntas*, that 'there is a kind of peace more fatal than the field of battle drenched with blood, and strewed with the bodies of the slain.' The patriotic fire may have flamed the higher for the holy oil of superstition poured upon it, but it was kindled by noble pride and generous shame and indignation, by the remembrance of what their fathers had been, and the thought of what their children were to be.'"

"In spite of the blunders, disasters, and treachery that have been rife in the land," said Lady Mabel, "more than one name has been added to the list of its heroes--Palafox and the Maid of Zaragoza have won immortal fame."

"And others less famous have deserved as well," said L'Isle. "Before Augustina, this second Joan of Arc, had stepped out of her sex, to display her heroism, she and others, behind the same shattered, crumbling wall, had been showing an equal heroism within their sex's sphere. Women of all ranks were zealous in the patriotic cause. They formed themselves into companies, some to assist the wounded, some to carry water, wine and food to those who defended the gates. The Countess Burita raised a corps for this service. She was young, delicate and beautiful. In the midst of the most tremendous fire of shot and shells, she was seen coolly attending to those occupations, which were now become her duty; nor through the whole of a two month's siege did the imminent danger, to which she incessantly exposed herself, produce the slightest apparent effect upon her; her step never faltered, her eye never quailed. What a partial thing is fame," he continued, "and how poor a motive to duty! The names of Palafox and Zaragoza are forever wedded. How few remember the old plebeian, *Tio Jorge*, who counseled and spurred on both governor and populace to their heroic defence!"

"When we remember all that the Spaniards have undergone in this war," said Lady Mabel, "we cannot but think that their atrocities in the new world have been visited on them at home."

"How far we must answer for the sins of our forefathers," said L'Isle, "is a nice question. We have some scriptural authority for asserting that responsibility; and as there is no hereafter for nations, they must be punished in this world, or not at all. I would be sorry to bear my share of the penalty of all that immaculate England has done. But I do not fear the fate of Spain for England:

'That royal throne of kings, that sceptred isle,
That earth of majesty, that seat of Mars,
That other Eden, demi-paradise;
That fortress, built by nature for herself,
Against infection, and the hand of war;

> That happy breed of men, that little world;
> That precious stone set in the silver sea,
> Which serves it in the office of a wall,
> Or as a moat defensive to a house,
> Against the envy of less happier lands.'

England against the world!" he exclaimed breaking off his quotation, in his enthusiasm, and laying his hand on his sword.

"You are certainly a patriot," said Lady Mabel, "if any amount of national prejudice can make patriotism. But yours is very like the cockney's, who despised all the world, beyond the sound of Bow bells. As to the fortress isle. (*Let me warn you to keep it well garrisoned against surprise.*) I believe there is an obscure little corner of it called Scotland, which both you and the poet have forgotten."

"I merely used *England* in a figure of speech," said L'Isle, "putting a part for the whole."

"I will not tolerate your figure of speech, as disparaging to old Scotland," she said. "But for us Scots—"

"Us Scots!" L'Isle exclaimed. "Why, it was but yesterday you told me how much you had angered Moodie by calling yourself an English woman."

"What of that? I would have you know that I have two sides to my natural character. I claim the right to present my Scotch or English side at will, and then you cannot see the other."

Fort San Christoval, on this side of the Guadiana, rose higher and higher before them. Gazing on

Badajoz and its castle on the other side of the river, L'Isle thought of the failures before it, and of the price in blood at which it had been bought at last. "We are not always successful in our sieges—at times undertaking them rashly, without the means of carrying them on. The sabre, and bayonet, unaided, take few walled towns. They need the help of Cranfield's art, and he cannot work without his tools."

"But we always beat the French in the field," said Lady Mabel.

"Always," said L'Isle. "There has been no instance of a real British army being beaten by a French one."

"None of late years," said Lady Mabel. "To find a victory over us they have to go as far back in the last century as Fontenoy."

"That is not a fair instance," said L'Isle eagerly. "We lost that battle chiefly through the backwardness of our Dutch allies; and Marshal Saxe, who was no Frenchman, but a German, beat us chiefly by aid of the valor of the Irish regiments in the French pay."

"That alters the case," said Lady Mabel; "but were we not beaten some years before that, at Almansa, here in Spain?"

"That instance is still more unfair," exclaimed L'Isle. "Our Peninsular allies ran away, while we fought their battle. Still, though the enemy were two to our one, the result might have been different. But the French had an English general, the Duke of Berwick, to win the battle for them, and we had a French commander, DeRuvigny, whom Dutch William had made Earl of Galway, to lose it for us."

"Then, after all," exclaimed Lady Mabel, "the Englishman won the field."

"Yes," to our cost," said L'Isle, bitterly. "What made it more provoking was, that we had at that very time the man to mate him;" and, standing up on his stirrups, he raised his clenched hand above his head, exclaiming: "O, for one hour of Peterborough to grapple with his countryman and redeem the day!"

"What is the matter with Colonel L'Isle?" asked Mrs. Shortridge, who was riding close behind with Cranfield.

"He is only leaping back to the beginning of the last century," answered Lady Mabel, "to reverse the issue of the battle of Almansa."

"Why, has not the colonel fighting enough before him," said Cranfield, laughing, "that he must go back so far for more?"

"Let us be content with what we have," said L'Isle joining in the laugh. "It is useless to dwell on old disasters but by way of shunning new ones. It has been our constant luck to go into battle shoulder to shoulder with allies who, except when in our pay, seldom stand by us to the end of the day."

The river was now at hand. Turning to the right before reaching San Christoval, they entered the *tete du pont*, and soon found themselves on a noble granite bridge of many arches. The voices of many singers drew their eyes to the banks of the river, where they saw all the washerwomen of the city, collected in pursuit of their calling, and lightening their labors with song, the burden of which, "Guadiana, Guadiana," fell often on the ear, while the sun-beams bleached the linen spread out on the banks of the stream, and tanned the faces of the industrious choir chanting its praise.

"This, then, is the Guadiana!" said Lady Mabel, peeping over the parapet. "I feel bound to admire its broad face, but miss the swift current and pellucid waters of the poetasters, to whose bounties the river god owes much of his fame."

"While you and our party loiter here, searching out the beauties of the Guadiana," said L'Isle, "I will ride on and secure our peaceful reception at the gate. A Spanish sentinel is often asleep, and apt to prove his vigilance by firing on whoever wakes him up."

Presently following L'Isle, who luckily found the sentinel awake, they reached the southern end of the bridge, and passing between two beautiful round towers of white marble, now tinted straw-color with age, they entered the northern gate of the city, and soon sought hospitality at the *Posada de los Caballeros.*

Putting up their horses here, they left the servants to see that a dinner was got ready; this meal, at a Spanish inn, depending less on what you find there than on what you bring with you. Three Spanish officers were lounging at the posada, one of whom immediately claimed Cranfield's acquaintance, and introduced his companions. Cranfield did not seem delighted to meet with him, nevertheless he presented them to the whole party with studied politeness. Captain Don Alonzo Melendez, with a handsome person, a swaggering air, and a costume more foppish than military, looked more like a *majo* of Seville than a soldier and a gentleman. His companions had much the advantage of him there, but he beat them hollow in assurance. Learning that curiosity alone had brought them to Badajoz, he at once took the post of guide. Finding that Lady Mabel knew enough of Spanish to make a good listener, he placed himself by her side. Cranfield escorted her on the other, and thus they walked forth. L'Isle, thrust into the background, accompanied Mrs. Shortridge and the rest of the party.

As they drew near the works, many marks of injury and devastation on the adjacent houses, brought the late siege prominently to their minds. Don Alonzo Melendez at once began to discourse grandiloquently on the subject. His narrative was so copious and inaccurate, that Cranfield soon lost all patience, and found it hard to keep from interrupting and contradicting him. Lady Mabel, detecting this, encouraged the Spaniard to the uttermost by displaying rapt attention, and full faith in his glowing narrative.

" I never before heard," said she to Cranfield, so graphic an account of the siege and storming of Badajoz."

"If our friend here talks about it much longer," said Cranfield, in English, "he will forget that we had any thing to do with it. The siege was, however, in one sense, the work of the Spaniards. If the traitor Imaz had not sold it to Soult for a mule load of gold, we would not have had to buy it back at the cost of so many thousands of lives. Nor were any of them Spanish lives," he added bitterly; "though some were Portuguese—for the only Spaniards at the siege were the renegados who aided Philippon and his Frenchman to keep us out."

"Every Spaniard is not traitor or coward," said L'Isle from behind. If the brave Governor Menacho had not been killed in defending the place, his successor Imaz could not have sold it a few days after to the French."

As they strolled along the ramparts, Don Alonso, with a strange forgetfulness of events within the year, lauded the impregnable strength of the works, as if Badajoz were still a virgin fortress. Cranfield, by way of rebuking him, pointed out to Lady Mabel the restorations he had made of the breached walls. She replied that "the patchwork character of his repairs were but too evident, as he had invariably omitted to use materials of the same color with the original works."

As they rambled through the city, Don Alonso failed not to point out the superior size and style of the buildings over those of Elvas, and Lady Mabel remarked that "in cleanliness, too, it far surpassed its neighbor.' Leading them to the cathedral, their guide compelled them to inspect minutely this heavy and cumberous building, while he eulogized it in terms that might have been suitable to St. Peter's, at Rome. "I am sorry," said he, "you cannot see it in all its splendor; but the gorgeous furniture of the altar and the rich ornaments of the shrines are not now exhibited."

"Why not?" asked Lady Mabel.

"In these troubled, sacrilegious times, the clergy think it best not to display the wealth of the church."

"They would find it difficult to display any thing but tinsel," said Cranfield. "It is two years since the golden crucifix, the silver candlestick, and the saintly jewelry, mounted on horseback and traveled into France."

"But the saints," said L'Isle, "knowing that the air of France would not agree with them, wisely staid behind."

As they were coming out of the cathedral, Mrs. Shortridge asked L'Isle the meaning of the words on a tablet near them: "*Oy se sacca animas.*"

"They give us notice," said L'Isle, "that to-day souls are released from Purgatory. But surely the notice is incomplete, not specifying whose souls they are. Their friends may go on spending money in masses for them after they are in Paradise."

"That would be throwing away their cash," said Mrs. Shortridge. "I have known good folks in London exercise their charity by releasing small debtors from prison. But their bounty bears little fruit, compared with that of the Papist, who, by opening his purse, rescues sinful souls from purgatory. But our works, as our faith, fall far short of theirs."

"And the Spaniards are foremost among the faithful," said L'Isle. "They are greedy of belief, even beyond what the church commands. Thus the mysterious origin of the Holy Virgin, which once convulsed the Spanish church, is here no longer a disputed point. It is the first article of their creed, as proved by their commonest term of salutation. On entering a Spaniard's house, you must begin with the words, '*Ave Maria Purissima*,' to which will be answered, '*Sin pecado concebida*.' Smithfield fires could not burn this dogma out of them, and they would become schismatics if the rest of Popedom were not treading on their heels. Yet to me this doctrine seems to sap the great Christian truth, that Christ is 'God made man,' for it pushes his human origin one generation further back. Did Scripture tell the name of the mother of the blessed Virgin, the next age might discover that she too was '*sin pecado concebida*.'"

"Since I have been in this land," said Mrs. Shortridge," I have seen scarcely a street, or even a house, which is without an image or picture of the blessed Virgin, and the images are often crowned with flowers."

"She is the goddess of these southern nations," L'Isle answered; "and styled the Mother of God.

Moreover, every pious Spaniard regards the Virgin in the light of his friend, his confidante, his mistress, whose whole attention is directed to himself, and who is perpetually watching over his happiness. With the name of Mary ever on his lips he follows his business, his pleasures, and his sins. It is in the name, too, of Mary," L'Isle continued, with an arch smile, "that the ladies write billetdoux, send their portraits, and entertain their gallants."

"Stop," said Mrs. Shortridge; "you are libeling our sex, and your love of satire makes you as bitter against Popery as old Moodie himself."

"It is, at least, no scandal to say that, under her patronage, small sins are easily absolved here, on the performance of certain duties of atonement."

"What are the duties of atonement?"

"Ave Marias, fasts, and alms. The alms go to the begging friars, or else to buy masses for the souls in purgatory."

Walking up the sloping street that leads to the castle, they found this Moorish edifice in a shattered condition, a few towers only standing whole amidst the ruins. From one of these, looking northward across the river which ran three hundred feet below them, they saw the strong fort of San Christoval towering above them, while they, in turn, overlooked the city, and beyond its walls, the plain to the south, not long since covered with vineyards, and olive groves, and the picturesque villas of the richer citizens of Badajoz—now its bare surface was furrowed with trenches, ridged with field works, and spotted with ruins. The devastating blast of war had left it the picture of desolation.

Lady Mabel, turning to ask L'Isle a question, saw him gazing gloomily down into the deep but dry fosse below them.

"What fixes your attention on that spot," she asked.

"Do you see where the earth shows, by its color differing from the adjacent soil, that it has been turned up not long since? Thousands of Britons, Portuguese, and French are buried there. They met but to contend, yet now lie peaceably together. I have more than one friend among them."

Mrs. Shortridge put her hand before her eyes, and Lady Mabel turned pale as she gazed earnestly below. "Come," she said, at length, "we have seen enough of bloody Badajoz. There are some feelings that may well kill the idle curiosity that led us hither."

Descending into the town, they walked into the great square, their party attracting much attention from several groups of citizens and of soldiers of the garrison. Captain Don Alonso Melendez stopped them here to point out various objects of interest, being evidently anxious to display himself as the patron and intimate of these distinguished strangers. He brought forward and presented to them two or three more of his brother officers whom he here met.

While he was thus engaged with others of the party, Lady Mabel found leisure to remark to Cranfield: "Short as is the distance from Elvas to Badajoz, I fancy I can perceive, without listening to the language around me, that I am among a new people."

"You may well be struck with the language," said Cranfield, "while listening to our patronizing friend here. But you must not take his discourse for a fair sample of Spanish style or facts."

"Of course not," said Lady Mabel. "Eloquence and intelligence like his are rare everywhere."

"I trust they are," said Cranfield, with a sneer. "But there is already an obvious difference observable here in the people, which becomes more marked as you proceed toward Castile. The Spaniard is taller and yet leaner than the Portuguese. He has a more expressive countenance, a striking sedateness of carriage, and a settled gravity of manner, especially when silent, which makes him seem wiser than he is. With much elegance of form, his meagre person shows that he is the denizen of a dry climate, which, every Spaniard will tell you, gives a peculiar compactness of structure to all its products: the wheat of Spain makes more bread, its beef and mutton are more nourishing, its wines have more body, and the men more enduring vigor than those of other countries. Certain it is that Spanish troops have often proved great marchers; yet of all nations they have the slenderest legs, and indeed they never use their own when they can substitute those of horse, mule, or *burro*."

"The heat of the climate discourages exercise on foot," said Lady Mabel.

"Or labor of any kind," said Cranfield. "The universal cloak sufficiently proves that they are not a working people."

"And imperfectly conceals that they are a ragged one," said she. "Had I old Moodie at my elbow, he would remind me that 'drowsiness shall clothe a man in rags.'"

Observing Cranfield gazing round the square with much interest, she said: "You must be quite familiar with this place."

"I shall never forget the occasion on which I saw it first," he answered. "I was one of two engineers attached on the assault to General Walker's brigade. While Picton was scaling the castle walls, and crowds of our brave fellows were dying in the breaches, we succeeded in forcing our way into the place over the bastion of San Vincente. Hard work we had of it, and the fight did not end there; for the enemy stubbornly disputed bastion after bastion on our flank, and our commander fell on the ramparts covered with so many wounds that his living seemed a miracle. The detachment I was with pushed forward into the town. 'The streets were empty, but brilliantly illuminated, and no person was to be seen; yet a low buzz and whisper was heard around; lattices were now and then opened, and from time to time shots were fired from underneath the doors by the Spaniards—"

"The French," you mean," said Lady Mabel.

"No; the Spaniards," persisted Cranfield. "And perhaps our talking friend there was one of them."

"Don Alonso is an Andalusian and a patriot," said Lady Mabel; and I will not have him so traduced."

"Be it so," replied Cranfield. "It is lucky for your patriot that he was not here. However, the troops, with bugles sounding, advanced up yonder street into this square, and we captured several mules going with ammunition to the trenches. But the square was empty and silent as the streets, and the houses as bright with lamps; a terrible enchantment seemed to be in operation; for we saw nothing but light, and heard nothing but the low whispers around us, while the tumult at the breach was like the crashing thunder. There, though the place was already carried on two sides, by Picton's column and ours, the murderous conflict still raged; we still heard the shots, and shouts, and infernal uproar, while hundreds and hundreds fell and died after fierce assault and desperate resistance were alike vain. We pushed on that way to take the garrison in reserve, but our weak battalion was repulsed by their reserve, and some time elapsed before the French found out that Badajoz had changed hands."

"But it was ours!" exclaimed Lady Mabel, "though too dearly bought.

"The carnage was dreadful," said Cranfield; "and when the full extent of that night's havoc became known to Lord Wellington, the firmness of his nature gave way for a moment, and the pride of conquest yielded to a passionate burst of grief at the loss of his gallant soldiers.—Then came the *væ victis*," continued

Cranfield. "We do not like to dwell on the wild and desperate wickedness which Badajoz witnessed on becoming ours. By the by, just where we stand stood the gallows."

"The gallows!" Lady Mabel exclaimed, stepping back from the polluted spot. "You could not hang the French. Did you hang the Spaniards who had fired on you."

"No; but Lord Wellington was compelled to hang some of his own heroes for making too free with what was theirs by right of conquest."

The young surgeon, who had been listening to Cranfield, now thought it time to lay some of his coloring on this picture of the siege, storming and sack of this unhappy city. He told some curious and thrilling incidents, but his profession getting the mastery of him, he soon got to the hospital, and, amidst ghastly wounds, horrid disfigurations, and dismembered limbs, began to bandage, slash, and saw, until Lady Mabel sickened at the tale. "Pray stop there; you make me shudder at your hospital scenes, which, in their endless variety of suffering are too like the Popish pictures of souls in Purgatory. I prefer going to dine at the posada, to stopping here to sup full of horrors."

They now returned to the posada and had their Spanish friends to dine with them—Lady Mabel seating Don Alonso beside her, and losing not a word of his grandiloquence. After the meal the party dispersed—most of them taking a siesta in order to get rid of two or three hot hours of the afternoon before they set out on their way back to Elvas. Their Spanish friends however, returned and persuaded them to postpone their ride until they had taken an evening promenade on the bridge, the favorite resort of the ladies of Badajoz and their cavaliers during the hot weather. Here they enjoy an extended prospect, and the cooling breezes that attend the current of a great river.

They found here many of the first people of Badajoz and many of the Spanish officers and their fair friends. Leaning against the parapet of the bridge, Lady Mabel forgot the idlers walking by, while she gazed on the scenery around, or watched the gliding stream below, and listened to L'Isle speaking of the Guadiana; of its mysterious disappearance near its source, its course betrayed only by the rich pastures overlying the subterranean streams, of its return to daylight in the lakes called its eyes: *Ojos de la Guadiana;* and following it to Portugal, to the *Salto de Lobo*, so called because a wolf might leap across the deep but narrow chasm between the overhanging rocks, he named the noted places on its banks, and quoted many a ballad of which it was the theme. Presently, finding themselves almost alone they followed their companions, to the bridge head, and joined the large company assembled in this outwork. The Spanish officers had provided music for their entertainment, and oranges and confectionary were handed about. Of the latter, the Spanish and Portuguese ladies, according to national habit, eat a great quantity. After a pause the musicians struck up a lively seguidilla, the gentlemen secured partners, Lady Mabel declining a dozen applications, and with difficulty ridding herself of Don Alonso, who could not understand how a lady who delighted so much in his conversation could refuse to dance with him.

The level space within this outwork was now crowded with couples, the Portuguese ladies entering fully into the spirit of the hour. Mrs. Shortridge and Lady Mabel stood aside, with L'Isle, and had the pleasure of witnessing a genuine *impromptu* Spanish ball in the open air. They were at once struck with the sudden gayety and activity of a people habitually so grave and inert. But as one dance followed another, the vivacity of the party increased. Many of the officers and some of their fair friends were from Andalusia, where music and the castinets are never heard in vain. Presently the tune was changed, and the excited dancers slid over into the fandango and volero, danced out to the life in so demonstrative, voluptuous and seducing a style, that Mrs. Shortridge declared such exhibitions abominable, and that they should be prohibited by law; while Lady Mabel shrinkingly looked on in bewildered astonishment. She had herself danced many a time, though not as often as she wished; but such dancing she had never dreamed of before.

At this moment the sun set, and the bells of the churches and convents across the water gave the signal for repeating the evening prayer to the Virgin. In an instant the gay crowd was arrested as if by magic. The music ceased; the dancers stood still; the women veiled their faces with their fans; the men took off their hats; and all breathed out or seemed to breathe a prayer to the protecting power who had brought them to the close of another day—all but the English officers, who, mingled with the devout dancers, stood looking like profane fools caught without a prayer for the occasion. After a short solemn pause, the men put on their hats, the women uncovered their faces, the music again struck up, and the throng glided off into gayety and revelry as before.

"I would not have lost this for any thing," Lady Mabel exclaimed; "It is so sudden and extraordinary a transition from the wild abandonment of revelry to absorbing devotion and back again to the revels. Without seeing it, I could not have imagined it. I have before witnessed and, at times, been impressed with this solemn call to the evening prayer, misdirected though it be. But here the effect is utterly ridiculous, to say the least."

"This may give you an insight into the Spanish character on more than one point," said L'Isle. "As to their love of dancing, and of the fandango in particular, it is said, though I do not vouch for it, that the Church of Rome, scandalized that a country so renowned for the purity of its faith, had not long ago proscribed so profane a dance, resolved to pronounce the solemn condemnation of it. A consistory assembled; the prosecution of the fandango was begun according to rule, and a sentence was about to be thundered against it. But there was a wise Spanish prelate present who knew his countrymen, and dreaded a schism, should they be driven to choose between the fandango and the faith. He stepped forward and objected to the criminal's being condemned without being heard.

The observation had weight with the assembly. He was allowed to produce before them a *majo* and a *maja* of Seville, who, to the sound of voluptuous music, displayed all the seductive graces of the dance. The severity of the judges was not proof against the exhibition. Their austere countenances began to relax; they rose from their seats; their legs and arms soon found their former suppleness; the consistory-hall was changed into a dancing-room, and the fandango acquitted.

Both ladies laughed heartily at this story, and L'Isle went on to say; "In spite of the exhibition before us, these people, in their serious hours, retain all the gravity and ceremonious stateliness in language and manner of their forefathers, in the time of Charles the Fifth and his glooming son, when the Spaniard was the admiration and dread of Europe.

"I have been told," said Lady Mabel," that you may, at this day, find many a Spaniard who might sit for the portrait of Alva himself."

"Yes," answered L'Isle, "It has been well said

that the Spaniard of the sixteenth century has vanished, but his mask remains."

Twilight was now failing them, and the party from Elvas hastened back to the posada. The horses had been brought out, and some of the ladies were already mounted, when Don Alonso Melendez came hastily up, having followed them to take a ceremonious leave. His parting words with his new friends, and especially his compliments to Lady Mabel, who did not allow herself to remain in his debt, delayed them some time. As they rode off, he waved his hat, and called out: "*Con todo el mondo guerra, y paz con Inglaterra!*"

"We taught them that proverb long ago," said Cranfield," by taking their galleons laden with plate from the New World."

"The Spaniard has a treasury of wisdom locked up in his proverbs," said L'Isle. What a pity it is he will not take some of it out to meet the current demands on him."

They soon again crossed the bridge, and entered the *tete du point*—but the dancers had vanished; their music was hushed; nor was its place supplied by the song of the morning. The chorus of "Guadiana—Guadiana," no longer arose from its banks. All was still, dark and desolate before them.

Meanwhile, Lord Strathern, though not given to over caution, was seized, as night drew on, with a sudden nervousness, at *Ma Belle's* taking a night ride across the borders of two such unsettled countries, infested with patriotic guerilleros, who sometimes mistook friends for foes. He entertained—in fact, cultivated—an unfavorable opinion of his neighbors, the Spanish garrison of Badajoz. He laid at their door every outrage perpetrated in the country around. —The party from Elvas would afford a rich booty in purses, watches, and jewelry; and he thought it quite possible that after some of their allies had entertained them in Badajóz, with ostentatious hospitality, others might waylay, rob and murder them before, or soon after they crossed the frontier. So, he hastily ordered Major Conway to send out a patrol of dragoons to meet them; and the Major sent off Lieut. Goring in a hurry on this service.

Now, Goring had passed the day chafing with indignation at hearing of the pleasant party, which he had not been asked to join; and his anger was not soothed by being despatched to meet it, at a late hour, when all the pleasure was over. Galloping on in this mood, with a dozen and more dragoons, behind him, he came to the Cayo, and after taking a look at the dark current, was about to cross, when he heard the sound of horses' feet, and the clattering of tongues drawing near on the other side. In the spirit of mischief, he followed the impulse of the moment. He ordered his men to form on the edge of the water, fronting the ford, to unbuckle their cloaks, and throw them over their helmets, and not to move or speak a word. The men took the joke instantly. The crescent moon, already distanced by the sun, was sinking below the horizon; the bank of the river threw its shade over them, and they stood below, a dark, undistinguishable mass.

Presently the party came straggling up, Dona Carlotta and her cavalier leading them, and feeling their way down to the water.

"This cannot be the ford," said he; the bank looks too steep on the other side."

"What is that black object across the water?" asked Cranfield, from behind. "Can the river have risen and the bank caved in?"

"It has too regular an outline for that," said L'Isle, who had now come up, and was trying to peer through the darkness. "Do you not hear the stamping of a horse across the water?"

"And a clattering sound?" said Cranfield, as a dragoon's sword struck against a neigboring stirrup.

"Lady Mabel," said L'Isle, eagerly, (she had pressed close up beside him,) "Pray ride back a little way, and take the ladies with you."

"I will, but what is the matter?"

"The road seems to be occupied. But go at once, and take them with you."

"I wish it were daylight!" said she, trying to laugh off her trepidation." "Adventures by night are more than I bargained for. Come ladies, follow me."

"Tom," said L'Isle to his groom," without turning his head, but gazing steadily at the dark object across the water, "Follow Lady Mabel."

"Better send the Doctor, sir," said Tom, doggedly. "He has not sword or pistol."

"Whoever they are," said L'Isle to Cranfield, "they have posted themselves badly for surprise or attack. Let us form here on the slope of the bank, and if they attempt to cross, fall on them as they come out of the water."

Officers and servants fell into line—a badly armed troop, with infantry swords, and some without pistols. Meanwhile, L'Isle sent Hatton's down to the edge of the river to challenge the opposite party.

"Now, Hatton's knowledge of foreign tongues was pretty much limited to those vituperative epithets which are first and oftenest heard in every language. He rode down to the edge of the water, and proceeded loudly to anathamatize his opponents in Portuguese, Spanish and French successively. Having exhausted his foreign vocabulary, he hurled at them some well shotted English phrases—but the heretics did not heed the damnatory clauses, even in plain English. Not a word could he get in reply from them. L'Isle literally and figuratively in the dark, grew impatient, and announced his intention to commence a pistol practice on them that would draw out some demonstration. He rode down to the water's edge, and was leveling a long pistol at the middle of the dark mass, when some epithet of Hatton's more stinging than any he had yet invented, proved too much for Gering's gravity. He began to laugh, and the contagion seized every dragoon of the party. The mask of hostility fell off, and they were instantly re cognized as friends, to the great relief of those on the other bank.

Provoked as they were at this practical joke, their position had been too ridiculous not to be amusing. After a hearty laugh, they hastened to bring back the ladies, who were not found close at hand, for Dona Carlotta and her friends had been posting back to Badajoz, and Lady Mabel had only succeeded in stopping them by the assurance that the road was doubtless beset, both before and behind them. When the two parties, now united, had taken their way back to Elvas, Lieutenant Goring found an opportunity of putting himself alongside of Lady Mabel.

She reproached him with the boyish trick he had just perpetrated. It might so easily have had fatal consequences. Goring, himself began to think it not so witty as he had fancied it.

"It was very provoking, though," said he, "to be left out of your pleasant party. I hope you will consider that, Lady Mabel, and forgive me for the little alarm I have given you."

"Not to-night," said she. "My nerves are quite too much shaken. But if I sleep well, and feel like myself again, I may possibly forgive you to-morrow.'

CHAPTER XVI.

(*Rosalind reading a paper.*)

From the east to western Ind,
No jewel is like Rosalind,
Her worth being mounted on the wind,
Through all the world bears Rosalind,
All the pictures fairest lined,
Are but black to Rosalind,
Let no face be kept in mind,
But the face of Rosalind.

Touchstone.—I'll rhyme you so, eight years together; dinners and suppers, and sleeping hours excepted; it is the right butter-woman's rank to market. AS YOU LIKE IT.

WHENEVER L'Isle took holiday from his military duties, he was pretty sure to take it out of his regiment, the next day. On parade, next morning, he inspected the ranks, bent on detecting some defect in bearing or equipment, and peered into the faces of the men, as if hunting out the culprits in the latest breach of discipline. Men and officers looked for a three hours' drill, to improve their wind, and put them in condition. But, to their great comfort, he soon let them off, and hastened back to his quarters. Arrived there, he called to his man for his portfolio, and at once sat down to write as if he had a world of correspondence before him. But it was plain to this man, who had occasion to come often into the room, that his master did not get through his work with his usual facility. He found him, not so often writing, as leaning on the table in laborious cogitation, or biting the feather end of his quill, or rapping his forehead with his knuckles, to stimulate the action of the organs within, or else striding up and down the room, in a brown study, over sundry half-written and discarded sheets of paper, scattered on the floor. L'Isle's servant wished to speak to him, but was too wise to disturb him in the midst of those throes of mental labor. But, when pausing suddenly in his walk, he pressed his forefinger on his temple, and exclaimed, "I had it last night, and now I have lost it!" his confidential man thought it time to speak. "What is it, sir, shall I look for it?"

L'Isle stared at him, as if just roused from a reverie, and bursting into a hearty laugh, bid him go down stairs until he called for him.

Down stairs he went, and told his two companions that their master was at work on the toughest despatch or report, or something of that sort, he had ever had to make in his life, adding, "I would not be surprised if something came of it."

"I have not a doubt," answered Tom, the groom, in a confident tone, "that the colonel has found out some new way to jockey the French, and is about to lay it before Sir Rowland Hill, or, perhaps my Lord Wellington himself."

Being men of leisure, they were still busy discussing their master's affairs, and had begun to wonder if he had forgotten that it was time to go to dinner, when L'Isle called for his man; but it was only to bid him send the groom up to him.

With an obedient start, Tom hastened up stairs. In a few minutes, he came down with an exceedingly neatly folded despatch in his hand. He seemed to have gained in that short interval no little accession of importance. He had quite sunk the groom, and strode into the room with the air of an ambassador.

"Now, my lads, without even stopping to wet my whistle," said he, "I will but sharpen my spurs, saddle my horse, and then—"

"What then?" asked his comrades.

"I will ride off on my important mission."

"Were you right?" asked L'Isle's gentleman. "Is that for Sir Rowland Hill?"

"Sir Rowland," answered Tom, carelessly, "is not the most considerable personage with whom master may correspond. And as the army post goes every day to *Coria*, he would hardly send me thither."

"Can it be for the commander-in-chief?" suggested the footman. "That is farther off still."

"You are but half-right," said Tom, contemptuously; "for it is not so far," and, holding up the letter, he pretended to read the direction: "'To his excellency, Lieutenant-General Sir Mabel Stewart, commander-in-chief of his majesty's forces in these parts.' If you had not been blockheads, you might have known it, from the extraordinary neatness of the rose-colored envelope, with its figured green border."

"I wonder where he got it?" said the footman.

"He brought them out with him from home," said Tom, as if he were in all his master's secrets, "for his love-letters to the Portuguese ladies—but never met with any worth writing love-letters to. And, now, my lads, hinder me no longer, I must ride and run till this be delivered to my lady, and your mistress, that is to be." He was soon in the saddle, and when there, rode as if carrying the news, that a French division, having surprised the dreamy Spaniards in Badajoz, was already fording the Cayo, without meeting even Goring's handful of dragoons, to check its advance.

L'Isle now hastened to the regimental mess, and, after dining, loitered there longer than usual, with a convivial set, until it was late enough to visit Lady Mabel.

He found her alone, in her drawing-room; her father being still at table, with some companions, the murmur of whose voices and laughter now and then reached L'Isle's ears.

"Lieutenant Goring, who is down stairs," said Lady Mabel, "has been amusing us at dinner with his version of our adventure at the ford of the Cayo; and a very good story he makes of it, giving some rich samples of Captain Hatton's polyglot eloquence. He, alone, seems not to have been in the dark; and saw all, and more than all, that occurred—nor does he forget you in the picture. But, papa cannot see the wit of it at all."

"*Burlas de manos, burlas de villanos.* There seldom is wit in practical jokes," said L'Isle; "but there was certainly more wit than wisdom in this."

"By-the-bye," said Lady Mabel, "our excursion yesterday has procured me a new correspondent. You will be astonished to hear who he is, and at the style in which he writes."

"Indeed!" said L'Isle, with heightening color. I hope he writes on an agreeable topic, and in a suitable style?"

"You shall judge for yourself," said Lady Mabel. "But the grandiloquence of the epistle, worthy of Captain Don Alonzo Melendez himself, calls not for reading, but recitation. Do you sit here as critic, while I take my stand in the middle of the room, and give it utterance with all the elocution and pathos I can muster. You must know that this epistle I hold in my hand, is addressed to me by no less a personage than the river-god of the Guadiana, who, contrary to all my notions of mythology, proves to be a gentleman, and not a lady." And, in a slightly mock-heroic tone, she began to recite it:

Maiden, the sunshine of thine eye,
   Flashing my joyous waves along,
The magic of thy soul-lit smile,
   Have waked my murmuring voice to song.

Winding through Hispania's mountains,
   Watering her sunburnt plains,
I, from earliest time, have gladdened
   Dwellers on these wide domains.

I have watched succeeding races,
   Peopling my fertile strand,

Marked each varying lovely model,
Moulded by Nature's plastic hand.

Striving still to reach perfection,
Ruthless, she broke each beauteous mould;
Some blemish still deformed her creature,
Some alloy still defiled her gold.

The Iberian girl has often bathed,
Her limbs in my delighted flood,
And no Acteon came to startle
This very Dian of the wood.

The stately Roman maid has loitered,
Pensive, upon my flowering shore,
Shedding some pearly drops to think,
Italia she may see no more.

While gazing on my placid face,
She meditates her distant home;
And rears, as upon Tiber's banks,
The towers of imperial Rome.

The blue-eyed daughter of the Goth,
Fresh from her northern forest-home,
In rude nobility of race,
Foreshadowed her who now has come.

The loveliest offspring of the Moor
Beside my moon-lit current sat;
And, sighing, sung her hopeless love,
In strains, that I remember yet.

The Christian knight, in captive chains,
The conqueror of her heart has proved;
His own, in far Castilian bower,
He bears her blandishments unmoved.

Thus Nature tried her 'prentice hand,
Become, at last, an artist true;
In inspiration's happiest mood,
She tried again, and moulded you.

Maiden, from my crystal surface,

May thy image never fade;
Longing, longing, to embrace thee,
I, alas! embrace a shade.

Fainter glows each beauteous image,
Thy beauty vanishing before;
I will clasp thy lovely shadow,
Fate will grant to me no more.

If the verses were not very good, L'Isle was ready to acknowledge it; but, in fact, he had not the fear of criticism before his eyes; for when did lady ever criticise verses made in her praise? But he had reckoned without his host. Though Lady Mabel recited them exceedingly well, in a way that showed that she must have read them over many times, and dwelt upon them, there was an under-current of ridicule running through her tones and action—for she had personified the river-god—and when she was done, she criticised them with merciless irony.

"This is no timid rhymster," she exclaimed, "but a true poet of the Spanish school: No figure is too bold for him. A mere versifier would have likened a lady's eyes to earthly diamonds or heavenly stars; the blessed sun itself is not too bright for our poet's purpose.—My timid fancy dared not follow his soaring wing; to me at the first glance, the 'stately Roman maid' was building her mimic Rome on the banks of the Guadiana with solid stone and tough cement, and I saddened at the sight of her labors. To come down to the mechanism of the verse," she continued, "besides a false rhyme or two, the measure halts a little.

—But we must not forget that the river-god is taking a poetical stroll in the shackles of a foreign tongue. In this case we have good assurance that the poet has never been out of his own country, and to the *eye* of a foreigner 'flood' and 'wood' and 'home' and 'come' are perfect rhymes. We must deal gently with the poet while 'trying his 'prentice hand,' hoping better things when he shall 'become an artist true;' and when we remember that to the national taste sublimity is represented by bombast, artifice takes the place of nature, and sense is sacrificed to sound, the love of the *ore rotundo* demanding mouth-filling words at any price, we cannot fail to discover the genuine Spanish beauties of the piece. I only wonder that in his chronological picture of the races he should omit to display the Phœnician, Jewish and Gipsy maidens to our admiring eyes."

"Heyday!" exclaimed Colonel Bradshawe, who now came in with Major Warren, while she was still standing in the middle of the floor, with the paper raised in her hand, "Is this a rehearsal? Are we to have private theatricals, with Lady Mabel for first and sole actress? With songs interspersed for her as *prima donna?* Pray let me come in as one of the *dramatis personæ.*"

"It is no play!" said Lady Mabel, much confused. I have just been throwing away my powers of elocution in an attempt to make Colonel L'Isle perceive the beauties of a piece of model poetry, moulded in the purest Spanish taste. I thought him gifted with some poetic feeling, but he shows not the slightest sense of its peculiar merits."

L'Isle, though much out of countenance, had kept his seat through the recitation, but now got up looking little pleased with it.

"Try me," said Major Warren. "You may be more successful in finding a critic."

"I never suspected you of any critical acumen," said Lady Mabel; "and so could not be disappointed."

"Do not overlook me," said Bradshawe. "Poetry is the expression of natural feeling, in a state of exaltation. Now, I am always in an exalted state of feeling in your company, and may be just now a very capable judge."

"No; one failure is enough for me," said Lady Mabel. "I am not in the humor to repeat it."

"Let me read it then," said Bradshawe, offering to take the paper from her hand.

Lady Mabel declined, and L'Isle tried to divert his attention. But Bradshawe's curiosity was strongly excited, and he made more than one playful attempt to get possession of the verses. Upon this, Lady Mabel went to the table near which L'Isle was standing, and pretended to hide them between the pages of one of the books there. L'Isle, anxious that they should be kept from every eye but hers, watched her closely. Could he believe his eyes? As she stooped over the table, she actually, unobserved, as she thought, slipped the verses into her bosom. Bradshawe pertinaciously began to search the volumes;

on which, Lady Mabel took up the largest of them, and with a grave face carried it out of the room, leaving L'Isle so well satisfied with her care for his epistle, that, by the time she came back, he was ready to bear, without flinching, any severity of criticism.

The rest of the company below being gone, Lord Strathern now entered the room. "Ah, L'Isle, I am glad to find you here; I was just about to send after you. I have this moment received a dispatch from Sir Rowland. He needs you for a special service, and this letter contains his instructions."

"Is it in verse, Papa?" asked Lady Mabel, coming close up beside her father.

"In verse, child? What are you dreaming of? Sir Rowland is a sane man, and never writes verses?"

"I thought it might be a growing custom to correspond in verse. The last letter I received was in regular stanzas."

"Who from?" asked Lord Strathern.

"A Spaniard—a genuine Spaniard, of the purest water," said Lady Mabel. "And, strange to tell, I never saw him but once in my life."

"The impudent rascal!" exclaimed his lordship. "I will have him horsewhipped by way of answer, a stripe for every line."

"Nay," said Lady Mabel, "a stripe for every bad line will be cutting criticism enough."

"Who is this fellow? Is it the Don Alonso Melendez you were telling me of?"

"Never mind his name, Papa. I am afraid you

might have him flayed alive, while the poor fellow deserves nothing but laughter for his doggerel." And while this doggerel was secretly pressed by her bosom, she stole a look at L'Isle, and was surprised to see how little galled he seemed to be by her ridicule.

"What is the burden of Sir Rowland's verses?" she asked, addressing him.

"Very true!" exclaimed L'Isle; "I had forgotten to read it." And breaking the seal, he ran his eye hastily over the letter. "I must leave Elvas at once, and be away some days," he said, with a look of dissatisfaction.

"Sir Rowland is very fond of sending you on his errands," remarked Lord Strathern. "And, hitherto you seemed to like the extra work he gave you."

"I would be gladly excused from it just now," answered L'Isle, and in spite of himself, his eye wandered toward Lady Mabel. Lord Strathern did not observe this, but said, jestingly: "I believe you have contrived to convince Sir Rowland that none of us can do any thing so well as you can," but there was a little tone of pique in the way this was said.

"I have made no attempt to do so," L'Isle answered. "But he has given me some thing to do now, and I must set about it at once." Taking leave of Lady Mabel, he held a short private conference with his lordship, and, when he went out to mount his horse, found Colonel Bradshawe already in the saddle, waiting for him. This annoyed him, for he instinctively knew Bradshawe's object, and looked to be ingeniously cross-questioned as to the verses which Lady Mabel had recited, and then criticised so unsparingly. Unwilling to let Bradshawe stretch him on the rack for his amusement, L'Isle assumed the offensive, and at once broached another matter which he had much at heart.

"I wonder when we will leave Elvas," he exclaimed, abruptly. "If we stay here much longer, we will be at war with the people around us. I never knew my lord so negligent of discipline. It evidently grows upon him."

"The old gentleman," said Bradshawe, carelessly, "certainly holds the reins with a slack hand."

"He is content with preserving order in Elvas," said L'Isle; "but turns a deaf ear to almost every complaint the peasantry make against our people."

"Many of them are lies," said Bradshawe, coolly.

"And many of them are too well founded," answered L'Isle. "You are the senior officer in the brigade, and a man of no little tact. Could you not stir my lord up to looking more closely into this matter."

"I will think of it," said Bradshawe, anxious to open a more interesting subject.

"Pray think of it speedily," said L'Isle. "There is no time to be lost, and I must lose no time now. The sun has set, and I must be in Olivenca by midnight."

"What will you do there?" asked Bradshawe.

"Bait my horses on my way into Andalusia," answered L'Isle, riding off at full gallop, leaving Bradshawe much provoked at his slipping out of his hands before he could put him to the question.

CHAPTER XVII.

Who cannot be crushed with a plot?

ALL IS WELL THAT ENDS WELL.

SIR ROWLAND HILL had sent L'Isle off to the southward, to ascertain the strength and condition of the reserve of Spanish troops moving up from Andalusia. One might think that these things could be better learned from the official reports of the *Conde d' Abispal* and the officers under him. But from the Prince of Parma's day to this, Spanish officers in reporting the number and condition of their commands, have made it a rule to state what they ought to be, not what they are, leaving all deficiencies to be found out on the day of battle. Sir Rowland, knowing this, now made use of L'Isle, whose knowledge of the Spanish language and character, and his acquaintance with many officers of rank, enabled him to ascertain the truth without betraying the object of his mission, or giving offence to these proud and jealous allies. Ten days had gone by when he again rode into Elvas, and in spite of the secrecy aimed at in military councils, many symptoms indicated that the campaign was about to open.

It was high time for the brigade to leave this part of the country. The soldiers were disgusted with the sluggish people around them, keen and active only in their efforts to make money out of their protectors. The Portuguese were exasperated at the insolence of their allies, their frequent depredations and occasional acts of violence, many of which went unpunished; for the English officers, always professing the utmost readiness to punish the offences of their men, were singularly scrupulous and exacting as to the conclusiveness of the proofs of guilt.

Lord Strathern's lax discipline may have aggravated, but had not caused the evil, which was felt throughout Portugal. The Regency, while proving itself unable to govern the country, or reform a single abuse, had shown its ability to harass their allies and embarrass the general charged with the conduct of the war. "A narrow jealousy had long ruled their conduct, and the spirit of captious discontent had now reached the inferior magistracy, who endeavored to excite the people against the military generally. Complaints came in from all quarters, of outrages on the part of the troops, some too true, but many of them false or frivolous; and when Wellington ordered courts-martial for the trial of the accused, the magistrates refused to attend as witnesses, because Portuguese custom rendered such attendance degrading, and by Portuguese law a magistrate's written testimony was efficient in courts-martial. Wellington in vain assured them that English law would not suffer him to punish men on such testimony; in vain he pointed out the mischief which must infallibly overwhelm the country, if the soldiers discovered that they might thus do evil with impunity. He offered to send, in each case, lists of Portuguese witnesses required, that they might be summoned by the native authorities; but nothing could overcome the obstinacy of the magistrates; they answered that his method was insolent; and with sullen malignity continued to accumulate charges against the troops, to refuse attendance in the courts, and to call the soldiers, their own as well as the British, 'licensed spoliators of the community.'"

"For a time the generous nature of the poor people resisted all these combined causes of discontent, * * * * * yet by degrees the affection for the British cooled, and Wellington expressed his fears that a civil war would commence between the Portuguese people on the one hand, and the troops of both nations on the other. Wherefore his activity to draw all military strength to a head, and make such an irruption into Spain, as would establish a new base of operations beyond the power of such fatal dissensions."

Throughout the war this great captain's hardest tasks had been to conciliate the jealous, vain-glorious Spaniard, to stimulate the laggard suspicious Portuguese, to enlighten the invincible ignorance of Regency and *Juntas*, in order to draw out and combine the resources of both countries with the scanty means afforded him by his own blundering government. He was required to do great things with small means, without offending one tittle against the laws, customs and prejudices of three dissimilar nations. He might toil, fret and fume, wearing himself to the bone, but could never get rid of this task of making ropes out of sea-sand. So much as to the state of the country. Let us return to our story.

L'Isle reached Elvas early in the day, and resolved to reward himself for his labors, by paying a visit to Lady Mabel; then after a conference with Lord Strathern, to sit down and write his report to Sir Rowland, on the state of the Andalusian reserve. He knew that Sir Rowland looked for a precise and pithy statement, and L'Isle mean this to be a model for all such communications. But fate may mar the wisest plan.

He found Lady Mabel and Mrs. Shortridge together, and soon perceived that the latter lady's head was full of an entertainment she was about to give.

"The commissary has warned me," she said "that from henceforth he will be ever on the move—that he must break up his household here, and send off his heavy baggage to Lisbon. In this he very politely includes his wife."

"I am truly sorry to hear it," said L'Isle, "but confess that first among a soldier's *impedimenta* must be reckoned his wife."

"I did not look for so blunt an assent to the commissary's opinion from you," said Mrs. Shortridge, somewhat nettled; "however, I am to go, and as many of the good folks of Elvas have been as polite to me as they know how, I wish to show my sense of it in parting. I have invited all my Portuguese friends, with a good sprinkling of red coats to meet them. I have put myself to infinite trouble and no little expense, meaning to have a grand evening, combining *turtulia*, concert and ball. I would show these people something of society and life, then vanish from Elvas in a blaze of glory. Now, as the rarest treat that I could offer, I had promised my guests that they should hear Lady Mabel in all her glorious richness of voice; and now she is seized with a sudden fit of modesty, and protests against being exhibited before a motly crowd like an opera singer."

Lady Mabel's reluctance was not feigned; and when Mrs. Shortridge called on L'Isle for assistance in overcoming it, he felt some scruples at lending his aid. But her companion and friend was about to leave her; it was painful to refuse her a favor on which she plainly laid great stress. Friendship and flattery at length prevailed, and Lady Mabel promised to do her utmost to charm the ears of the natives, on condition that L'Isle should be at hand as her interpreter, and say to them for her a dozen polite and half as many witty things for every song she sang, in order that these foreigners might not mistake her for a mere singer.

L'Isle pledged himself to be at her beck throughout the evening, and to furnish wit and politeness without stint. This obstacle overcome, Mrs. Shortridge was delighted, and talked gaily of her arrangements and anticipations for the appointed night. L'Isle entering into her humor, busied himself in drawing out a programme for Lady Mabel's performance, and after turning over all the music at hand, made a list of songs long enough to have cracked her voice forever. It was late when he suddenly remembered that he had occasion to see Lord Strathern, and he tore himself away to seek him.

L'Isle found his lordship in the business room of his quarters, and quite at leisure, although seated by a table on which lay sundry papers in no business like order. Most of them were despatches, returns and other military documents. But among them was a goodly pile of communications from the *Juiz de fora* of more than one neighboring *comarca*, written in eloquent but denunciatory Portuguese, being, in truth, philippics aimed at sundry individuals or parties, belonging to his command.

The old soldier had not treated them with absolute neglect. After having the first two or three duly translated to him, and making himself familiar with the tenor of this kind of document, he had prepared a concise form of reply: regretting that any of his Majesty's soldiers should be guilty of any act of violence, depredation or impropriety in the country of their friends and allies, and proposing that the accusers should come forward and prove the charges before a court-martial, according to British laws. A copy of this stereotyped answer, turned into good Portuguese, was always at hand to be dispatched in reply to each new complaint, as soon as it reached headquarters. Thus the correspondence cost little trouble there, for Lord Strathern had an easy-going philosophy, which, like an ambling pad, carried him smoothly over the rough and intricate path of diplomacy, policy, and military exigencies. He knew it was impossible to give perfect satisfaction to the Portuguese, and unlike his commander, he eschewed all such attempts to make ropes out of sea-sand.

L'Isle's entrance roused Lord Strathern from a pleasant reverie over his cigar.

"Why, L'Isle! are you back again? You certainly have the gift of appearing just when you are wanted. Is not that the case with a character called Mephistophiles?"

"Yes, my lord; but he is a devil," said L'Isle, drily.

"I beg your pardon. I did not mean to make an unsavory comparison. But here is another billet-doux from Sir Rowland awaiting you."

L'Isle, taking the dispatch handed to him, broke the seal and read it deliberately, then said: "Does Sir Rowland think I keep an extra stud of horses, to do the riding that properly belongs to his own staff?"

"Why, where is he sending you now?"

"To Badajoz, on an errand similar to that on which I went into Andalusia."

"To Badajoz? That is no distance at all; at least nothing to grumble at," said Lord Strathern. "You are growing lazy, L'Isle. Why Mabel would ride that far after a rare flower. Just think you are chasing a fox, who takes the high road, and never doubles once between this and Badajoz."

"That would be a fox of a new breed," suggested L'Isle.

"I confess," said his lordship, "I never started one of the kind. But Sir Rowland's staff have their hands full just now. To lighten their labors, I have had to furnish more than one officer for special duties. You surely would not have Sir Rowland send an aid all the way from *Coria*, merely to see if those Spanish fellows in Badajoz are in a state to march without disbanding, or without plundering the country as they move through it!"

"Talking of marauding, my lord," said L'Isle; "I wish the the taste for that diversion was confined to our Spanish friends. It is becoming every day more necessary to check the excesses of our own people. We cannot send out a party into the country around, but on their return they are dogged at the heels by complaints and accusations. When we march hence, we shall leave a villainous name behind us."

"Oh, we will never come back here again," said Lord Strathern, carelessly. "Moreover, two-thirds of these complaints are groundless, and the rest grossly exaggerated."

"The sacking of the farmer's house on the border needed no exaggeration," said L'Isle.

"I tell you that was done by the Spaniards,'" exclaimed Lord Strathern.

"Yet worse cases than that have occurred, and gone unpunished," urged L'Isle.

"Because they never could prove the charge, and

point out the culprits," replied his lordship. "The country is full of *rateros.* They commit the crimes and our fellows bear the blame."

"That is often true; but I have met with one little case in which the offenders can be pointed out."

"Well, let me hear it," said Lord Strathern, leaning back in his chair, as if compelled to listen, but anxious to be rid of the subject.

"I stopped for a while on my way back," said L'Isle, "at a little venda on this side of *Juramenha.* The people of the house were shy and sullen. I had to ask many questions before I could induce them to speak freely, but at length out came a charge against some of our people. Three nights ago five of our men had come to the house, and, calling for wine, sat down to drink. They soon became riotous, and their conduct so insulting to the man's wife and daughters, that they ran away to hide themselves. When he required them to pay the reckoning and quit the house, they promised most liberal payment, and seizing, bound him to a post in his own stable, where they gave him fifty lashes with a leathern strap, valuing the stripes at a *vintem* apiece."

"The witty rascals," said Lord Strathern; "I would like to repay them in their own coin."

"Moreover," continued L'Isle, "on the man's son making some resistance to their treatment of his father, they bound the boy, too, and gave him a dozen *vintems'* worth of the strap for pocket money."

"The liberal rascals!" said Lord Strathern; "they

deserve a handsome profit on their outlay. But how do you know, L'Isle, that this story is true?"

"There is no mistake about the flogging," exclaimed L'Isle. "They used the buckle end of the strap, and I myself saw the marks, some not yet scarred over."

"That silent witness may prove a good deal; I cannot call it tongueless," said his lordship, "for I suppose the buckle had a tongue."

"I can vouch for that by the mark it left behind," said L'Isle. "Both father and son swore that they would know the fellows among a thousand. But the man dare not come to Elvas to search them out, as the scamps promised faithfully to make sausage meat of him should he venture near the town."

"If the cowardly rascal will not come forward and lodge a complaint," said Lord Strathern, "what the devil can we do?"

"We can bring him here and protect him," said L'Isle, "while he hunts out the culprits. If necessary, I will take him before my regiment, and let him look every man in the face, to see if he can identify the offenders in the ranks; and so with other regiments."

"What! muster the whole brigade for such a poltroon to inspect them!" exclaimed Lord Strathern. "What are you dreaming of, L'Isle? It would be offering a bounty for accusations against the men. Half these rascals would swear away a man's life for a *crusado*."

"Perhaps so, my lord. But by cross-questions and

examining them apart, the truth may be wrung from even lying witnesses."

"Impossible, with these people; the truth is not in them. Come, L'Isle, no one knows better than you, who are so much in Sir Rowland's councils, that we are on the point of moving from this part of the country. The little disorders that have occurred here, can be followed by no ill consequences."

"We carry the worse consequences with us," said L'Isle, pertinaciously. "Little disorders, my lord! The peasantry round Elvas do not talk of them so. They say that their property is plundered, their women insulted, and themselves at constant risk in life and limb."

"What! do the rascals talk of us in that way? even while we are protecting them," exclaimed Lord Strathern, springing from his chair. "We have spent more money among them than their beggarly country is worth in fee simple; and they are no more thankful than if we had occupied it as enemies. I wish they had among them again, for a few weeks, that one-handed *Loison* with his cut-throat bands, or pious *Junot*, who loved church plate so well."

"It is bad enough to be robbed by their enemies, they say," suggested L'Isle, "but they did not expect it from their friends."

"Pooh," said Lord Strathern, "the Portuguese, of all people, ought to know what real military license is. The French taught them that. As for our fellows, what if they do at times drink a little more wine than they pay for, or even take a lamb or kid from the flocks they protect, or kiss a wench before she has consented; is that any thing to make a hubbub about? The lads should be paid for drinking their muddy *vinho verde*, and as for the girls, all the trouble comes of their ignorance of our tongue, so that they have to be talked to by signs."

"You must be jesting, my lord. To overlook small offences is to license greater."

"I license none; I punish whatever is clearly proved, but will not play grand Inquisitor, and hunt out every little peccadillo. With your notions, L'Isle, you would bring the men to confession every morning and make the service worse than purgatory. Must I answer for it if a girl squeaks out, half in jest, and half in earnest?"

L'Isle was provoked to see that Lord Strathern was aughing at him, and said, earnestly, "You cannot have forgotten, my lord, the state of the army at the end of the campaign. Little has yet been done to bring this brigade up to the mark, and little will be achieved by it in the coming campaign in its present state. Now is the time to check the licentious spirit by making some severe examples."

"I will do no such thing," said Lord Strathern, coolly. The occasion does not call for it. We will be in the field shortly, and want all the bayonets we can muster. The brigade is too weak to spare men from the ranks to put into irons."

"I did not suppose," said L'Isle, "that the warning

my Lord Wellington gave us not long since, would be so soon forgotten.

L'Isle alluded to the circular letter Wellington had addressed to his subordinates, at the end of the campaign, in which he had politely dubbed half of his officers idlers, whose habitual neglect of duty suffered their commands to run into ruffianism. Perhaps their commander was suffering under a fit of indigestion when he wrote it. It certainly caused a general heart-burning among his officers. Lord Strathern, among others, had found it hard to digest, and now angrily denounced it unjust.

"Well, my lord," said L'Isle, with more zeal than discretion, "by the end of the campaign our men may be in a state to be improved by a touch of discipline from *Julian Sanchez* or *Carlos d'Espana*, unless they reject them as too much like banditti!"

"And I am captain of the banditti!" exclaimed lord Strathern, in a sudden rage. "As you do not *yet* command the brigade, let me beg you, sir, to go and look after your own people, and keep them up to the mark, lest they become banditti!"

"I always obey orders, my lord," said L'Isle, with suddenly assumed composure; "I will go and look after my own regiment, and let the rest of the brigade march"——

"Where, sir?" thundered Lord Strathern.

"Their own road," L'Isle answered, and bowed himself out of the room. He walked sedately through the long corridor that led to the entrance of this monastic house, then, yielding to some violent impulse, sprang into his saddle, and plunging his spurs into his horse's flanks, dashed out of the court and through the olive grounds at a killing pace. His astonished groom stared at him for a moment, then followed with emulous speed. As L'Isle turned suddenly into the high road, a voice called out: "Don't ride me down; I'm no Frenchman!" and he saw Colonel Bradshawe quickly but coolly press his ambling cob close to the hedge, to avoid his charge.

"You seem to be in a hurry, L'Isle. Hallo! here is another!" said the colonel, giving his horse another dexterous turn, to shun the onset of the groom. "What news has come? Or have you joined the dragoons? Or are you merely running a race with your man here?"

"Neither, sir," said L'Isle, who had pulled up and turned to speak to his comrade. His flashing eye and excited manner, his thoroughbred steed, chafing on the bit and pawing the ground, were in striking contrast with the unruffled Bradshawe on his sleek cob, whose temper was as smooth as his coat.

"The fact is," said L'Isle, in what was meant for an explanatory tone, "I have just had a serious conversation with Lord Strathern—"

"Which grew quite animated before it came to an end," interjected Bradshawe, coolly.

"In which I took the liberty of expressing my opinion," continued L'Isle—

"Rather strongly on the subject of discipline, military license, and the articles of war," interjected Bradshawe again.

"You are happy in your surmises, sir," said L'Isle, stiffly; for Bradshawe's imperturbable manner chafed him much in his present mood.

"Surmises! my dear fellow. Do I not know your opinions and my lord's? You believe the rules and regulations were made to be enforced *ad literam*, and he thinks they are to be hung up *in terrorem*. My lord," added Bradshawe, in a calm, judicial tone, is the more mistaken of the two."

"Since you so far agree with me," said L'Isle, "would it not be well for you to remind his lordship that it is time to enforce some of the rules and regulations for the government of his Majesty's troops, if he would have his brigade consist of soldiers, and not of robbers."

"It is very desirable to keep up the distinction between the two professions," said Bradshawe. "One has a strong tendency to slide into the other. Pray, tell me what arguments you have been using with my lord."

L'Isle, with an effort at calmness, repeated the substance of the late conversation, much to Bradshawe's amusement; for in him a genuine love of mischief rivaled his epicurean tastes.

"On one point, my lord had the advantage of you," said Bradshawe. "It is his privilege to bid you look after your regiment; not yours to bid him look after his brigade."

"True," said L'Isle, bitterly. "But as you, though my senior, are not my commander, I trust there is no insubordination in my telling you that the brigade is left to look after itself, and is going to the devil as fast as it can."

"As individuals," said Bradshawe, "that is the probable destination of most of us."

"We will have to get Julian Sanchez, or the Empecinado, or some other guerilla chief, to undertake its reformation," continued L'Isle, in great heat. "I forgot to suggest to my lord, that before we march away, we ought to levy a contribution, as a bounty for the blessings we bestow on the neighborhood in leaving it."

"A capital idea," said Bradshawe, "but by no means original. The French always do so when they change their cantonments; that is, if there be any thing left in the country around. If our hands were not tied, we might yet learn some clever arts from Monsieur. Junot's system was to drive up all the farm cattle of the neighborhood just before he marched off; then allow them to be redeemed at a low cash price. He found it a capital way to extract the last hidden crusado."

"You have mastered the enemy's system thoroughly," said L'Isle, with a sneer. "But as our hands are tied, we cannot imitate them. Perhaps it would better become your position in the brigade, for you to try and rouse his lordship to the necessity of checking the license that is growing daily."

"I would gladly do so," said Bradshawe; but being no Oxford logician, have not your irresistible power of convincing him. You have handled the matter so fully and ably, that I need only repeat faithfully every word you have said. You may depend upon me for that." And, turning his horse, he rode gently off toward headquarters, while L'Isle galloped up the hill to Elvas.

Bradshawe found Lord Strathern in as great a rage as the comrade he had just parted with; so he amused himself with drawing out from his lordship a recital of their late conversation, which he repaid with a sketch of L'Isle's roadside conference with himself. The old soldier was only the more provoked on finding that, freely as L'Isle had spoken, he could hardly charge him with insubordination, or twist his hot arguments into a personal insult. Soothing and chafing him by turns, Bradshawe did not permit the subject to drop until they were interrupted by a courier with despatches.

"What is all this! Post upon post! There must be some thing in the wind!" said my lord, as he broke the seal, which was Sir Rowland Hill's.

"Our pleasant winter here is over, said Bradshawe, with a sigh. "We will be moving shortly, and then hot marches and cold meals, sour wine and bad quarters, or no quarters at all, will be the order of the day. I trust we shall move through a more plentiful country than we did last year."

"It has not quite come to that yet," said Lord

Strathern. Here is an order for me to meet Sir Rowland at Alcantara, at ten, the day after to-morrow. I am to take you and Conway with me, for he has special instructions for you both. And here is an order for that modest fellow L'Isle to attend and report the state of the Andalusian reserve. I expect Conway to dinner. You had better stay and meet him."

In due time Major Conway appeared, and dinner was announced. Mrs. Shortridge had gone home, so that only two guests sat down with Lady Mabel and her father. No man made himself more agreeable in his own house and at his own table than Lord Strathern usually did, for hospitality was with him an article of religion. But to-day my lord was not in a religious frame of mind. He was moody and silent, or growled at his servants, and gave short answers to his guests; so that Major Conway, after sundry attempts to engage him in conversation, gave it up, and joined Bradshawe in his efforts to entertain Lady Mabel. At length the cloth was removed, the servants withdrew, and the gentlemen sat over their wine; yet Lady Mabel, not trained to a nice observance of little conventionalities, lingered there, watching her father's moody brow.

"So L'Isle has got back," said Major Conway.

"The impudent coxcomb!" exclaimed Lord Strathern.

Conway started. But Lady Mabel started as if a snake had bitten her. She said nothing, however;

perhaps she could not had she tried. But Conway exclaimed: "My lord, perhaps I did not hear you rightly."

"You did Major Conway. I say that L'Isle is an impudent coxcomb. The most presumptuous fellow I know. I will find or make an occasion to give him a lesson he much needs."

"Why, my lord, what has L'Isle done?" asked the Major.

"Done!" said Lord Strathern angrily. "He has said a great deal more than I will tolerate." And, having broached the subject, he told the story of L'Isle's interview with himself, and his remarks to Bradshawe, pronouncing his whole conduct presumptuous and impertinent. Losing his temper more and more, he exclaimed: "Sir Rowland's absurd partiality has spoiled the fellow utterly!"

"Sir Rowland must not bear all the blame," said Bradshawe, interposing; then added slyly: "No wonder L'Isle's head is turned, considering who all have helped to spoil him."

"So they have; and you have spoiled him more than any one else," exclaimed Lord Strathern turning suddenly on Lady Mabel. "I hear of nobody but Colonel L'Isle. This Colonel of yours has been growing more and more intolerable—

"My Colonel, papa? I assure you I lay no claim to him," said Lady Mabel, hastily disclaiming all interest in poor L'Isle.

"Why do you have him so much about you, then, and quote him so often?"

"Why, my lord," said Bradshawe, again interposing, "Lady Mabel cannot but see and hear much of L'Isle, while she sees so much of Mrs. Shortridge, their mutual friend."

Lady Mabel was truly thankful for this diversion. It gave her one moment to think, and that was enough. In her father's present mood, L'Isle could not escape gross insult at their next meeting. She felt that the best way to molify his anger was to take up his quarrel vigorously herself. So, warming herself into a fit of indignation becoming the occasion, she exclaimed: "It is no fault of mine that I see so much of Colonel L'Isle. Why do you make him so often your guest? As Colonel Bradshawe says, I have no fit companion here but Mrs. Shortridge, and he is often with her. As to his presumption, it is not so new to me as you suppose. I have often laughed at him for his vanity in thinking that nobody can do anything as well as himself. I have had to check him before this for presuming to find fault with your management of the brigade; but did not imagine he would have the impertinence to insinuate to your face that he could command it better than you do."

"By Jove!" exclaimed Lord Strathern, "indirectly, he as good as told me so."

"So it seems," said Lady Mabel indignantly. "I am your daughter, and resent such boyish impertinence more even than you do. I will take the earliest opportunity to express to him my opinion on that point most emphatically."

Bradshawe was discreetly silent, drinking in every word. He did not actually hate L'Isle; he liked Lady Mabel well; but he loved the mischief a-brewing, and watched her game, for he saw plainly that she was playing one. Conway sat wondering what all this would lead to, anxious, yet afraid, to say a word in extenuation of poor L'Isle's offences.

"By the bye," exclaimed Lady Mabel, "I have promised Mrs. Shortridge my utmost aid in entertaining her guests to-morrow night; and the better to enable me to give it, Colonel L'Isle is pledged to be in constant attendance as my interpreter. I must write at once, and let him know that I shall dispense with his services."

"Write to the fellow at once," growled Lord Strathern, "and do not let him misunderstand the tenor of your note."

"But he has gone to Badajoz," said Bradshawe. "Still, if he has an appointment with you, Lady Mabel, he will assuredly be back in time."

"But, my lord," said Major Conway, "you have an order for him to attend Sir Rowland, at Alcantara the morning after, so that he would have to give up the pleasure of waiting on Lady Mabel at Mrs. Shortridge's, even though she did not discard him in this summary manner."

"Then Mabel shall summon him to attend her, according to promise, in spite of Sir Rowland's order!" thundered Lord Strathern, with all the perverseness of an angry man.

"But suppose he pleads Sir Rowland's order in excuse," urged Conway.

"It shall not serve him. Mabel shall treat it as a fresh piece of impertinence, and cut him forever."

"Suppose he attends Lady Mabel, and neglects Sir Rowland?"

"Then Sir Rowland shall know how lightly he holds his orders."

"That is being very hard upon L'Isle," said Conway.

"Not as hard as he deserves," said Lord Strathern with a bitter laugh.

"It is probably very important," urged Conway, "that Sir Rowland should know at once the real state of this Andalusian reserve. Much may depend upon it."

"Tut," said Lord Strathern contemptuously. "What matters L'Isle's being able to tell him whether or not they look like soldiers? If you had been long in Spain, you would have known that the fighting has to be done by us."

"O yes," said Bradshawe. "Whatever they may do on parade, the fighting always falls to our lot."

Lady Mabel had listened to this dialogue with intense interest, and no little confusion of mind. She was very angry with L'Isle, and that perhaps made her feel how important he had become to her. She was not quite prepared to cut his acquaintance, and turn her back on him forever, and now thought she saw her way through the difficulty.

"You are driving my friend L'Isle to the wall," said Major Conway. "I know him to be a *gallant* man; but however painful the sacrifice may be to him, I think he will feel compelled to waive his engagement with Lady Mabel, and wait on Sir Rowland Hill."

"Let him, if he dare," said Lady Mabel, with an emphatic stamp of her foot.

"I applaud your spirit, Lady Mabel," said Bradshawe mischievously. "It is lucky for L'Isle that the Stewarts of Strathern are not now represented by a son. As it is, L'Isle will have to make his submission with the best grace he can."

"I trust Lady Mabel will accept it in some other shape than slighting Sir Rowland's order," said Conway. "L'Isle will not do that."

"That, and nothing else," said Lady Mabel resolutely—almost angrily. "I hold myself to be quite as good as Sir Rowland, and the first appointment was with me."

"Sir Rowland will have to yield precedence to you, Lady Mabel," said Bradshawe. "If L'Isle knows the penalty, he will have to attend on you."

"Begging Lady Mabel's pardon," said Conway, "L'Isle will do no such thing."

"Conway," said Lord Strathern, with a sneer, "this punctilious friend of yours is very exacting—toward other people. But I will bet you fifty guineas that he keeps Sir Rowland waiting for news of a batch of ragamuffins not worth hearing about."

"My funds are rather low just now," said Conway, "to hazard fifty guineas on a bet."

"I thought you would not back him but in words," said Lord Strathern, in a contemptuous tone.

"Nay," said Conway, stung by his manner, "I know that where duty is concerned, L'Isle is a punctilious man. To obey every order to the letter and the second, is a point of honor with him, and I will risk my money upon him."

"Done," said Lord Strathern; "and now, Mabel, use your wits to keep the fellow here, and make a fool of him; and I will expose and laugh at him, as he deserves, at Alcantara."

"But this is a regular plot against poor L'Isle," objected Conway.

"Plot or no plot, it is understood that you give him no hint," said Lord Strathern.

"Certainly not," exclaimed Bradshawe, rubbing his hands together. "Conway, you must not blab."

"I suppose I must not," said Conway, with a very grave face, chiefly for L'Isle, but partly for his fifty guineas. "But this is a serious matter. It may be of vital importance for Sir Rowland to know at once if the Andalusian reserve"—

"The Andalusian reserve," said Lord Strathern, interrupting him, "will never let themselves be food for powder."

Lady Mabel now slipped out of the room, to hide her confusion and anxiety; and Major Conway, finding my lord not in a mood to please or be pleased, soon took leave, followed by Bradshawe in high glee, though he suppressed the outward signs of it until he had turned his back upon the hospitable mansion.

CHAPTER XVIII.

"Here on the clear, cold Ezla's breezy side,
My hand amidst her ringlets wont to rove;
She proffered now the lock, and now denied—
With all the baby playfulness of love.

"Here the false maid, with many an artful tear,
Made me each rising thought of doubt discover;
And vowed and wept till hope had ceased to fear—
Ah me! beguiling, like a child, her lover."

SOUTHEY, *from the Spanish.*

Lord Strathern's anger was not unlike a thunder-storm, violent and loud, but not very lasting. It had spent its worst fury last night; but Lady Mabel still heard the occasional rumbling of the thunder in the morning, while seated, with her father, at an unusually early breakfast; for he had before him no short day's journey over the rough country between Elvas and Alcantara. Sleep may have dulled the edge of his anger against L'Isle, but he had not yet forgotten or forgiven him. As he kissed his daughter before he mounted his horse—for she had followed him into the court—he said: "Do not forget that fellow L'Isle, Mabel; keep him here, and make a fool of him, and I will expose and laugh at him to-morrow in Alcantara."

Now, Lady Mabel had forgotten neither L'Isle, nor

his offences. She was indignant at his presumptuous censure of her father, as unjust and disrespectful to him, and showing too little consideration for herself. In short, it was, as Colonel Bradshawe had insinuated, an indignity to the whole house of Stewart of Strathern. It must be resented. Yet she could not resolve to turn her back upon him, and discard him altogether, as she was pledged to do, as one alternative. She thought it a far fitter punishment to compel him to keep his appointment with her, and make Sir Rowland wait, fretting and fuming for the intelligence he longed for, and which L'Isle alone could give him. She reveled in the idea of making L'Isle turn his back on military duty to obey her behest:

"How she would make him fawn, and beg and seek,
And wait the season and observe the times,
And spend his prodigal wit in bootless rhymes."

But then L'Isle was so punctilious on points of duty, and Major Conway had been so confident that she could not detain him in Elvas, that she begun to doubt it herself, and resolved to spare no pains to gain her end. So she at once sat down and penned an artful note; then calling for her fine footman, dispatched him with it to L'Isle's quarters, after schooling him well that he was to give it to the colonel's own man, with strict injunctions to put it in his master's hand on his return—if possible—before his foot was out of the stirrup; certainly, before he got any other letter awaiting him.

Meanwhile, L'Isle was zealously fulfilling his mission at Badajoz. He had made such good speed the evening before, that though the sun had set on him in Elvas, some lingering rays of twilight still fell on the round Moorish tower of white marble, on either hand, as he entered the bridge-gate of Badajoz.

No sooner had he alighted at the posada, than he wrote a note, and sent it to the governor of the place, saying, that having just come back from Andalusia, whither he had been sent on an important mission by Sir Rowland Hill, and not doubting that the Spanish dignitary would be glad of news from that province, he would wait on him at breakfast next morning. This done, and learning that many of the Spanish officers were to be found at another posada, he hastened thither, soon meeting acquaintances—and making more—among them. He knew well how to approach the Spaniard, mingling the utmost consideration with his frank address, and taking pains to make himself agreeable, even to that puppy, Don Alonso Melendez, whom he found among them. Many of them were at cards, and the dice were not idle. L'Isle soon found a place among the gamesters, and took care to lose a few pieces to more than one of his new friends; a thing easily done, they being in high practice, and he little skilled in these arts. Having thus made himself one of them, he, like a true Englishman, set to drinking, contrived to get about him some of the graver and less busy of the gentlemen present, and, while discussing with them the best wine the house afforded, he adroitly turned the conversation to the topics on which he sought information. He did not go to bed, at a late hour, without having learned much as to the garrison of Badajoz, and of the few precautions taken for the safety of this important fortress.

Early in the morning, L'Isle called on the governor, and found him in his dressing-gown, just ready for his chocolate. The Don was well pleased to hear L'Isle's account of the force coming up from Andalusia, of his interviews with officers high in command in it, and his comments on the spirit, activity, and endurance of the Spanish soldier. This led to further conversation, in which L'Isle, while sipping chocolate with the Spaniard, took occasion to abuse the French roundly, which was agreeable enough to his host; but he quite won his heart by the unfeigned contempt and abhorrence he expressed for the *Afrancesados*.

L'Isle soon found that, in spite of his unsoldierly undress, the Don was a sturdy old fellow, who chafed at being shut up in a garrison, surrounded by defensive walls and moats. He longed to take the field and become the assailant.

"I trust we will all be in the field shortly," said L'Isle, echoing his sentiment. "But we have wily foes to deal with. All their great successes have been won by surprise, aided by traitors among us. They are now evidently anxious to anticipate us, and if we delay long, there is no knowing where the first blow may fall. I wonder," said he, with a puzzled look, "why they keep so large a force at Trujillo, and have such strong detachments foraging on this side the mountains of Toledo? A few marches may unite them near us."

"Do you suppose that they are thinking of Badajoz?" asked the Spaniard, looking as if L'Isle had seized him by the shoulders, and roughly waked him up.

"Marshal Soult has an eye this way, and would give more than his little finger to have it again," said L'Isle; "for nothing would cramp our movements more than the loss of it. They have now, indeed, little chance of success, we know," he added, bowing to the governor, "but may think it worth trying. Their leaders think nothing of risking the loss of a thousand men or so, on the slenderest chance of a great prize. The conscription fills up all these gaps."

"No doubt; no doubt. But we will watch the rascals closely," said the governor.

"I dare say," said L'Isle laughing, "you have a spy or two in Trujillo, besides the lynx-eyed, keen-eared scouts you keep on the roads, and in the villages around you."

"We get intelligence—we get intelligence," said the Spaniard evasively. "But as the French are now moving, it will be well to bestir ourselves, to find out what they are at."

These, and other hints, that L'Isle threw out—not as advice, but inquiries and chance suggestions, being mingled with deferential attention to all the Spaniard had to say—neither startled his vanity, nor chafed his pride. He was pleased with L'Isle, talked frankly to him, and presented him ceremoniously to his officers, who now began to wait upon him. When L'Isle was about to take his leave, he urged him to return to dinner, and charged a favorite officer to show L'Isle everything he wished to see in Badajos, that he might be enabled to report the condition of this stronghold to Sir Rowland Hill.

"I must communicate with Sir Rowland so speedily," said L'Isle, "that I must be content with the pleasure of having breakfasted with your Excellency;" and with marked respect he took leave of the governor and his suite, having been treated—in diplomatic phrase—with "distinguished consideration." Indeed, had Sir Rowland seen and heard him during his audience, he would have patted him on the back, and thanked his stars for giving him so able and adroit an ambassador. Were it possible to become wise by the wisdom of another, Badajos would have had a watchful governor. Prolonged watching is no easy task, but L'Isle knew that if the Spaniard could be roused to a week of vigilance, the urgent need of it would be over.

He spent an industrious morning, making himself agreeable to his companion, while inspecting the resources of the place, and the day was well worn away when his guide and escort took leave of him at the posada. His business here finished, he wished to leave Badajoz at once; and on looking for his groom, found him ensconced in the kitchen, providently dining on a rabbit, stuffed with olives, and draining a bottle of wine, baptized *Valdepenas*—addressing the landlord's tawny daughter with a flattering air, and smacking his lips approvingly, after each mouthful, whether solid or fluid, while he abused both food and wine in emphatic English, throwing in many back-handed compliments to the lady's beauty, and she stood simpering by, construing his words by his manner.

On seeing his master enter hastily, Tom, who had laid in all the wine, and most of the food set before him, got up respectfully to receive his orders; while with a full mouth he mumbled out: "Prayer and provender hinder no man's journey."

"You abridge the proverb in practice," said L'Isle, "leaving out the prayer to gain time to take care of the provender." Then sitting down at the table, he took out a paper and began to note down what he had observed in Badajoz. "There is nothing very tempting here," said he presently, glancing his eye over Tom's scanty leavings, "but a luncheon will not be amiss; so I will take what I can find, while you saddle the horses."

It was late in the day when L'Isle left Badajoz; but instead of posting back to Elvas, as he had come from it, he rode slowly on, sometimes lost in thought, at times gazing on the scene around him. Many objects along the road brought vividly back to him the incidents of that pleasant excursion, so lately taken in company with Lady Mabel. Here she had turned her horse aside for a moment, to pluck some blossoms from this carob-tree, which stands alone on the sandy plain around it; here, on the bank of the Cayo, was the spot where she had pressed so close up beside him for protection, in the dark, on the first alarm of danger before them; there stood the old watch-tower, which they had examined together with interest, speculating on its history, lost in by-gone ages; crossing the stream here, further on, were the prints of her horses hoofs on the steep, pebbly bank, as she had turned suddenly from the road, to ride up to the mysterious old ruin.

Were these pleasant days over? L'Isle knew that Lord Strathern had taken violent, perhaps lasting offence at his strictures; and he himself was too indignant at the summary way in which his commander had cut short his protest, and dismissed him and the subject, for him to make any conciliatory advances. Knowing, too, Lady Mabel's devotion to her father, and her tenacity where his character and dignity were concerned, there was no saying how much she might resent L'Isle's offence, when it came to her knowledge. He could hardly, just now at least, frequent headquarters on his former footing.

He was so much engrossed by these unpleasant thoughts, that it was in vain officious Tom several times rode up close upon him, making his own horse curvet and caper, hoping to attract his master's attention, and remind him that he was loitering on the road long after his dinner hour. L'Isle went on at a foot-pace up the hill of Elvas, until, from a neighboring hedge, a nightingale, for whose ditty the hours of darkness were too short, began his plaintive song. Many a time had L'Isle paused to listen to such minstrelsey ; but now his ear, or something else, was out of tune:

> "Except I be with Silvia in the night,
> There is no music in the nightingale."

Rousing himself, he cantered through the gate, and hastened to his quarters.

Now, it was some time since L'Isle's servants had picked up the notion, that in no way could they please him half so well as by obeying the slightest hint from Lady Mabel. So his man came promptly out, armed with her note, and thrust it into his hand before he had left the saddle. Entering his quarters hastily, he broke it open, and read it with infinite satisfaction.

(Lady Mabel Stewart sends her compliments to Col. L'Isle. She has a presentment that her pleasant sojourn in Elvas draws to its end. Like Mrs. Shortridge, she is ambitious to leave among her Portuguese friends, the most favorable recollection of herself. So to-night she will spare no pains, but will dress, look, sing and act her best, and be as agreeable as she can to the natives at Mrs. Shortridge's house. She relies, confidently, on Col. L'Isle's attending her as interpreter, and saying a thousand witty and pleasant things in her name. This, too, may be her last opportunity of thanking him for the many, many delightful excursions enjoyed under his guidance and protection. She may never repeat, but can never forget them !)

This note relieved L'Isle of a load of anxiety. It was plain that Lord Strathern had gotten over his anger, and meant to have no quarrel with him; or, more gratifying still, would not have the whole house of Strathern involved in it, and so had given no hint of it to his daughter. It was too the first note he had ever received from Lady Mabel, and sportive as its tone was in the beginning, there was something of feeling and even sadness in its close. L'Isle well knew, while Lady Mabel had only chosen to assume it, that the time for leaving Elvas was indeed at hand. Yet a few days, and a few things were more uncertain than his again meeting Lady Mabel on this side of the grave.

A few golden hours had yet to fleet by. Who would throw away a happiness because it is fleeting? L'Isle had sunk into a delightful reverie, anticipating the pleasures of the evening, when his man of method laid before him the despatch from his other correspondent, Sir Rowland Hill.

He read it hastily, and angrily threw it on the floor. He thought himself an ill-used man! "Be in Alcantara by ten to-morrow!" I will do no such thing! I have been in the saddle for weeks. My horses are worn out," (he chose to forget a fresh horse in the stable.) "Up late last night and worried all day about affairs over which I have no control, and fellows who will fail us at need. Sir Rowland must wait till dinner time to-morrow for news of these dilatory Spaniards. If he has to deal much more with them, it will be a useful lesson to learn to wait."

He now went to his chamber to dress in order to attend Lady Mabel. When he returned to his parlor, seeing Sir Rowland's insulted despatch still lying on the floor, he condescended to pick it up and stow it away in his pocket with his notes on the state of the Andalusian reserve and the garrison of Badajoz, and then rode off in the happiest mood to head-quarters. But when he dismounted there, his conscience pricked him. An ambitious soldier, zealous in the cause for which he fought, he, not long since, would have felt one moment's forgetfulness, or the slightest neglect of the service, to be treason against his own nature. He now turned back from the door to bid the groom leave his own horse in Elvas, and take the fresh horse on to the little town of Albuquerque, and expect him at the posada there before the dawn of day. Having, by this provision for riding post, quieted the compunctious visitings of conscience, he entered the house.

Lady Mabel kept him waiting some time, purposely, for delay was now her policy. Soon, however, he heard her talking in the next room, and the abrupt and crabbed tones of the voice which answered her, betrayed Moodie in one of his objecting and protesting moods. Lady Mabel was giving sundry injunctions to an unwilling agent. At length the old Scotch grieve, like one of his own ill-conditioned steers, would neither lead nor drive; for when she bid him to put the clock back an hour, he flatly refused, calling it acting a lie, as the wily Gibeonites did to Joshua.

"Or as Jacob and Rebecca did to blind old Isaac," Lady Mabel suggested; but even the example of the patriarch could not move him, and Lady Mabel had to make time move backward with her own hand.

At length she entered the room radiant with beauty and with smiles, for Moodie's obstinacy had not ruffled her in the least. She was so sorry to have kept Colonel L'Isle waiting, and so much afraid he would have to wait a while longer, as the old Lisbon coach and the mules, with their harness, were not put together so speedily, as the London turn-out of a fashionable lady. "I am to blame," she continued, "for not having looked to it before, for Antonio Lobo, my impromptu postillion, is less skilled in the management of my vehicle, than of the olive trees among which he has lived until he has taken the color of their ripe fruit."

To fill up the time she now asked L'Isle's opinion of her dress, seeing him eye it with some surprise. Turning gracefully about and showing it off to him from different points of view, she told him that, as a last compliment to her Elvas friends, she had, for once, adopted their costume.

"Improved upon it, rather," said L'Isle, for she had not closely followed the local costume where it did not please her. Then running on, from one lively topic to another, she amused L'Isle so successfully that he felt it to be an interruption when the footman came in to say that the coach was ready. After depositing her guitar in state, on a pile of music, on the front seat, L'Isle at length found himself beside Lady Mabel in this venerable vehicle, long used to bear a noble burden, having belonged to a Portuguese Marquis, who on the first approach of Junot's invading horde, had run off to Brazil, leaving his coach, his estate, his country, and perhaps his honor behind him. Slow and dignified, as became its character, was its progress up the hill of Elvas; for one pair of the team of mules which had brought it from Lisbon, had returned to their duty in the quartermaster's department, and their comrades, left to their own unaided efforts, found the coach almost as hard to handle as a nine-pounder. But in the dove-like, billing and cooing humor in which L'Isle was, time flew on the wings of the carrier-pigeon, and they arrived at Mrs. Shortridge's house too soon for him, though all the guests, but themselves, were there already. Two or three score of Portuguese, most of them ladies, and nearly as many English officers filled the rooms.

Some of these gentlemen looked surprised at seeing L'Isle, thinking he had already left Elvas. Lieutenant Goring, who was showing off his tall lithe person and dragoon uniform to the best advantage, beside his short and sturdy friend, Captain Hatton, seemed annoyed at L'Isle's presence, and Hatton shared his feelings. L'Isle stood in the way of their paying court to Lady Mabel, and Goring, at least, had reckoned on his absence.

"I had hoped," said he, "that we were rid of the Colonel for once. He is an abominable monopolist."

"He is so," said Hatton," for Lady Mabel's smiles belong to the brigade."

"And the light dragoons quartered with it," interjected Goring. "But here he is, basking in the sunshine, and keeping us shivering in the shade, when he ought to be on the road to Alcantara. Sir Rowland is expecting him. Major Conway seemed quite anxious that he should be there betimes in the morning, and, doubtless, had some good reason for it.

"Why do you not give him a hint?" asked Hatton, perhaps he has forgotten it."

"He is your colonel, and the hint would come better from you."

"Thank you, said Hatton. But in our regiment, it is contrary to the etiquette to hint to the colonel that he is neglecting his duty."

"But it seems," said Goring, "that the rule does not apply to the brigade. The major tells me that L'Isle has freely censured my lord's remissness, and urged him to enforce more stringent discipline."

"How did my lord take it?"

"Like a slap in the face," answered Goring. "At least he treated it as a great piece of presumption, and L'Isle was thoroughly angered at the rough answer he got. Indeed, Conway thinks that there is nothing but ill blood between them."

"That does not look much like it," said Hatton, glancing at Lady Mabel, with L'Isle at her elbow.

'Let us go and beat about the bushes; we may start some thing worth chasing!"

The two friends, looking like a greyhound and a bull-terrier coupled together, proceeded to hunt in couple, by thrusting themselves into the cluster of gentlemen around Lady Mabel. Hatton, with a little start of admiring surprise, praised the taste displayed in her dress, regretted her being so late in adopting it, it so became her. He looked round, appealing to the bystanders, all of whom assented to his opinion, except the discriminating Goring, who asserted that it was not the costume which became Lady Mabel, but Lady Mabel who set off the costume, and he carried the popular voice with him. "No head looks so well under a Turk's turban as a Christian's," he continued, "and no native could show off the national dress here like a genuine English beauty." Lady Mabel had learned to listen complacently to the broadest language of admiration.

There were handsome women present—for Elvas could boast its share of beaufy—but none to rival hers; the more conspicuous, too, from being loveliness of a dif ferent type, and not likely to be overlooked among the dumpy Portuguese ladies, few indeed of whom equaled her in height. Lady Mabel would have been no woman had she not enjoyed the admiration she excited; but she remembered the business of the night, when Goring, bowing to L'Isle, spoke of the unexpected pleasure of seeing him here.

At once interrupting him, she exclaimed: "It is

probably the last time we shall have the pleasure of meeting our friends of Elvas, so I at least have come to devote myself exclusively to them. Do, Colonel L'Isle, take pity on a dumb woman, and lend me a Portuguese tongue." And gliding off among a party of the natives present, she entered into conversation with them, calling continually on L'Isle to interlard her complimentary scraps with more copious and better turned periods.

Mrs. Shortridge, too, kept her interpreter, the commissary, close at her elbow, and the quantity of uncurrent Portuguese she made him utter to her guests, in the course of the night, amounted to a wholesale issue of the counterfeit coin of that tongue. From the assiduity of both ladies in courting the natives, one might have thought that they meant to settle at Elvas, or that they were rival candidates canvassing the borough for votes.

It was a young and gay party assembled here, and Mrs. Shortridge's floor was soon covered with dancers. In private houses the national dances are often executed in a modified and less demonstrative style, at least early in the evening, than elsewhere. Still the dancing in Elvas and Badajoz were near neighbors to each other. But a change had come over Mrs. Shortridge, and now she made no protest, and saw little impropriety in displays which she had denounced a few days ago. Fashion is the religion of half the world; the mode makes the morals, and what it sanctions cannot be wrong. The commissary, not so easy a convert, sneeringly remarked that the exhibition was very suitable to ballet dancers and such folk, plainly classing most of his guests in that category; while Lady Mabel, with bare-faced hypocrisy, glided about among her foreign friends, lamenting that her English clumsiness cut her off from taking her part in a diversion, and in the displays of grace and feeling, which, she said, with double meaning, were unbecoming any but women of the Latin races.

The night was hot, and dancing made it hotter. So Mrs. Shortridge called upon Lady Mabel to fill up the interval of rest, and gratify the expectations of their friends with some of her choicest songs.

But yesterday so large an audience would have abashed her; now she scarcely saw the throng around her in her eagerness to gain her end by prolonging the amusements of the night. She sent L'Isle for her guitar, made him turn over her music, never releasing him for a moment, while she sung no Italian, French or English songs, but some of those native and cherished requidillas, the airs and words of which find here so ready an access to all hearts; and she executed them with a skill, melody, and pathos, that flattered and charmed the Portuguese. The guitar, though the cherished friend of serenading lovers of the old Spanish school, was truly but a poor accompaniment to such a voice; but L'Isle saw that, like the harp, it had the merit of displaying to advantage, the roundest, fairest, and most beautifully turned arms he had ever gazed upon.

The dancers were again upon the floor; the night sped on, and Lady Mabel made free use of her interpreter in ingratiating herself with the Portuguese. L'Isle, true to his pledge, taxed his powers to the utmost to be witty and agreeable in her name; at times a little overdoing his part. Thus, at supper, when an elaborate compliment to Dona Carlotta Seguiera, drew a reply as if it had originated with himself, he stripped it of part of its merit by saying that he was merely the mouth-piece of Lady Mabel's sentiments. When Dona Carlotta expressed her surprise that Lady Mabel's short English sentence should make so long a speech in Portuguese, he explained it by Lady Mabel's peculiar faculty of uttering a volume in three words.

Supper and the dance that followed were over; Mrs. Shortridge's great night drew to a close; and many of the company asked for one more melody from the sweet songstress before they dispersed. While turning over her music, Lady Mabel seemed to hesitate in her choice, and L'Isle thought that her hand trembled as she selected a sheet.

As the fruit of his musical gleanings in the peninsula, Major Lumley had lately sent her a parcel of old Spanish songs, among which she had found a little piece, a mere fragment, but exquisitely touching in melody and sentiment. Her father had been much taken with it, but no one else had heard it from her lips. Like a volatile perfume, that escapes in the attempt to pour it from one vessel to another, such things defy translation. How, too, Lady Mabel gave it vocal life, may be imagined, not described. She sang it with a truthfulness of feeling that seemed to grow with each succeeding line. For the mere words, we can only find this slender version for the English ear:

In joyous hall, now thronged with young and fair,
Your roving eye marks every beauty here;
I harbor not one doubt or jealous fear;
Constant your heart; it beats for me alone.

In woodland glade, when armed for sylvan war,
You mark the antlered monarch from afar,
Your sportive toil cannot my pleasure mar;
Constant your heart; it beats for me alone.

In summer night, gazing on starry sky,
And on yon radiant queen, who rides on high,
Your fancy seems to roam, yet hovers nigh;
Constant your heart; it beats for me alone.

But hark! you trump! you start as from a dream;
From your bright eyes the warrior flashes gleam;
All else forgotten. War is now your theme;
Constant my heart; it beats for you alone.

'Midst charging hosts, the foremost rank is thine;
In saddened bower, the thrilling fear is mine;
You glow with ardor, I in sorrow pine;
Constant my heart; it beats for you alone.

Could L'Isle's vanity be beguiling him? The tremor of her voice, her saddened troubled look, the beaming glances of her eyes, which hovered about him, yet shunned to meet his gaze—they all betrayed her. She was, perhaps half consciously, identifying him with the object of the song. Her audience were delighted, but L'Isle was entranced, and no longer a responsible man.

The guests were now fast leaving the house, and Lady Mabel, having much to say to Mrs. Shortridge, was among the last. L'Isle attended her down stairs, and was about to hand her into the old coach, when she drew back timidly.

"How dark it is, with that cloud over the moon. I am afraid Antonio Lobo is scarce postillion enough to drive down that steep rough road without accident."

L'Isle instantly recollected, that having escorted Lady Mabel to the party, it was his privilege to see her safe home again. Bidding the footman keep the coach door open, he sprang into the house for his hat, and in a moment was again seated by her side. The lumbering vehicle rolled out of the *praca* and down the sloping street to the western gate of Elvas. As the guard there closed the gate behind them, and shut them out from the light of the lantern, they seemed to plunge into "outer darkness." Lady Mabel's nervous terrors came back upon her with redoubled violence.

The fosse under the drawbridge seemed a ravenous abyss, and the deep road cut through the *glacis* and overhung by the outworks appeared to be leading down into the bowels of the earth. The road, too, down into the valley was steep, winding and much cut up by use and the heavy winter rains.

"I have been so much on horseback lately," she

said, apologizing for her fears, "and so seldom in a carriage, and this is such a rickety old thing, that you must excuse my alarm. Besides, I do not know that Antonio ever played the part of postillion before. Why, the coach will run over the mules," she exclaimed presently, as it glided down a steep spot; then springing up and leaning out of the window, she called out in plaintive Portuguese, "Antonio, my good Antonio, beware of that short turn in the road, or we will all go tumbling down the hill together! Excuse my terrors, Colonel L'Isle, but some late occurrences have shaken my nerves sadly."

Surprised at her unusual timidity, L'Isle tried to calm her fears, and taking her hand, endeavored to keep it, while he assured her that every Portuguese peasant was familiar with mules and mountain roads from boyhood. With a little laugh, she, struggling, rescued the captured member, saying, "I shall need both my hands to scramble out with when the coach breaks down or overturns, whichever happens first," and after this she was more chary of her demonstrations of terror, to escape his demonstrations of protection.

"If you doubt honest Lobo's ability to drive you safe home," said L'Isle, "though I do not, perhaps your own man may be more skilful."

"What! cut down my two yards of footman into a postillion?" exclaimed Lady Mabel; "on a mule, too! Why, he would rebel against such degradation!"

"It would be promotion," said L'Isle, laughing, "to

put a footman into the saddle; and William would be of use for once in his life."

"Neither I nor nature demand usefulness of him. His whole capital consists in being a tall footman, who becomes his livery; and he fulfills his destiny when both he and it excite the admiration of the Elvas ladies."

The coach presently turned into the olive yard, and drew up before the old monastic pile without accident. L'Isle was surprised to see the inhabited part of the building brightly lighted up at this late hour. Old Moodie, looking graver and more sour than ever, was at the open door. L'Isle handed Lady Mabel out of the coach, and she coolly took his arm, showing that he was expected to hand her up stairs, before taking leave of her. Moodie followed them into the drawing-room, and said abruptly, "Well, my lady, will you have supper now?"

"Certainly, if it be ready. By-the-bye, Colonel L'Isle, I did not see you take the least refreshment at Mrs. Shortridge's—not even half a pound of sugar-plums, like the Portuguese ladies."

"I followed your example; for you yourself fasted."

"I was too busy talking my best and my last to my Portuguese friends," said Lady Mabel. "But when and where did you dine?"

"Dine?" said L'Isle, hesitating, then recollecting his luncheon; "about two o'clock, in Badajoz."

"A Spanish dinner, I'll warrant, at a Spaniard's house!" she exclaimed, throwing up her hands.

"You must be faint with hunger. Why," she added, taking up a light, and holding it close to him, "you do look pale and famished; as if you had dined like a Portuguese beggar's brat,—on a crust, rubbed over with a *sardinha*, to give it a flavor. I cannot let you go away in this condition. If you starve yourself so, you will degenerate from a beef-eating red-coat, into a rationless Spanish soldier."

"There is no danger of that," L'Isle answered. "But how do you happen to have a supper ready at this hour?"

"It shows what a slave of habit Moodie is. Because he has a supper got for papa and his friends every night, he could not omit it; though papa is far away, and he knows that I never touch it. But here he comes to announce it. For once it is well timed, and you must do it justice, unless you would make both Moodie and myself your enemies for life."

"Supper is ready, my lady," said Moodie. Then grumbled aside to her, "If you wait awhile longer it will serve for breakfast."

"Pray send Jenny to me; and then, Moodie, I will not keep you up longer," said Lady Mabel, for she was anxious to get rid of the old marplot.

They went into the next room to supper, and she seated L'Isle sociably beside her. It was truly a tempting little supper party, without one too many at table. Lady Mabel had now been long enough in the army to feel at home there. Why should she not, like any of her comrades, bring home a friend to sup with her? Especially when that friend is the pleasantest fellow in the brigade? Having or affecting an appetite, she set the example to L'Isle, and urged him to make up for the meagre fare of the day. The table looked as if Lord Strathern and three or four of his friends had been expected to take their seats at it; and when she bid the footman hand wine to Colonel L'Isle, he promptly placed three decanters on the table.

"William mistakes me for Colonel Brahshawe," said L'Isle smiling, as he glanced at them.

"That is Moodie's doing," said she. "He provides liberally, one bottle for you, and two for himself, I suppose."

Jenny Aiken now came into the room, very neatly dressed, and, evidently not at all surprised at her mistress's summons. Upon this Lady Mabel bid William go, as he would not be wanted."

"I have not a doubt, Colonel L'Isle, that you prefer a Hebe to a Ganymede."

"Infinitely," said L'Isle; "and I only wonder how great Jove himself could differ with me."

"Then let Jenny refill your glass, that you may drink the health of the Portuguese ladies, to whom you said so many witty and pleasant things this evening.

"I only translated them," said L'Isle, bowing gaily to her.

"May I be ever blessed with such an interpreter," said Lady Mabel, "and I may, without fear, set up for a wit." And she repeated some of the best things he had said in her name, and seemed to enjoy them so much, that L'Isle, who, like some other people, had

> "A *heart*
> Open as day to melting *flattery*,"

became almost as much charmed with himself as he was with his companion. Thus they amused themselves, recalling the little incidents of the evening; Lady Mabel turning satirist, at the cost of all her friends, not sparing even Mrs. Shortridge, in her attempts to play the Rome hostess, and ridiculing, without mercy, the commissary's awkward efforts at Portuguese eloquence and politeness. Then recalling and laughing at the extravagant compliments paid her after each song, she sung snatches of several of her favorite pieces, but had the grace not to allude to 'Constant my Heart;' while L'Isle longed for an occasion, yet hesitated to tell her how much better he liked it than all the others. In the midst of her extravagantly high spirits, checking herself suddenly, she said: "I see that you are surprised at me, but not more than I am at myself. Have you ever heard of our Scottish superstition of being *fie*—that is, possessed by a preternatural excess of vivacity? No? It is deemed the sure forerunner of evil at hand,—a sudden and violent death; some dire misfortune; perhaps a sad and final parting of—of the dearest friends. I own," she added, with a deep sigh, "I cannot free myself from this superstition of the country."

"I will not share it with you!" L'Isle exclaimed. "And you must shake it off. What were life without hope, and high hope too!" and seizing her hand he kissed it respectfully but with a fervor which indicated the direction his hopes had taken.

"For shame, Colonel L'Isle!" she exclaimed, laughing, while she snatched her hand away. "See how much shocked Jenny is at this liberty taken with her mistress!"

L'Isle had forgotten Jenny Aiken's presence. He turned to look at her, and the Scotch Hebe was plainly more amused than shocked at what she was witnessing. Had L'Isle forgotten also his appointment to-morrow morning at Alcantara? Perhaps not. But had Sir Rowland Hill now appeared and demanded his opinion of the Andalusian levies, L'Isle would have told him that he had no leisure to think of him or them.

But all sublunary pleasure has an end. Supper was over, and L'Isle could devise no excuse for lingering here, but the pleasure of listening to Lady Mabel, who seemed willing to amuse him as long as he staid. After a pause, divining that he was about to take leave of her, she said suddenly: "What an unreasonable fellow Sir Rowland Hill must be! Because he cannot find any one to execute his delicate commissions half so well as you do, he must be thrusting them all upon you! Does he take you for a Popish saint, endowed with pluripresence, and able to be in Andalusia, at Badajoz, Elvas, and Alcantara, all at one time?"

"Not exactly so," said L'Isle, a good deal flattered at this speech. He has indeed tasked me well, at times doing other men's work; but it is all in a good cause, you know; and I never objected to these tasks till now——My Lord, I hear, set out for Alcantara early this morning, taking Bradshawe and Conway with him."

"Yes! they rode merrily off this morning," said Lady Mabel in a gay tone. "A summons to Alcantara breaks the monotony of their life here, and they were eager to meet Sir Rowland. I hear that these conferences with his officers always conclude with a capital dinner. That sallow Major Conway, with his fastidious appetite, and his Calcutta liver, will appreciate the excellence of the *cuisine*. I have heard Colonel Bradshawe dilate, with enthusiasm, on Sir Rowland's choice selection of wines. Papa, too, will meet some new people there, which will give him an opportunity of once more undergoing his three years of siege, famine, and bombardment in Gibraltar thirty years ago, and of uttering a new edition to the expedition to Egypt, in which he will again put Sir Ralph Abercromby to a glorious death in the arms of victory. They tell me, Sir Rowland, too, dearly loves these occasions for repeating his favorite lecture on strategy and grand tactics. But you must have heard it so often, that you can repeat it *verbatim* to me, if you have nothing more entertaining to say."

"I hope I could find topics more agreeable to us both," said L'Isle, laughing and blushing. "But unluckily I have in my pocket Sir Rowland's order to meet him there, and have intelligence he is waiting for. I am afraid he will have to wait."

"I am afraid, he will," said Lady Mabel, coolly, "for I do not see how you are to get out of the house now. By this time Moodie has bolted, barred, and locked every door and window below, hidden the keys, and gone to bed in his usual condition. He never can find them again, until his head gets clear in the morning."

"What!" exclaimed L'Isle, "that respectable old man drunk every night!"

"Not *every* night!" said Lady Mabel. "But have you forgotten in what condition he came back with us from Evora?"

"True. But I thought that an accident, and more the effect of sickness than drinking. He seemed quite sober when you came home, and a graver and more sedate man I do not know."

"O, he is a Presbyterian, you know, and the more liquor he swallows the graver and more sanctimonious he becomes."

"That may be. Still Lady Mabel, I must find some way of getting out of the house. Already I shall be too late at Alcantara."

"I am afraid Sir Rowland will not drink in your news at breakfast. But if it be good, it will come in capitally after dinner, by way of dessert."

"After dinner!" said L'Isle hurriedly. "I must be there many hours before that!"

"Then I am sorry to have kept you here so long. I suppose Jenny and I must keep watch by ourselves all night, for I cannot keep those heavy-headed fellows awake."

"Awake and watching!" exclaimed L'Isle.

"Yes—awake and watching," Lady Mabel answered. "If you could stay we would not insist on your sitting up with us. I could have Papa's room made ready for you; and if I knew that you were asleep in Papa's bed, with your drawn sword on one side, and a pair of his pistols, cocked, on the other, I would not be in the least afraid."

"Afraid of what?" asked L'Isle in astonishment.

"Of these robbers, who go plundering and murdering all over the country by night!" said Lady Mabel, her large blue eyes opening wide in well-feigned terror.

"Oh, don't talk of them, my lady!" said Jenny, with a stifled scream, and an affected shudder.

"Have you not heard of them?" Lady Mabel asked in a tone of surprise.

"I cannot say I have—at least of any depredations here at Elvas."

"But we are outside of Elvas—to our sorrow; and the monks, great engineers as they have elsewhere proved themselves, have constructed but a very weak fortress in this building. Our garrison is weaker still. Papa carried off his two most efficient servants. William is a simpleton, Tomkins a craven, and Moodie, though bold as a lion, is an old man, already bound hand and foot, and gagged by his strong enemy."

"But where is the Portuguese part of your household?" L'Isle asked.

"Being thieves in a small way," said Lady Mabel, "we always, at night, lock them out of this part of the building. While the robbers were cutting our throats up-stairs, they might be stealing our silver below. We have an anxious time here, I assure you. It is as much as I can do to keep poor Jenny from going off into hysterics; she will not go to bed lest she should be robbed and murdered in her sleep. It is lucky that I, being a soldier's daughter, have a little courage."

"Courage!" exclaimed L'Isle, "I am astonished at your sudden timidity. Why, there is a sentinel day and night here at headquarters."

"But out of sight and hearing at the other end of this old rambling monk's roost," said Lady Mabel, "mounting guard over papa's musty despatches."

"And the fellow now there," said Jenny, "told me he could not quit them—no, not if we were robbed and murdered twice over. I could scream now, only that I'm afraid the villains might hear me!"

While L'Isle looked suspiciously at the maid, not so good an actress as her mistress, Lady Mabel glanced her eye at the clock. Apparent time called it one, real time said it was two hours after midnight. She felt sure of her game, and need wear the mask no longer. She had been acting a long and trying part, and began to feel tired, and now showed it by letting her terror subside into one or two little yawns, which became her so well, that L'Isle never thought her more lovely than now when she was getting tired of his company.

It was high time to get rid of him. But now a real fear come over her, and she shrunk from his searching glance with unfeigned timidity. Still the thing had to be done; so nerving herself to the task, she stepped close up beside him, and looking confidingly in his face, said: "I am truly sorry to have kept you here so long, and hope you will not find Sir Rowland fretting and fuming at the delay of your news; but I was so anxious to have your protection, having just learned that these horrid ruffians are not *guerilleros* from the Spanish band at Badajoz, but some of your own regiment disguised as banditti."

L'Isle started back one step. In an instant, from the fairy land of hope and love, his Eden of delights, with every soothing and intoxicating influence around him, he found himself transported to a bleak common, stripped of his dreamy joys, exposed to the ridicule of the enchantress, and soon to be pelted with the pitiless jests of all who might hear of his adventure. He looked at Lady Mabel, almost expecting to see her undergo some magic transformation. But there she stood unchanged, except that there was a little sneer on her lip, a glance of triumph from her eye, an expression of intense but mischievous enjoyment in her whole air, and, what he had never observed before, a strong likeness to her father.

Striving quickly and proudly to recover himself, L'Isle said, with admirable gravity, "You have convinced me, Lady Mabel, that it is my especial duty to protect you from my own banditti. I will not leave you, not close an eye in sleep, while a shadow of danger hangs over you. But," he added, slowly drawing near to a window, and gently opening it, "I have observed that house-breakers always choose the darkest hours to hide their deeds of darkness. For to-night the danger is over. The moon is overhead, and not a cloud obscures the sky. We English may envy these Southern nations their nights, though not their days." Half a dozen nightingales were now pouring out their rival melodies in the grove. Looking out on the landscape before him, its features softened rather than concealed by the sober silvery light, he repeated:

> "How sweet the moonlight sleeps on yonder bank,
> * * * * In such a night as this,
> When the sweet wind did gently kiss the trees,
> And they did make no noise—in such a night
> Troilus, methinks, mounte . the Trojan walls,
> And sighed his soul toward the Grecian tents,
> Where Cressid lay that night."

While repeating these lines, he measured with his eye the distance to the ground. The comfort-loving monks had provided lofty ceilings and abundant air for their apartments under the scorching sun of Alemtejo. But in L'Isle's angry, defiant mood, he would have leapt from the top of Pompey's Pillar, rather than stay to be laughed at by Lady Mabel. Seating himself on the window-sill, he turned and threw his legs out of the window.

"For Heaven's sake, Colonel L'Isle, what are you dreaming of?"

"I am dreaming that, happy as Ulysses, I have listened to the Syren, and escaped her snares."

She had sprang forward as he spoke, and now threw out her arms to draw him back. He eluded her clasp, and dropped to the ground on his feet, but fell backward, and did not at once rise again. She shrieked, and then called out in a piteous tone: "Speak to me, Colonel L'Isle. For Heaven's sake, speak. Say you are not injured—not hurt."

"Console yourself, Lady Mabel," said he, rising slowly. "I have not broken my neck, and shall not break my appointment. And, now, I must bid you good-night; or shall I say good-morning?"

As L'Isle turned, he spied old Moodie standing in the open gateway of the court, with a light in his hand, and knitting his shaggy brows. He looked neither very drunk, nor much afraid of robbers, but trembled with rage on seeing L'Isle's mode of breaking out of the mansion. With a strong effort of self-control, L'Isle walked off without limping, and was soon lost in the gloomy shades of the olive and the orange grove.

Lady Mabel had played out the comedy, and now came—reflection. What had she done? How would it tell? Above all, what would L'Isle think of her? What were his feelings now? And what would they be when the exact truth—the whole plot—was known to him? Every faculty hitherto engrossed in the part she was playing, until this moment she had never looked on this side of the picture? Now, bitter self-reproach, womanly shame, and tears—vain, useless tears—filled up the remaining hours of the night. Jenny Aiken's feeble attempts at consolation were worse than futile, and she was sent off abruptly to her room for misconstruing the cause of her mistress' grief. Lady Mabel found little relief in remembering her father's injunction, to play her part well, and not fail of success. She was hardly soothed even by the resolution she took to rate that father soundly for the gross impropriety he had permitted, induced—nay, almost commanded—her to perpetrate.

CHAPTER XIX.

Don Pedro.—By this light he changes more and more. I think he be angry, indeed.

Claudio.—If he be, he knows how to turn his girdle.

Benedict.—Shall I speak a word in your ear?

Claudio.—God bless me from a challenge.

MUCH ADO ABOUT NOTHING.

SIR ROWLAND HILL, with a stout division, had been posted during the winter at Coria, facing Marshal Soult in the valley of the Tagus—holding him to bail not to disturb the peace and quiet of the British army cantoned along the frontier. The Marshal had now swallowed or pocketed all that he could find in the rich, but hapless vale of Plasencia, and of late had been casting hungry glances on the country south of the river. This had induced Sir Rowland to ride over from Coria to Alcantara, to look to his line of communication with the southern provinces. This old city had been long sinking into decay; the French General, Lapisse, spent one night in it four years ago; and well nigh completed the work which time had begun. Still its position and its famous bridge, one arch of which had been blown up, and had now been hastily repaired, made it an important point at this time.

In a Gothic hall, which looked as if it had not long since been visited by the Vandals, but which had of old been often thronged with members of the once chivalrous order of Alcantara, now as effete in knighthood as that of Malta; a military secretary was writing at a small table, at the dictation of Sir Rowland Hill, who stood near, perchance, as good a knight as ever trod that floor. Cfficers came in to him, and were sent out again on various missions. Lord Strathern was seated by a larger table at the other end of the room, conversing gaily with his fellow-travelers from Elvas, and waiting Sir Rowland's leisure.

Sir Rowland presently looked at his watch, and raising his voice, inquired—"My Lord, has L'Isle come yet?"

"Not yet," Lord Strathern answered with a smiling countenance, while Sir Rowland's expressed disappointment. He knew that the commander-in-chief was about to order a combination of simultaneous movements. Every part of the allied force from Gallicia to Andalusia had its task allotted, and he was anxious to know how far the *Conde di Abispal's* could be relied on.

"L'Isle is usually before his time," said Sir Rowland. "Do you think he got my order yesterday?"

"I have little doubt of it," said my lord.

"But I doubt his being here soon," said Bradshawe, dipping in his oar to trouble the waters. "He had to go last night to a concert in Elvas."

"A concert detain him! I do not understand that."

"Nor I, Sir Rowland," said Bradshawe. coolly. "I only heard it without pretending to understand it."

Sir Rowland looked puzzled, but his unfinished dispatch claimed his attention, and he turned again to his secretary.

Meanwhile Lord Strathern was in high spirits. "The hour has come, but not the man!" he said, and began to triumph over Conway, and laugh at L'Isle so merrily, that he would have soon found it in his heart to forgive the latter all his offensive strictures on him. But, suddenly, his merriment gave place to a look of surprise and disappointment. Conway, turning to ascertain the cause, saw L'Isle walk into the room as if he had come hither at his leisure; yet, something in his bearing, betrayed that his pride was in arms.

"I am glad to see you, L'Isle," said Sir Rowland. "I were loath to close my dispatch without adding the intelligence you might bring me. By the bye, some of these gentlemen thought that you would not be here so soon."

"They must have supposed that I had not received your order, sir," said L'Isle, glancing haughtily round on Lord Strathern; "but, having got it, I am here."

"It seems to have cost you hard riding though, and more fatigue than you are yet equal to," said Sir Rowland, remembering his late wounds. "And you have had a fall," he added, observing some marks on his clothes.

"Not from my horse," said L'Isle, shortly and

somewhat bitterly. "But it is of no consequence," and he hastened to produce his notes and furnish Sir Rowland with the information expected from him.

Besides the unerased marks of a fall, L'Isle's clothes were travel-stained, and his face was pale, less, perhaps, from fatigue and loss of sleep, than from the violent excitement and revulsion of feelings he had lately undergone. But he soon withdrew Sir Rowland's attention from himself to his full and precise account of the state of the Andalusian reserve, and the garrison of Badajoz.

"I am glad to find that this body of Spanish troops are not, like too many Spanish armies, men of straw, an army on paper," said Sir Rowland. "The French are trying to occupy so extended a position here in Estremadura, that our Andalusian friends may do capital service in harassing their out-posts, and cutting off their convoys."

"If they can be kept out of the plains, and induced not to fight," said L'Isle, smiling. "But the Spaniard is always seeking to surround the enemy, and force him to battle."

"At all events," said Sir Rowland, "I can now give Lord Wellington a definite and reliable account of their condition;" and, making a sign to L'Isle to accompany him, he walked across the room and seated himself at the larger table. Here he held a somewhat prolonged conference with Lord Strathern, in which the other gentlemen were, at times, called upon to take part. When compelled to speak, L'Isle distinguished himself by giving admirable specimens of the lapidary style, not one spare word. Sir Rowland had many questions to ask and instructions to give; but, these over, he gave a less professional turn to the conversation, and then said: "I hope, my lord, you and these gentlemen will share my poor dinner to-day; but remember, I am not at home in Alcantara, and cannot feast you, as you do your friends at Élvas; neither can we sit long and drink deep, as I must return to-night to Coria."

"We will dine with you with pleasure," said Lord Strathern. "Pray, Bradshawe, who could have told Sir Rowland that we sit long and drink deep at Elvas?"

"Some thirsty fellow," said Bradshawe, "who had drained the last drop from his last bottle."

"Oh, my lord," said Sir Rowland, laughing, "I meant no insinuation. But I must finish my despatch," and he returned to his secretary.

While Lord Strathern and his companions awaited Sir Rowland's leisure, L'Isle sat moodily apart, turning an unsocial shoulder toward his lordship, giving him a glimpse of his back.

Lord Strathern smiled; he saw the earth stains, and saw, moreover, evident marks of anger and chagrin in L'Isle's demeanor. His curiosity was strongly excited, and he resolved to make the silent man find his tongue.

"Pray, L'Isle how came you to let your horse slip from under you, and measure your length in the road?"

"You are mistaken, my lord," said L'Isle, formally; "my horse did not throw me."

"You are so used to success that you will acknowledge no failure, not even a fall from your horse, or your hobby-horse. Perhaps you got tired, and took a nap by the roadside, which accounts for your getting here no sooner.

L'Isle was too angry to trust himself with an answer, but Major Conway, turning to Bradshawe, said gaily: "Colonel L'Isle is here soon enough for me; he is within the time, and I have won the fifty guineas."

L'Isle started. Here was a revelation! His last night's adventure was no secret. There were more parties to the plot than he had imagined.

"Sir!" said he, turning upon Conway, with a cold, hard manner. "Am I to understand that you have done me the honor to bet on my movements?"

"Here is gratitude for you," exclaimed Conway, pacifically appealing to his companions, and his voice attracted Sir Rowland's attention. "Here have I been showing for him the height of friendship, hazarding my best friends, my guineas, on his infallible fulfillment of duty; and my full faith in him is received as an outrage."

"I suppose, sir," said L'Isle, turning on Bradshawe, with freezing politeness, "it is you who have so obligingly afforded my volunteer backer so singular an opportunity of proving his friendship?"

"I cannot claim the credit of it," answered Bradshawe, with easy urbanity. "I am not even a stake-holder in the game; though, as a mere looker-on, I confess having watched it with keen and and growing interest." And with a little wave of the hand he passed L'Isle gently over to Lord Strathern.

L'Isle looked from the imperturbable colonel to the pacific major, who professed to be so zealously his partisan, and back again to the former. Not seeing how he could fasten a quarrel on either, he turned somewhat reluctantly on Lord Strathern, who complacently awaited him.

"As for you, my lord, I might have felt surprise at your making me the subject of such a bet, but it is lost in astonishment at the means you took to win it!"

"And, after all to lose it," said Lord Strathern, in a mocking, dolorous tone. "Is it not provoking?"

"No scruple," continued L'Isle, "seems to have stood in your way, my lord, in the choice of either means or agent."

"On the contrary," said Lord Strathern, blandly, "I always scrupulously choose the best of both."

"You must have contrived this plot," L'Isle persisted, "though the chief actor be in Elvas. But I will say no more here."

"A few words more, I pray," said Lord Strathern, smiling. "I understood that you were to have been detained in Elvas. How the devil did you get away?"

L'Isle turned abruptly away, seeing that the more anger and mortification he showed, the more gratified Lord Strathern seemed to be. Rising from his seat, he walked up to Sir Rowland, who had been watching him with much curiosity, and said: "I suppose, sir, you have no further use for me here. If so, pray excuse my absence from your table to-day, as I have occasion to return at once to Elvas."

Sir Rowland bid his secretary go and send off the despatch at once; then looking fixedly at L'Isle, said: "I may need you here for a day or two."

L'Isle bit his lip till the blood came, while Sir Rowland, stepping over to Lord Strathern, asked in an undertone: "What is the matter with L'Isle, my lord? he seems strangely out of humor."

"The truth is, Sir Rowland," said his lordship, in a confidential tone, "somebody in Elvas has been quizzing L'Isle, and a man of his vanity cannot stand being quizzed."

"Quizzed!" said Sir Rowland. "Does quizzing make a man mad?"

L'Isle dared not trust himself longer in Lord Strathern's company; he wanted time to recover his self-command; so he again addressed Sir Rowland: "That I left Elvas so suddenly, and unprepared for a prolonged absence, matters little, Sir Rowland; but I have been so little with my regiment of late, that—"

"Let your major take care of it a few days longer," Sir Rowland answered, in a positive tone.

"You had better let L'Isle go, Sir Rowland," said Lord Strathern. "He is afraid to lose sight of his regiment, lest they become banditti."

L'Isle's flushed cheek and compressed lips, showed

that he felt the taunt, while Sir Rowland exclaimed, in surprise: "Are they so unruly? Then you must look to them yourself, my lord, for I shall keep Colonel L'Isle a while with me. The truth is, L'Isle, I divine your urgent business at Elvas. Some one there has given you gross offence, and you seek revenge under the name of satisfaction. There is always sin and folly enough in these affairs; but here, within sight of the smoke of the enemy's camp, and now, when we are about to fall upon them, these personal feuds are criminal madness. I would put you under arrest, sooner than let you post off to Elvas on so bloodthirsty an errand."

Sir Rowland uttered this speech with an air worthy of his Puritan uncle, of Calvinistic memory; but, in spite of the respect due to the speaker, it was too much for the gravity of his hearers. Lord Strathern and his companions burst into a roar of laughter, and even L'Isle, amidst all his anger, felt tempted to join them.

"Gentlemen," said Sir Rowland, in grave astonishment, "I like a joke as well as any of you. "Pray explain this, that I may share your enjoyment."

Bradshawe, with an effort, cut short his laughter, to say: "As a neutral party, Sir Rowland, I will be Colonel L'Isle's surety, that in whatever mood he may set out for Elvas, as soon as he finds himself in the presence of his enemy there, he will be gentle as a lamb."

"You deal in mysteries; who in Elvas is so safe from L'Isle's resentment?"

"Nobody but Lady Mabel Stewart."

"Lady Mabel Stewart!" exclaimed Sir Rowland, looking at Lord Strathern. "If a lady contrived this plot, I shall never unravel it; so you must do it for me."

"Perhaps the explanation," said Bradshawe, "would come more gracefully from my lord."

"If I knew the details of it," said Lord Strathern, interrupting his hearty laughter, for he seemed resolved, at all hazard, to recover his fifty guineas, in sport, out of L'Isle. "I can tell but the beginning; and then, Sir Rowland, you can squeeze the rest out of L'Isle himself."

"By all means," said Sir Rowland. "L'Isle, take a seat, and learn to stand fire. You must not dodge from a volley of laughter, that happens to be aimed at yourself."

"L'Isle reluctantly sat down, while Lord Strathern said: "Have you ever discovered, Sir Rowland, that L'Isle is a monomaniac?"

"No! On what point?"

"Discipline! He is a little touched here," said my lord, laying his finger on his temple, "on the subject of discipline. He never eats heartily, nor sleeps quietly, but after detecting the breach of a dozen of the rules and regulations made for the government of his Majesty's troops. He fancies that they were made expressly to afford him the pleasure of detecting the breach of them."

"Is this disease prevalent in your brigade, my lord?" Sir Rowland inquired in a sarcastic tone.

"By no means; I have kept it down; for my method, looking to the spirit, not the letter of the law, discourages it greatly."

"I have seen something of your method, my lord," said Sir Rowland, smiling; "but cannot say that I have mastered its peculiar merits."

"That is very likely," said Lord Strathern, complacently. "As every art has its mysteries—so each man may have some peculiar gift in the application of his art; even though taught by the same master, no two men's handwriting are exactly alike; so each of us may have some inimitable peculiarity in his soldiership. It is certain that L'Isle, not understanding my more enlarged and liberal system, wished to force me into his own narrow notions, and when I would not yield to him, he intimated to me that I was training up banditti. I had to recommend to him the study of one of the articles of war, which he had overlooked. It treats of subordination, and of each man's minding his own business. Neither of us was very successful in keeping his temper; and, indeed, being a good deal ruffled, I afterward spoke pretty freely of L'Isle's conduct to these gentlemen, who dined with me. Mabel shared my feelings, and, with my consent, set a trap for him, hoping to teach him that he himself might be caught tripping. How he escaped in time to get here you must learn from himself."

"Come, L'Isle, we have heard the prologue," said Sir Rowland; "be not bashful, but give us the comedy."

What was L'Isle to do? It was evidently something more than curiosity that made Sir Rowland so earnest to sift this matter. He could hardly refuse all explanation to him—and he felt that it would never do to give an account of Lady Mabel's behavior, to himself, as he had construed it. Lord Strathern, too, did not exactly know what he was urging him to do. Suddenly recollecting Lady Mabel's note, L'Isle drew it from his pocket, and handed it to her father, for his private reading. To L'Isle's astonishment, Lord Strathern read it out with great *gusto*, and commented on it.

This was capital bait for the trap. "And pray, Mr. Interpreter, how did you and your principal get through the evening?"

"You see the dilemma, Sir Rowland," exclaimed Bradshawe, with glee. "Here was a conflict of duties. Colonel L'Isle had to obey two commanders at one time, which Scripture tells us is difficult, if not impossible."

"L'Isle seems to have achieved the impossible," said Sir Rowland; "for I know you are too *gallant* a man, L'Isle, to neglect a lady's order for mine."

Sir Rowland's manner, though not his words, were urgent for an explanation; and L'Isle being now fairly in for it, with an effort, gathered his wits together, and opened the narrative of his last night's adventure. He recounted Lady Mabel's successful efforts to amuse and occupy him into a forgetfulness of the flying hours; her artful delays before setting out; their slow but pleasant drive up hill to Elvas; the animated and well-sustained part she had played throughout the evening; her wit, her satire, and her singing, and his labors as interpreter, acknowledging many foolish things of his own, in his efforts to be witty and amusing according to contract. He described her well-feigned fear of returning home in the dark without an escort, the brilliantly lighted house and well-timed supper, at which, unconscious of the flight of time, he sat listening to her diverting talk, including her piquant sketch of Sir Rowland's glorious dinners and tactical lectures, and the value his officers set on each. Here his auditors had each an opportunity of laughing at each other, and being laughed at in turn.

L'Isle strove to make Lady Mabel appear witty, amusing, and adroit; he gave edge to her satire—keenness to her wit; but carefully rounded off all the more salient points of her acting. He said nothing of her singing "Constant my heart," at him. He did not hint at his taking her hand in the coach, or kissing it at the supper table; but dilated on her skillful libel on old Moodie's sobriety, and her well acted dread of the house-breaking banditti, from whom he could best protect her, as they are no other than his own men.

Though L'Isle did not get through his narrative with the best possible grace, he was doubly successful in it; at once greatly amusing his auditors, yet exhibiting Lady Mabel only as a witty girl, who had merely played the part allotted to her with mischievous pleasure and consummate tact. But he attained this at the cost of showing himself an easy dupe to her arts, and getting well laughed at for his pains. It cost L'Isle no small effort to do this. It was, in fact, a heroic, self-sacrificing act; for he was not used to being laughed at, and there is something highly amusing in compelling a man to tell a story which makes him more and more ridiculous at every turn. But while showing so much consideration for Lady Mabel, so far was he from beginning to forgive her ill-usage of him, that the constraint he had put upon himself only embittered his feelings toward her.

As to Lord Strathern, he was delighted with the account of *ma belle's* cunning manœuvres and witty speeches, even to the point of laughing heartily at her satire on himself; and he reveled in L'Isle's ill-concealed mortification, exclaiming: "What a pity the plot failed by Mabel's unmasking too soon. That and your good horse enabled you to keep your appointment at the risk of your neck. Why, L'Isle, you might have become a ballad hero. Mabel would have put your adventure in verse, and set it to music, and you would have been sung by all our musical folks, from Major Lumley down to the smallest drummer-boy. You are a lucky fellow; but this time your luck has lost you fame."

"And how did you get away at last?" asked Sir

Rowland, fully convinced that L'Isle had been a prisoner, under lock, bolt and bar.

The earth-stains on L'Isle's clothes might have testified that he had gotten a bad fall in jumping out of a lady's window, at two o'clock in the morning. But this is a scandalous world. L'Isle remembered Bradshawe, without looking at him, and evaded the question.

"I found old Moodie, lantern in hand, at the open gate, looking as if he had drank nothing but vinegar in a month, the picture of sour sobriety!"

Sir Rowland had striven in vain not to join in the laugh; but, in spite of himself, was much diverted at L'Isle's adventure. But he was provoked at the usage his favorite colonel had incurred, for the best of faults—too much zeal for the service; and he longed to discuss with Lord Strathern the propriety of setting traps for his own officers, when posting, with important intelligence, to their common commander. But there was a lady in the case, and Sir Rowland was afraid to broach the subject; Lord Strathern, too, though his subordinate was nearly old enough for his father—a man of high rank, and a known good soldier; so he put off the discussion to a more convenient season. As to L'Isle, Sir Rowland had been watching him closely, and saw something in his eye and bearing that betrayed too much exasperation for him to be trusted to return at once to Elvas. So, Sir Rowland invented, on the spot, a special duty for him, and bid him accompany him, that evening, to Coria.

CHAPTER XX.

RALPH.—Help down with the hangings.
ROGER.—By and by, Ralph.
I am making up the trunks here.
RALPH.—Who looks to my lady's wardrobe? Humphrey!
Down with the boxes in the gallery,
And bring away the couch-cushions.
SHORTHOSE.—Will it not rain?
No conjuring abroad, nor no devices
To stop this journey.
—*Wit without Money.*

Away, you trifler!—Love?—I love thee not:
I care not for thee, Kate; this is no world
To play with mammets, and to tilt with lips:
We must have bloody noses, and cracked crowns,
And pass them current, too. Godsme, my horse!
—*Henry IV.*

LORD STRATHERN returned the next day to Elvas, and found his daughter very desolate, and full of more than filial anxiety to see him. She was alone, for the Commissary had, the day before, sent off his heavy baggage toward Lisbon. Lady Mabel would, at any time, have grieved at parting with a true-hearted friend like Mrs. Shortridge; but now other troubles weighed heavy on her, and so aggravated her obvious grief, while the chief cause was hidden, that her kind friend was deeply moved and greatly flattered at perceiving it. Had she staid longer in Elvas, Lady Mabel would have confided her troubles to her, knowing that, though she might not think wisely, she could feel rightly, and give both advice and sympathy. But after a struggle of hesitation, she let Mrs. Shortridge depart in ignorance, receiving from her many kind messages and adieus for L'Isle.

Perhaps it was best that it should be so; for, had the good lady learned the usage her favorite had met with, she might, for once in her life, have boiled over with indignation.

"Well, *Ma Belle*," said Lord Strathern, as soon as he was alone with his daughter, "so that fellow, L'Isle, beat us, after all, at our own game. I did expect that your woman's wit would have carried it through successfully."

"Would to Heavens, papa, my woman's wit, as you call it, had been sufficient to keep me out of it altogether. How could you think of putting such a part upon me? I never would have dreamed of it, if you had not urged—insisted on my detaining him here. What is Colonel L'Isle to me, that I should manœuvre to keep him in Elvas, when Sir Rowland Hill expects him in Alcantara? And as for my resenting your quarrels with him, there is an impropriety in it, and yet more in the mode you made me adopt. I am ashamed of myself—I am ashamed of you, papa, for conceiving it."

"And to fail, after all," said Lord Strathern. "And yet, by L'Isle's own account, you played your part well."

"His account!" exclaimed Lady Mabel. "To whom?"

"To us all—Sir Rowland, Bradshawe, Conway, and myself. He was disposed to be sulky and silent, at first; but, with Sir Rowland's help, we drew it all out of him."

"Drew it all out of him!" said Lady Mabel, in a faltering tone. She gasped for breath, and her cheek grew pale. But the next moment the blood rushed into her face, and she exclaimed: "What! Did Colonel L'Isle give you a full account of the party—of all that occurred that evening?"

"Full and minute. He was very reluctant to tell, as we were all laughing at him; but Sir Rowland is a good inquisitor, and made him speak out, and at length. I did not know he had so good a memory, or you so much wit."

"For Heaven's sake, papa, what did he tell you?" Lady Mabel sat watching her father with eager eyes, her hands firmly clasped, and her heel impatiently tapping the floor, while she strove to master her almost uncontrollable confusion and anxiety.

"Why, he handed me your note," said Lord Strathern. "Perhaps he meant it for my eye alone; but it was such capital bait for the trap, that I read it aloud. He then seemed to make up his mind to conceal nothing. He told us of your artful delays, your slow-paced coach crawling up-hill; of your efforts to entertain Mrs. Shortridge's company, and keep him employed as interpreter; your songs and your care to prolong the amusements of the evening; your affected fears at riding home in your old coach with your new postillion. He described your supper-party, and repeated your entertaining conversation, your libel on Moodie, gone drunk to bed, and your satire on Sir Rowland and the rest of us; your well-acted terror of robbers, and your triumph over him when you thought the game was won. If you had not been over-confident and too hasty, Mabel, we would have had L'Isle on the hip."

"Was that *all* he told you?" asked Lady Mabel.

"Why? Was there any thing more to tell?" inquired her father.

Lady Mabel drew a deep, long breath. "Then he said nothing about my—my singing—'Constant my heart' to him?"

"How!" exclaimed Lord Strathern. "Did you sing 'Constant my heart' *at* him?"

"How could I help it, papa, it came in so pat to the purpose?"

"The devil it did! It seems you did not mean to fail, by under acting your part. It is lucky he forgot to mention it. Was there any thing more?"

"And he said nothing about squeezing my hand in the coach," asked she, hesitatingly, "when I showed so much fear of its overturning?"

"Squeezing your hand?"

"Or of his kissing it, after supper?"

"What! Had he got on so far? And pray, madam, what did you tell him?"

"Tell him!" said Lady Mabel. "I was acting a part, you know, papa; so I told him his presumption had put Jenny Aiken quite out of countenance."

"By Jove! you were acting your part with a vengeance! Why not tell him, at once, never to kiss your hand when a third person was present?"

"How can you talk so, papa? I meant no such thing. But what account did he give of his leaving the house?"

"Merely that he hurried away when you unmasked the plot to him; hastened to Elvas to get his horse, and post off to Alcantara."

"Then he said nothing of his leaping out of the window?"

"Did he leap out of the window?"

"Or of my trying to hold him back?"

"What!" exclaimed Lord Strathern, starting up. "Did he escape by jumping out of the window, and you try to detain him?"

"The height was so great, I feared he would break his neck."

"Damn his neck!" said Lord Strathern, striding up and down the room. "Better a neck cracked than a reputation. Things have come to a pretty pass. You singing love-songs at him, he squeezing and kissing your hand—perhaps going further. In these cases, women never tell the whole truth! When he would escape by a leap from your window, you try to keep him by strength of arm. You get on finely, madam! Three months in the army have done wonders for you. Three months more will accomplish you so thoroughly, that you will be fit for no other society through life. I will tell you what, Mabel, I will not lose a moment, but bundle you up, and pack you off to your aunt, while you are yet worth sending!"

Between shame and indignation at this unjust assault from such a quarter, poor Lady Mabel burst into tears, and rushed off to her room, where she locked herself up, resolving never again to leave it until she commenced her journey homeward. It was not long before her hasty father repented of his coarse and violent attack on her, in a case in which the heaviest fault was his own. He came rapping at her door, and by dint of apologies, remonstrance, and commands, brought her out, and induced her to spend the evening in his company. And a very uncomfortable evening it was to both of them.

Two days after this, L'Isle rode into Elvas, and brought orders with him that set the town astir. Such a breaking up of all the comfortable and luxurious arrangements of messes and quarters had not been lately seen. For Elvas was the Capua of the brigade, which had to lighten itself of many an incumbrance, including much of what Shortridge termed its heavy baggage, in order to bring itself to a condition to march. There was many a woeful parting, too, and scandal says that the ladies of Elvas might have laid the dust with their tears. But we will leave these stories to Colonel Bradshawe.

All was confusion in the household at headquarters. Lord Strathern had to bestir himself, to get both his brigade and himself ready to march by one route, and Lady Mabel had to prepare for her journey by another. It was now that Moodie's worth shone manifestly forth. The old coach and harness were overhauled and put in order. He secured, we believe, by impressment, another pair of mules and two postillions. Every leaf of the *hortus siccus* was carefully packed, and put into the hands of an *arriero*, bound for Lisbon, and Jenny Aiken and William, the footman, were pulled and shoved about in a way that convinced them that it was time to be moving; yet he found plenty of time to spur up my lord's own servants, and push forward their preparations. Busy as Lord Strathern was, he failed not to remark Moodie's prompt, methodical, and energetic labors. He pronounced him the prince of quartermasters, and a heavy loss to the army. "The old fellow would evacuate a fortress, or conduct a retreat with the precision of a parade, and not leave even a dropped cartridge to the enemy behind him." In fact, had Marshal Soult sworn to sack Elvas to-morrow, Moodie could not have been more on the alert in getting Lady Mabel ready to leave it. Not that he was afraid of a Frenchman—he would willingly have faced him, and made his mark upon him—but when all might be lost, and nothing gained by staying, Moodie, like Xenophon, was proving his soldiership by a speedy, yet orderly retreat. He was carrying off Lady Mabel, *via* the villages of Lisbon and London, to his stronghold of Craggy-side, where, he trusted, she would be safe from L'Isle and Popery.

Many signs of a speedy flitting were now seen about head-quarters. Lady Mabel sat melancholy and alone in her half-dismantled drawing-room. To-morrow, she is again to enter the desert of Alemtejo, on her way back to Lisbon. What a relief she would have found in busy preparations, even for that dull journey, now robbed of all the charms of novelty and expectation; but Moodie's industrious alacrity had deprived her even of this resource. She was ready, and, instead of busy preparations, had only sad thoughts to occupy her. About to part with that father, of whom she had known more in the last three months than in all her life before, for hitherto her's had been but a child's knowledge of him—loving him and proud of him—for the defects she began to see she viewed but as minor blemishes, foreign to his nature, and due solely to that long career in which he had known no home, nor companionship, but what he found in garrison and field; she could not conceal from herself the new career of danger he was about to run. Everything she heard indicated that he was now to march to fields where war's wild work would be urged on with a fury, and on a scale for which the last five campaigns, great as their results had been, were but the preparation. She shuddered to think that, yet a few days or weeks, and the veteran of near forty years of service may lie on his last field. This, perhaps, was not her greatest grief, but she strove to make it so, and sat gloomily and anxiously awaiting her father's return from Elvas.

Presently she heard the sound of horses' hoofs clattering on the pavement of the court. Rising from her melancholy posture, she was going to meet her father, when, on opening the door, Colonel L'Isle stood before her.

All the incidents of the last evening they had spent together, particularly those which he had so carefully suppressed from the narrative wrung from him, rushed upon her memory. Her folly and his generous forbearance stood facing each other. Casting her eyes on the floor, and grasping the handle of the door, to steady her tottering frame, she could only gasp out, "I expected my father."

"My lord is very busy in Elvas, and so indeed was I," said L'Isle, coolly; "but, as I march at sunrise to-morrow, I felt bound to borrow a few minutes from duty to take my leave of Lady Mabel Stewart."

She now recollected herself enough to let go the handle of the door, and make room for him to enter, and, by a motion of the hand, invited him to take a seat.

Taking a chair near her, L'Isle ran his eye round the well-remembered room. Perhaps he was thinking of his last visit here—perhaps remarking its dismantled, comfortless condition. It was not more changed than he was. All his earnest frankness of manner was gone. He seemed to have borrowed a leaf from Colonel Bradshawe's book; and his air of cool self-possession, his imperturbable manner, under the present trying circumstances, would have excited that gentleman's admiration, but it added a chill to the discomfort of Lady Mabel's position.

Had he been angry, indignant, haughty, or sullen, it would have been an infinite relief to her. She might have known how to deal with him, and perchance have soon brought him round to a very different mood. Now L'Isle evidently waited with cool politeness to hear some sound from her lips; and she at length stammered out, "I am very sorry that you are going—that is, that papa and all of you are going so soon."

"Our pleasant sojourn in Elvas is over!" said L'Isle, carelessly, "and Elvas is a pleasant place. Your stay here, too, has been quite an episode in winter quarters. We cannot thank you too much for the enlivening influence of your presence among us. I, for one, will ever carry with me a vivid recollection of it."

Lady Mabel bowed. How cold and formal did this sound in her ears..

"To do ourselves justice," continued L'Isle, "some of us have not been remiss in our efforts to enable you to pass your time pleasantly. I dare say now, were I to hold myself to a strict account, I could reckon up many an hour stolen from the dull routine of duty to devote it to Lady Mabel's service."

"I am surely deeply indebted to you for the hours

you so borrowed to bestow on me," Lady Mabel answered, much at a loss what to say, and looking every way but at L'Isle. "When I look back, I cannot but be surprised at the amount of my gains, the knowledge and amusement I have crowded into three short months, and chiefly through you."

"That time has passed, however," said L'Isle; "I can no longer be at hand to afford you amusement. And as for knowledge, although older than you, and knowing more of life, the world, and perchance of books, I doubt whether you have been the greatest gainer in our intercourse. But feeling a deep interest in you, I sincerely hope that you may gain one precious lesson through me."

"What is that?" asked Lady Mabel eagerly—for the first time looking fully at him.

"Never again heartlessly to throw away a friend!!" L'Isle said this more gravely than bitterly. Then rising, he bowed respectfully but formally, and was turning to go away.

Can she let him go without one word? But what can she say? She, at length, gasped out, "It was papa's doing."

"Your father's doing!" exclaimed L'Isle, with well-feigned astonishment. "Then Lady Mabel is an automaton," he added scornfully, "and I, blockhead that I am, never found it out till now! But I am thankful for wisdom even that comes too late. I now know Lady Mabel and myself."

Was not Lady Mabel now disarmed and defenceless? Completely at his mercy? By no means! In this extremity she sheltered herself behind her strongest defences. She covered her face with her hands, and burst into tears.

Was ever man more embarrassed than L'Isle? His proud, scornful air, vanished like a snow-flake in the fire—and forgetting all that had passed, he was seizing her hands to draw them away from her face, when old Moodie abruptly entered the room, and called out, "Colonel L'Isle, you are wanted in Elvas?"

"What the devil are you doing here?" said L'Isle, turning round quickly, and placing himself so as to hide Lady Mabel's face.

"My duty," said the old man sternly, "and they have sent for you to attend to yours!" for he saw that something had gone wrong; and he longed to get L'Isle out of the house.

Looking into the passage, L'Isle now saw an orderly, whom Moodie had officiously brought up-stairs from the door, and he hurried out to receive the man's message, and send him off. This done, he hastily re-entered the room to speak to Lady Mabel. But he was too late! The bird had flown, and her old Scotch terrier was covering her retreat, shutting the door of the next room behind her, and spitefully locking it in L'Isle's face.

At sunrise, the next morning, L'Isle marched his regiment out of Elvas. Setting his face sternly northward, he never once looked back on the serried ranks which followed him, until the embattled heights of La Lippe had hidden Elvas and its surroundings. Turning his back upon the past, he strove to look but to the future; but at the very moment of this resolve, memory cheated him, and he caught himself repeating a line of Lady Mabel's song:

> "All else forgotten, War is now my theme."

and the thrilling music of her intonation seemed to swell upon his ear. He hastily exchanged his quotation for a greater poet's words:

> "He that is truly dedicate to war,
> Hath no self-love."

If it be possible to forget, he will have ample opportunity, amidst the crash of armies and the crumbling of an empire, to erase from his memory Elvas, and its "episode in winter quarters." From the heights of Traz os Montes, Wellington was now to make an eagle's swoop upon the north of Spain, and a lion's spring upon the herd, driven into the basin of Vittoria. The march now begun was to lead thence to the blood-stained passes of the Pyrennees, to Bayonne, Orthes, and Toulouse, and later, to Paris, from the field of Waterloo. But who shall measure, step by step, over conquered enemies and fallen friends, this long eventful road?

> "To die beneath the hoofs of trampling steeds,
> That is the lot of heroes upon earth!"

CONCLUSION.

He that commends me to mine own content,
Commends me to the thing I cannot get.
I to the world am like a drop of water,
That in the ocean seeks another drop;
Who, falling there to find his fellow forth,
Unseen, inquisitive, confounds himself.

COMEDY OF ERRORS.

THREE eventful years have passed, and a general peace is giving rest to exhausted Europe. The war has cut off many a brave man; but it remained for peace to terminate the military career of a rising soldier in L'Isle's person; and sad to say, before he was either Major general or knight of the Bath; though sought in many a dangerous path, he had not found his golden spurs.

Regiments have been disbanded, his comrades are scattered, and he himself has nothing to do, not even the poor resource of having to study economy on half-pay, or of looking for more additional means to eke out a living.

It is the curse of those entirely engrossing pursuits, which excite all our enthusiasm, and task every energy, and of which the statesman's and the soldier's callings are the best examples, that, when they fail us, we can find no substitute. All things else are, by comparison, stale, flat, and unprofitable. Can the brandy drinker cheer himself with draughts of small beer? Screw up his nervous energies to their accustomed tone with slops?

Tired to death of fox-hunting, pleasant shooting, and country neighbors; all the means of excitement around him exhausted, L'Isle lounged in the library at C——d Hall, with half a dozen open but discarded volumes before him, revolving in his mind all possible means of occupation. At one time he would resolve to travel the world over, and get up a personal narrative, attractive as that of Humboldt, and views of nature, that should look through nature's surface to the recognition of Nature's God, whom the philosopher seems never to have found in all his works. At another time, in order more effectively to counteract the ill effects, on mind and habits, of the soldier's exciting and unsettled life, he resolves to subject himself to still severer regimen: not to go rambling about the world, an idling philosopher, but to tie himself down to one spot, and take violently to a course of high farming; grow the largest turnips, breed the fattest South-downs, and the heaviest Devonshires, and carry off agricultural prizes as substitutes for additional Waterloo medals.

But this was too severe a contrast to his late mode of life, and the prospect soon disgusted him utterly. Having strong influence to back him, he now thought of getting a seat in Parliament, and for a moment the prophetic cries of 'Hear! hear!' arose from both sides of a full House of Commons. But he knew that the occasion, even more than the man, makes the orator; and in 'this weak piping time of peace,' these cost-counting, debt-paying days, he foresaw no occasion that could call forth the thunders of Demosthenes or Burke.—But although a new light shines in upon him, and he suddenly makes up his mind that, since he can no longer take the field, because all the world is tired of fighting, and yet more of paying the bills run up in that expensive diversion, he will write the narrative of the campaigns in which he had taken part, without letting the '*quorum pars magna fui*' fill too large a place in the picture.—Where can he find so much of the materials needed in the construction of his work as in London? So to London he went.

The season was at its height, and the town was full. L'Isle's object required that he should not only examine many musty papers, but see many persons; as some of his gayer friends soon found him out, and induced him to look in upon the inner circles of London fashionable life, to which his early and long absence from England had kept him a stranger.

It so happened that Lord Strathern had come up from his moors, where the winter had got too cold for him (the climate had changed much since he was a boy), to visit the clubs and meet old comrades. But these proved too much for the old veteran, who soon had to shut himself up, in order to stave off an attack of his old enemy, the gout. He would not, however, permit Lady Mabel to stand the siege with him. The consequence was, that not long after L'Isle had come up to London, he found himself in one of Lady D——'s thronged rooms, within four steps of Lady Mabel.

In three years she had become, if we may be pardoned the bull, more like herself than ever, for she was now all that she had promised to be. She shone out in a richer and riper beauty, and a more sedate and womanly deportment set it off, retaining not the least trace of that somewhat cavalier manner she had picked up in the brigade. She was more than three years wiser, and certainly more dangerous than ever.

L'Isle had long and studiously schooled himself to the conviction that his fair and fascinating companion in Elvas was, after all, but a heartless woman. Yet his vanity, to say nothing of any other feeling, had never quite gotten over the rude shock it had received on Mrs. Shortridge's great night there. His first thought was to withdraw from the dangerous neighborhood. But he blushed at his own cowardice; and the moment after, having caught her eye, he, self-confident, made his way through the crowd, and greeted her politely as an old acquaintance. It was plain that she was a little nervous on his approach; her lips were compressed for a moment, and she drew more than one deep breath, while watching him closely, and carefully modeling her manner by his. Yet no stranger could have inferred, from word or look, that they had not met for years, still less that they had ever met on terms of intimacy. If L'Isle needlessly prolonged the conversation, to the annoyance of the gentlemen at her elbow, his sole object was to prove to her, beyond the possibility of doubt, by his easy self-possession, that he had now, at least, attained to a sublime indifference where she was concerned.

The ice once broken, accident seemed to throw them frequently into the same company. L'Isle doubtless needed relaxation from his historical labors; and a London season had at least the attraction of novelty for him. He was, too, just the man to win friends among the ladies; yet he still made it a point, whenever he met Lady Mabel, to bestow on her a few minutes cold attention and indifferent notice, for old acquaintance sake.

Lady Mabel stood in no need of these attentions. It was not her first season; and many a butterfly, that hovered about that garden which blooms in winter at the West-End, had hailed with delight the reappearance of this rare flower. And she liked to have them buzzing about her; it was her due, and yielded pleasant pastime. Yet while busiest dealing sentiment, jest, and repartee among them, she now had always an ear and a word for L'Isle, when he condescended to bestow a few minutes cold consideration on her.

Her gentlemen in waiting wondered at her having so much to say to L'Isle. She seemed to be under an obligation to be at leisure for him; and Sir Charles

Moreton, who was argus-eyed where Lady Mabel was concerned, ventured to ask: "What pleasure can you find in talking to this austere soldier? His smile is a sneer; he warms only to grow caustic, and his cynical air betrays how little he cares even for you."

"Were you ever clogged with sweet things?" asked Lady Mabel. "At times I tire of bonbons, and long for vinegar, salt and pepper. My austere friend deals in these articles."

She seemed to have found a special use for him, treating him as a complete thinking machine, of high powers of observation, inflection, thought and reason, but not susceptible of aught that savored of feeling, sentiment or passion. She quietly threw the mantle of Mentor over his shoulders, deferred to his judgment, had recourse to him as a store-house of knowledge; and seemed so fully impressed with the fact that he had a head, as utterly to forget the probability of his having a heart. With a strange perversity, L'Isle was at once flattered and annoyed at the use she made of him. It was an unequal game he was playing, like a moth fluttering round a candle. His temper began to be worn threadbare, and oftener than ever he repeated to himself, "She is a heartless woman!"

In this mood L'Isle was listening, with a curled lip, to an animated discussion between Lady Mabel, Sir Charles Moreton, and another gentleman, as to the merits of a new actress, a dramatic meteor, then briefly eminent on the London boards. The Honorable Mr.

L——, who was a *savant* in the small sciences that cater to amusement, pronounced her the Siddons of the day; Lady Mabel called her a ranter, then, as if alarmed at her temerity, appealed as usual to L'Isle.

"No one can be a better judge of acting than Lady Mabel," said L'Isle. "But for her opinion, I would call your favorite an indifferently good actress."

Thus to "damn with faint praise," displeased Mr. L—— more than positive censure, and he exclaimed: "Then you never saw her play Jane Shore. The illusion is perfect. The house is deceived into forgetting the drama, to witness the living and dying agonies of the desolate penitent. Who can equal her?"

"Many," answered L'Isle; "and Lady Mabel can do better."

"Lady Mabel! She doubtless excels in everything. But I never saw her act."

"I have," said L'Isle bitterly. "The illusion of Mrs. ——'s acting is limited to the spectators. Lady Mabel deceives him who acts with her."

Lady Mabel turned pale, and then red, while the two gentlemen stared at her and L'Isle alternately. Suddenly exclaiming, "There is my friend, Mrs. B——. I have not seen her for a month. I must go and speak to her," she accepted the arm of the *savant* in small things, and hastened after her friend, who had appeared so opportunely.

"You set little value on Lady Mabel's favors," said Sir Charles, looking inquisitively at L'Isle. "You have certainly offended her greatly."

"Do you think so?" said L'Isle coldly. "Then I suppose I must apologize and beg my peace."

"If you do it successfully," said his companion, "I will be glad of a lesson from you in the art."

L'Isle was angry with himself. Not that he felt that he owed Lady Mabel any amends. But he had never until now made the slightest allusion to certain scenes in the past. Pride had forbidden it. And he was still reproaching himself with his want of self-control, when, on entering another room, he saw Lady Mabel seated between two old ladies, having ensconced herself there to get rid of the small *savant*.

She no longer looked discomposed or angry, nor did she turn her eyes away on his approach. She almost seemed to wish to speak to him. So he offered his arm, and they walked toward the room he had just left.

"I know that you are too proud," she said, "to ask my pardon for the attack you made on me just now. So I wish to tell you that I have already forgiven it."

"That is truly generous," said L'Isle, with haughty irony. "You prove the adage false which says, 'The injurer never forgives.'"

"Say you so? I see then that you have gone back years to dig up old offences. Although I remember, to repent of them, I trusted that you would have willingly forgiven and forgot my folly, or only recall it to laugh at it. I know now," she said, stealing a look at him, "that you are of an unforgetting, unforgiving temper." Then looking away, she added, "I thought better of you once."

"There are some things," answered L'Isle, but in a softened tone, "not to be forgotten, nor easily forgiven."

"I assure you," said Lady Mabel, with the air of a penitent, "I have been terribly ashamed of myself ever since. Had I known that you still viewed my thoughtless conduct as a serious wrong to you, I would willingly have made you any apology, any reparation."

"Apologies would hardly reach the evil," said L'Isle. "But any reparation! That is a broad term."

"Any, I mean, that you ought to ask, or I to make."

"There would be no absolute impropriety in my asking a good deal," said L'Isle, in tones that reminded Lady Mabel of some witching moments in Elvas, "I will not make the blunder of asking too little," he added resolutely. "Let me first ask when you will be at home to-morrow—at three?"

"Certainly at three; more certainly at two," she answered in a low tone.

"And most certainly at one," said he joyously. "I like your superlative degree of comparison."

"I only meant," she said, yet more confused, "that I am more likely to be at home alone at two." And turning quickly away, she took a vacant seat beside one of her friends, to whom, while fanning herself, she complained of the heated room. She seemed, indeed, quite overcome by it, which accounted for her labored breathing and heightened color.

* * * * * * * * *

"After all," said Lady Mabel, some days after the

morning on which L'Isle found her at home alone, "I was neither so good an actress, nor so great a hypocrite as you took me for. My offence was not so much that I simulated, as that I ceased to dissemble."

L'Isle readily embraced the faith that she was no actress but a true woman, nor did he ever waver from it. But she did not always find so easy a convert. Old Moodie, true to his nature, baffled all her efforts to convince him of his errors. It is true that he became in time, somewhat reconciled to L'Isle, but to his dying day he continued to laud that special providence, which had snatched Lady Mabel from the land of idolatry, at the very last moment before her perversion to Rome.

Lady Mabel was not the woman to forget old friends; and now, that she could recur with pleasure to her recollections of Elvas, she sought out that companion who had so amiably filled the part of duenna and chaperon. She and Mrs. Shortridge fought all their battles over again, by retracing, step by step, varied excursions and toilsome journey, while enjoying all the comforts of an English home. But it never does to tell all that we do, still less, to lay open the spirit in which we do it. Lady Mabel never let Mrs. Shortridge fully into the secret history of the last dark treacherous scene in the episode in winter quarters.

Lord Strathern was much pleased to find that L'Isle had greatly modified his opinion, as to the mechanical nature of an army, and hoped in time to dispel certain other erroneous notions, to which he had formerly clung so stubbornly. It is not known whether or not L'Isle ever finished his narrative of the Peninsular campaigns. It is certain that he never published it. The author often labors harder than the ploughman; and when a man is made happy, he becomes lazy. Let the wretched toil to mend his lot, or to forget it.

www.ingramcontent.com/pod-product-compliance
Lightning Source LLC
Chambersburg PA
CBHW032317280326
41932CB00009B/845
* 9 7 8 3 7 4 4 6 6 4 3 8 7 *